The New Antisemitism

ספר זה מוקדש לד״ר אינסה ברשדסקיי והצוות הרפואי של
מרפאת ביקור רופא, סניף ראשון לציון, ולד״ר אבי פוקס והצוות
הרפואי של יחידת לב ביניים בבית החולים קפלן ברחובות, אשר
הצילו את חיי ואפשרו לי לכתוב את הספר הזה

The New Antisemitism

The Resurgence of an Ancient Hatred in the Modern World

SHALOM LAPPIN

polity

First published in 2024 by Polity Press

Polity Press
65 Bridge Street
Cambridge CB2 1UR, UK

Polity Press
111 River Street
Hoboken, NJ 07030, USA

ISBN-13: 978-1-5095-5856-8

A catalogue record for this book is available from the British Library.

Library of Congress Control Number: 2023948030

Typeset in 11 on 14pt Warnock Pro
by Fakenham Prepress Solutions, Fakenham, Norfolk NR21 8NL
Printed and bound in Great Britain by CPI Group (UK) Ltd, Croydon

For further information on Polity, visit our website:
politybooks.com

Contents

Preface   vi

1 Introduction: Democracy in Crisis   1
2 The Roots of Antisemitism in Western Culture   33
3 The View from the Right   54
4 The View from the Left   81
5 The View from Radical Political Islamism   109
6 The Israeli–Palestinian Conflict Re-naturalized   127
7 The Jewish Response to the Crisis   157
8 Notes for a New Progressive Politics   179

Notes   196
References   207
Index   223

Preface

The entry of antisemitic themes into mainstream political discourse in the West over the past two decades has been accompanied by a significant rise in anti-Jewish hate crime. There has been widespread discussion of these developments in the press and among academics. Much of it has tended to view antisemitism as an independent phenomenon, in isolation from the context in which it arises. In fact its resurgence is conditioned by the crisis in democracy and social cohesion that has been affecting many countries over this same period. Writing this book has given me the opportunity to consider the connection between antisemitism and the political effects of economic globalization, specifically the sharp rise of inequality in income that has accompanied globalization. It has also permitted me to explore the way in which the long history of anti-Jewish hostility embedded within Western culture facilitates the ease with which antisemitism crosses a variety of ideological boundaries, in a way that other forms of racism do not.

I am grateful to my editor, Ian Malcolm, for invaluable guidance and constant support. My wife, Elena, my children and my grandchildren have given me generous amounts of love, good humour, and patient encouragement during the months that I was absorbed in working on this volume. I wish to thank Daniel Burston, Raphael Cohen-Almagor, Mark Glouberman, Alan Johnson, Matt Kramer, Susie Linfield, Benny Morris, Peter Nicholas, Mori Rimon, Haim Rubenstein, Richard Sproat, Nigel Vincent, Garvan Walshe, Anthony Warrens and an anonymous reviewer for much useful advice. My son Yaakov has provided extremely helpful critical feedback on draft chapters. Needless to say, I am solely responsible for the ideas presented in this book, and any errors that it may contain.

Several chapters of the book were written in Israel in the winter of 2022–3, while I was recovering from emergency open-heart surgery there. I owe an enormous debt of gratitude to the medical staff who saved my life. I appreciate their remarkable level of professional competence, and their deep compassion, more than they can know. I also thank family and friends who gave me much-needed support in this time. It is greatly valued.

During this period a large Israeli democracy movement emerged, organizing regular demonstrations of hundreds of thousands of people from a large cross-section of the population. Against initial expectations, they have sustained a surprisingly effective opposition to the Netanyahu government's ongoing assault on the country's democratic institutions and independent judiciary. After a lifetime of activism I found myself confined to the role of observer as these dramatic events unfolded. It was moving and gratifying to cheer on my family and friends as they joined the demonstrations. The future of the country depends on the success of this movement.

One of the main conclusions that I reach in the book is that an effective response to antisemitism requires a new progressive politics that addresses the underlying causes of the current crisis in democracy. Such a response must be grounded in an understanding of the history of antisemitism.

It is important to recognize where it comes from, and why it is pervasive as a response to the social dislocation generated by rapid change.

I completed the manuscript for this book shortly before the large-scale Hamas terrorist attack of 7 October 2023, and the conflict that followed it. These events have significantly altered the situation in the Middle East. They have also had a very deep impact on Jews in the Diaspora, and the environments in which they are living. I have tried to update some of the chapters to take account of these events, which remain ongoing. I have been forced to limit myself to brief observations, as a proper treatment of these developments would require another study. At this point it seems that many aspects of the international reaction to the attack and its aftermath amplify some of the tendencies and patterns previously identified in the book.

Shalom Lappin
London
December 2023

1

Introduction: Democracy in Crisis

On the evening of 11 August 2017 a group of White supremacists carrying torches marched through the streets of
Charlottesville, Virginia shouting 'Jews will not replace us.'
This was the opening event of a Unite the Right weekend
rally. The following day, a far-right activist drove his car into
a crowd of counter-demonstrators, killing Heather Heyer.
President Trump responded to the clash by condemning
violence and hatred 'on both sides'. He did not mention
the previous evening's torchlight parade, and the antisemitic
chants that it featured. In the days that followed the riot, he
reiterated his view that White nationalist rioters and anti-
racist protestors bore equal responsibility for the situation.
He never abandoned his claim of moral equivalence between
the two groups, insisting that there were 'fine people on both
sides'.

The comedian Dave Chappelle hosted *Saturday Night Live*
on 13 November 2022. He devoted his opening monologue
to the problems that Ye (the rapper and fashion icon formerly
known as Kanye West) had recently encountered due to a
series of strongly anti-Jewish posts on social media. Chappelle
opened his remarks by taking a piece of paper from his pocket

and reading a formulaic condemnation of antisemitism, in comic mode, to knowing chuckles from the studio audience. He followed this with the sentence, 'And that, Kanye, is how you buy yourself some time.' This was greeted with loud laughter and applause. The monologue went on to explore the issue of Jewish control of Hollywood, with the clear suggestion that there are some topics one cannot afford to speak about freely. Chappelle's performance drew criticism from the Anti-Defamation League, and others. His defenders argued that he was parodying bigotry, while pushing the boundaries of comic expression through edgy sophistication. It would have been interesting to observe their response to a monologue that commented on racism directed at other ethnic groups, in the same 'edgily sophisticated', 'boundary-pushing' way.

These two events, from opposite parts of the political and cultural spectrum in America, indicate the extent to which ideas that had been safely confined to the margins of political life in the postwar era have now entered the mainstream in recent years. The expanding tolerance of antisemitic discourse in the public domain corresponds to a sharp spike in anti-Jewish hate crime in America, the UK and continental Europe.[1] It is generally the case that an increase in racist rhetoric is accompanied by a rise in racist violence.

There have been numerous studies of antisemitism in recent years. Lipstadt (2018) looks at the resurgence of anti-Jewish bigotry on both the right and the left through an examination of the conspiracy myths of Jewish power that drive it. Julius (2010) provides an exhaustive history of antisemitism in England. Rich (2016), Hirsh (2017) and Baddiel (2022) deal with different aspects of left-wing antisemitism in Britain. Rich (2023) discusses the history of antisemitism as a set of recurring myths and prejudices embedded in European culture, with Britain as the focus of his study. In this book I will explore the emergence of contemporary antisemitism in the context of extremist anti-globalist movements. These movements are reacting to deep economic changes that have been generating wrenching social dislocations over an extended period of time. Attempting to understand the politics of anti-Jewish racism in this framework will, I hope, illuminate its close connections with other forms of bigotry, while throwing into sharper relief those distinctive properties that render it unique. This perspective will also clarify at least some of the factors that root this toxic prejudice so deeply within the cultures of Western and Middle Eastern societies.

1.1 The Rise of Extremism

We are living through a time of ongoing political and social turmoil, which has extended throughout much of the world over the past decade. Democracy is under siege in Europe, the United States, parts of Latin America and India. Far-right parties and extreme religious movements have moved from the periphery of many societies into the mainstream.

In America Donald Trump and his supporters retain a commanding influence within the Republican Party. They have been using it to effectively undermine the integrity of large swaths of the country's electoral and judicial institutions. Both China and Russia are ruled by stridently nationalist autocracies pursuing increasingly aggressive policies of repression at home and expansion abroad. Vladimir Putin's regime is waging a bloody war of aggression against Ukraine in the centre of Europe. Previous paradigms of stable progressive government, like Sweden, now prominently display neo-fascist parties poised on the edge of political power. Italy and France exhibit similar patterns. Hungary is under the control of Viktor Orbán, a pro-Putin authoritarian who has dismantled the independent judiciary and imposed partisan state control of the press. Recep Tayyip Erdoğan uses Islamist ideology to advance Turkish nationalism and the suppression of dissent. Narendra Modi has substituted extreme Hindu sectarianism for secular democracy in India. After being narrowly defeated in a recent presidential election, former Brazilian president Jair Bolsanaro continues to pursue his version of a Trumpian agenda in opposition. Many other countries and regions show variants of this dynamic.

In addition to far-right ethno-nationalism, varieties of far-left and radical Islamist movements have become increasingly influential in shaping the contemporary political landscape. In Europe and America a postmodernist identity politics of the left, formulated as 'anti-colonialism', has entrenched itself in large parts of academia, publishing and the entertainment industry. Across Muslim-majority countries different strands of Islamism have largely replaced post-colonial secular nationalism as a dominant ideology of government, as well as of opposition.

Conflict and extremism are not new phenomena, even in periods of relative cohesion. What is remarkable about the current era is the extent to which deep social unrest is driving radical political movements and undermining trust in established institutions across such a large and diverse set of environments. These movements, and, in some countries, the regimes that they have produced, threaten to destroy liberal democratic institutions. They are promoting ethnic conflict, and they are generating instability on a very large scale.

It is possible to identify at least four elements common to most of the extremist movements that are seizing control of the public domain. First, a distinctive sense of grievance lies at the core of their appeal. Their supporters feel that they have lost control over central aspects of their lives and their social contexts. This sentiment infuses these movements with the militance and the escalating violence that they exhibit.

It defines the rancour that they bring to current political discourse.

The second factor is a collapse of faith in established political parties and existing institutions to meet the challenges that are now overwhelming them across a wide range of areas. Such challenges include sustaining an equitable level of prosperity, handling immigration, managing cultural diversity and coping with climate change. Increasing numbers of people are coming to the view that conventional political and economic arrangements are aggravating rather than solving these problems. They are embracing previously unthinkable alternatives that lie beyond the consensus on which public life in the postwar era in the West, and in many other areas, has depended.

Third, extremists of the right, the left and radical Islamism are staunchly anti-elitist. They attribute the failure of current governments and institutions to the machinations of various groups, who operate the machinery of the state, the economy and the mainstream media for their own benefit, rather than for the public good. For this reason these movements are frequently (and often misleadingly) described as 'populist.' Their anti-elitist posture provides fertile ground for conspiracy theories, which they use to recruit support, and to define the targets of their campaigns.[2]

Finally, these groups have made identity politics a focus of their respective agendas. They stress the ethnic, cultural and gender aspects of the oppression that they claim to oppose. They present themselves as threatened by other groups of a different identity, who either make up the ruling elite, or are imported and used by it, to dispossess them.

The rise of extremism provides the more general context in which I am considering contemporary antisemitism. It has become an increasingly prominent theme in the politics of all three types of extremist movements. The far right in Europe and America targets ethnic and religious minorities, with people of colour, immigrants (particularly Muslim immigrants) and Jews identified as the main threat. Large parts of the far left have moved from criticism of Israeli state actions to vilification of the overwhelming number of Jews who are committed to Israel's existence and wellbeing. They paint them as agents of a nefarious lobby that controls the press, financial institutions and Western governments. They use the language of extreme 'anti-Zionism' to avoid the terminology of 'Jewish control', which is embedded in the far right. In fact, their ideas converge at the same point. Many radical Islamists take the idea of a Jewish/Zionist conspiracy of control as integral to their own project of establishing societies based on the hegemony of Islamic law, free of Western influence. In this respect, antisemitism is a unique form of racism. It runs across political and cultural lines. The myths of malicious Jewish power that encode it are shared by the three dominant forms of extremism driving the current assault on democracy.

Those committed to democracy and pluralism are now very much aware of the crisis that has engulfed us. They are reacting with varying degrees of alarm, resistance and, in some cases, despair. They have enjoyed some successes in opposing extremist movements, such as Trump's defeat in 2020, but they have not managed to wrest control of the political momentum in the current contest. For the most part, democrats remain on the defensive in the face of the growing authoritarian challenge. In order to effectively meet this challenge it is not sufficient to identify it, and to oppose it. We need to understand what is driving the rise in extremist movements. Only then will it be possible to formulate an alternative social and political vision that undercuts the forces sustaining their appeal. It is these forces that have invigorated the virus of antisemitism from a relatively somnolent state in the West in the postwar order into a potent pathogen infecting mainstream politics in the current decline of this order.

1.2 The End of the Postwar Era

The first half of the twentieth century was ravaged by two world wars, with a depression and the rise of fascism, Nazism and Communism, in the years between them. Determined to avoid a repetition of this cycle of mass destruction and destitution, the Western architects of the postwar era established a set of institutions designed to create prosperity and ensure stability. These included, among others, the Marshall Plan for rebuilding the destroyed economies of Europe, a programme to reconstruct Japan and the Bretton Woods system for international monetary exchange and capital management. Bretton Woods included the establishment of the International Monetary Fund and the World Bank.

The postwar years of 1945–72 saw substantial economic growth, an increase in labour productivity and low unemployment throughout much of the world, particularly in the West.[3] This was accompanied by a rise in living standards and a reduction of social and educational gaps in many countries. Both the West and the Soviet bloc experienced an expansion of manufacturing and rapid technological development. In the West, unions were relatively powerful, and job security was widespread.

This was the highwater mark of liberalism and the expansion of the welfare state in the West. The developing world went through decolonization. It saw the emergence of nationalist governments committed to both rapid development and independence from colonial rule. The Union of Soviet Socialist Republics (USSR) moved from Stalin's regime of terror to a more settled, bureaucratic form of Communist rule. Competition between the West and the Soviet Union froze relations between them into an extended period of stasis. While the 1960s brought significant cultural change and political conflict to the West, this remained a period of relative economic and social stability, in which a liberal democratic consensus stayed intact in Western Europe, America and many other countries.

The period of prosperity and cohesion came to an end in 1973, when a sharp increase in the price of oil generated high inflation, falling growth and rising unemployment. By the end of the decade these developments contributed to extended periods of Conservative government under Ronald Reagan in the US and Margaret Thatcher in the UK. Their administrations reduced the redistributive social programmes and the progressive tax systems that their predecessors had implemented. They also restricted the power of labour unions, and union membership declined significantly after this time. All of this was done in the name of an ideology of minimal state 'libertarianism'. It was marketed with the promise that removing constraints on capital would yield increased growth, which would benefit all classes from the top down.

By the end of the 1980s, Mikhail Gorbachev's experiment with political reform culminated in the collapse of Communism in Eastern Europe, and the dissolution of the USSR in 1991. Many commentators in the West hailed this event as establishing free-market-based liberal democracy as a universal, inevitable economic and political order. Fukuyama (1992) described it as the end point of historical evolution. But by the time that Fukuyama's book appeared, Yugoslavia had broken up into its constituent republics and descended into a sequence of bloody civil wars that lasted until 2001. History did not stop, but it continued through a series of major upheavals.

The rapid move to an unconstrained free market economy in the former Communist countries of the USSR and Eastern Europe created social upheaval. Massive privatization of state assets in the Russian Federation under Boris Yeltsin gave rise to a small class of wealthy oligarchs, who took control of large areas of economic and political life. Vladimir Putin rose to

power in the chaotic frontier economy that radical privatization generated. He proceeded to re-establish state control
over large sections of the economy, and he moved to totali-
tarian rule through selective alliances with groups of oligarchs,
who are beholden to him.[4]

In 2007–8, an international financial crisis produced a severe
recession, aggravated by the austerity policies of many governments, particularly those of the UK and the European Union
(EU). This recession lasted into 2009. More recently, the Covid
pandemic of 2019–21 caused a major economic contraction
and social disruption. It was followed by a rebound that has
fuelled high inflation. The energy crisis that Putin's war in
Ukraine has unleashed is aggravating inflation. The increasing
frequency of extreme weather events due to climate change
(extended droughts, forest fires and flooding) are intensifying
these shocks.

Several of the major economic disruptions that occurred
at the end the of twentieth century and the beginning of the
twenty-first were the direct result of policy decisions. Some of
these were initiated by centrist governments of the liberal left.
In 1999, the Clinton administration deregulated the financial
markets with the Gramm–Leach–Bliley Financial Services
Modernization Act. This law largely neutralized Roosevelt's
Glass–Steagall Act, enacted in 1933 to prevent banks from
engaging in speculative lending and investment. Clinton then
approved the Commodity Futures Modernization Act in
December 2000. This legislation exempted derivatives from
federal government control.[5] The New Labour government
of Tony Blair and Gordon Brown pursued similar policies of
financial deregulation during the same period. The crash of
2007–8 was preceded by smaller-scale, more local meltdowns
in Savings and Loans associations, extending from the
mid-1980s through to the mid-1990s. These were also made
possible through congressional legislation removing many of
the constraints on the lending industry in the 1980s.

Deregulation was instrumental in creating a highly globalized market for capital investment, loans and derivatives. Hedge funds and investors are able to chase short-term profitable returns across the world, buying and selling financial products anywhere, virtually without constraint. This rapid movement of large amounts of capital around the world has had a profound effect on the development of national and regional economies.

Brexit is another instance of a government policy decision that generated significant economic damage. Its implementation coincided with the disruptions of Covid, and so it was initially difficult to assess its impact accurately. As the pandemic began to recede, the extent of Brexit's negative influence on the British economy has become increasingly apparent. The effects include a substantial reduction in the UK's trade with both EU and non-EU countries, a decline in the level of foreign investment that it attracts, a rise in the price of imported goods and an acute labour shortage across a wide range of services and industries.[6]

The deregulation of financial markets that produced the crashes of the 1980s, the 1990s and 2008 was driven by the interests of bankers and investment agencies. It facilitated economic globalization. By contrast Brexit was motivated by anti-globalist sentiment. It was packaged as the promise to reclaim 'sovereignty' from the EU. Its advocates harnessed nationalist and isolationist impulses to achieve electoral endorsement, with these frequently spilling into xenophobia in the course of the referendum campaign.

From our current perspective, we can see that the early 1970s marked the end of the postwar era. At the conclusion of the first quarter of the twenty-first century we are witnessing the unravelling of the institutions that sustained the stability that those years afforded. Many people who grew up in the postwar era tend to see the features of this period as the norm. They regard the increasing chaos of the following years as exceptional departures from that norm. In fact there are good reasons to doubt this assumption. Piketty (2014) provides extensive evidence from tax receipts and other financial records, in a variety of countries, across several centuries, in support of the view that the postwar era was highly exceptional as a time of extended growth and reduction in income inequality. The economic profiles of earlier historical periods more closely resemble those of the years that have come after this era. To get a better sense of what might be conditioning the political breakdown on display now, it is worth considering some of the deeper, long-term structural patterns that extend over many years.

1.3 Globalization and Inequality[7]

Economists have identified two major periods of globalization over the past two centuries. Figure 1, from Petri and Banga (2020), shows the historical trend of world trade as a percentage of world gross domestic product (GDP) from 1820 to 2020. It rose from 10 per cent in 1820 to a peak of 15 per cent in 1910, and then fell in the first half the twentieth century as a result of the two world wars and the intervening depression. The second wave began in 1970, reaching a peak of 25 per cent in 2008. It declined in the wake of the financial crash, and then recovered to a plateau of ~22 per cent. The pandemic and recent economic disruptions, as well as political tensions between Western countries and China, have produced a levelling-off of the trajectory.

   Both periods of globalization were in part driven by technological innovation, and they involved major economic change. During the nineteenth century and early twentieth steamships and railways revolutionized transportation. The telegraph, followed by the telephone, transformed communication. Mass production lines allowed for the large-scale manufacture of standardized goods in a relatively short period of time. The

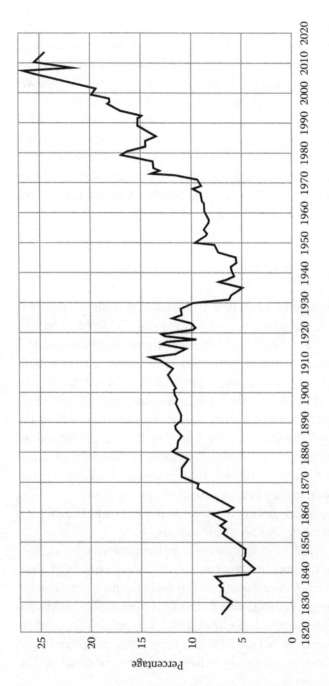

Figure 1: Value of world exports as a share of world GDP. From Petri and Banga (2020), using data from Fouquin and Hugot (2016).

second wave of globalization was facilitated by computers and digital communication, more efficient shipping (containers and cargo flights), improved manufacturing systems and high-yield intensive agriculture.[8]

The graph in Figure 2, from Chancel and Piketty (2021), shows the global Gini inequality index for the years 1820 to 2020.[9] The trajectories in the growth of inequality, and their peaks, as well as their troughs, run roughly parallel to those of the globalization graph in Figure 1.

Chancel and Piketty distinguish two dimensions of inequality, one between countries, and the other within countries. The first is measured in terms of relative GDP, on the basis of the simplifying assumption that the residents of each country earn the same income. The second is determined through distribution of income in each country, normalizing all countries to the same level of GDP. Their data for the past two centuries reveals a surprising and important pattern. While both types of inequality rose during the first period of globalization, they diverged in the second, moving in opposite directions. Between-country inequality declined sharply from 1980 through to 2020, while within-country inequality rose during this time. Their graph, given in Figure 3, shows this divergence clearly.

Globalization in the nineteenth century and early twentieth took place under the colonialist regimes of European countries. They used their colonies in America, Africa and Asia as sources of raw materials and markets for manufactured products, as well as a reservoir of cheap (often enslaved) labour. The rapid industrialization that Europe and North America experienced generated inequality along both dimensions. A large gap opened up between industrialized Western countries and the rest of the world, much of which they had colonized. The distribution of income within Western countries also became increasingly unequal, with the concentration of capital in the property- and capital-owning classes.

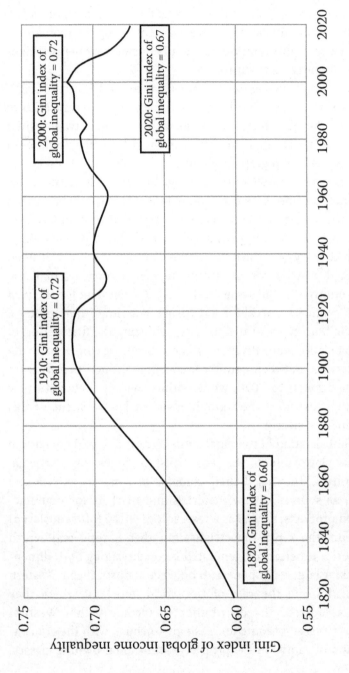

Figure 2: Global Gini index 1820–2020. From Chancel and Piketty (2021).

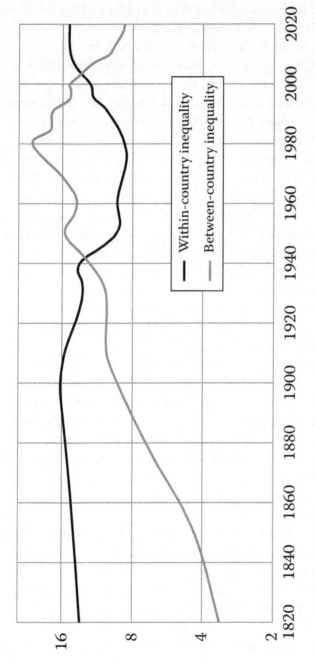

Figure 3: Inequality between and within countries, measured as the ratio of the top 10 per cent average income to the bottom 50 per cent average income. From Chancel and Piketty (2021).

However, the global effect of this inequality was smaller than the trend to inequality among countries.

In the second wave of globalization, there has been a substantial movement of industrial production from the West, most noticeably the US and the UK, to East Asian countries, in particular China and India. This has reduced the difference in GDP between some of these developing countries and the West. It has lifted large numbers of people in Asia out of poverty, However, this process has greatly exacerbated inequality both within Western countries and in the developing countries that have benefitted from substantial growth.

Service industries have replaced manufacturing as a major source of employment in the West. Wages have remained stagnant or declined for much of the middle and working classes. Job security has become elusive, and working conditions have become precarious, with benefits disappearing.[10] Manufacturing towns in many of these countries have been hollowed out, and rural populations have suffered a decline in their relative living standards.

By contrast, the top 10 per cent of the global hierarchy has benefitted from a significant rise, with the top 1 per cent now controlling a very large proportion of the world's income. This has produced a cleavage between people with higher education and technical skills on one side and the lower sectors of the income and education scale on the other. The former are concentrated in urban/suburban centres, while many of the latter are either in rural areas or in poorer inner-city neighbourhoods.

The differential effects of the growth that globalization has generated are frequently represented by an 'elephant' curve.[11] This chart displays the rising share of growth in the Asian economies, concentrated in the bottom 50 per cent of the income percentile, followed by a sharp decline in the middle and lower classes of the developed economies, at the 70–90 percentiles. The top 10 per cent and 1 per cent exhibit a steep rise. The line of the graph traces the outline of an elephant with a trunk at the right. Chancel and Piketty's version of this chart is in Figure 4.

Milanovic (2023) observes that the rapid rise of China's GDP over the past two decades has reduced global inequality, while intensifying inequality within countries, particularly in the West. Middle- and working-class income groups in Western countries have slipped down the global income distribution percentiles during this period, while the wealthy have retained their relative international positions. Milanovic also notes that because India, Africa and Latin America have not experienced the sort of economic growth that China has, they have not contributed significantly to a reduction in between-country inequality. They remain at the lower end of world income, although India has experienced an improvement in its situation.

We have been representing inequality as differences among percentiles of income distribution. It is worth noting that these differences are accentuated when one measures wealth, rather than income. This is natural, given that most wealth is income accumulated through time.[12] The distinction between the two is clearly shown in Figure 5, which gives Chancel et al's (2022) graph for global income versus wealth distribution in 2022.

An additional feature of this issue worth noting is the rapid decline of publicly owned wealth, and the concomitant rise of private wealth, since 1980, in both the developed and the developing world. Alvaredo et al. (2018) describe this trend in detail. It is the direct result of large-scale privatization of assets and services. One of its consequences is that governments have increasingly limited resources for providing universally accessible public services, available to lower-income groups. The privatization of rail, water and energy companies in the UK, as well as the sale of British local council housing, illustrates this phenomenon.

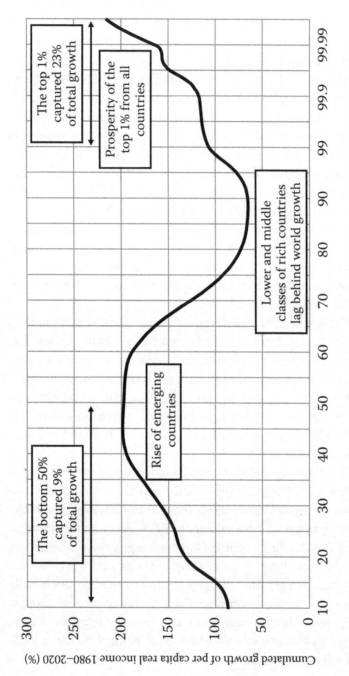

Figure 4: An elephant curve of global income distribution from 1980 to 2020. From Chancel and Piketty (2021).

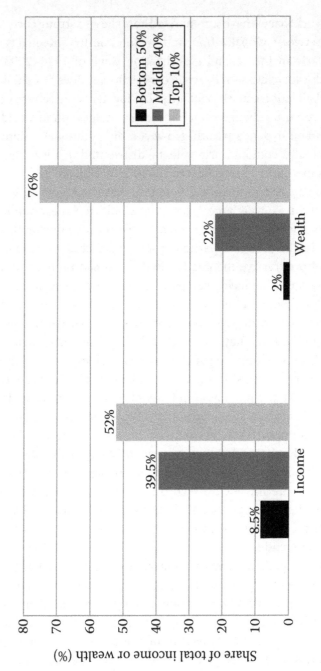

Figure 5: Global income and wealth distribution for 2022. From Chancel et al. (2022).

The work that we have summarized here shows a strong correlation between globalization and within-country inequality, particularly in the second globalization wave of 1970–2008. While the correlation indicates a connection, it does not show that globalization causes inequality. The former is the vehicle of major economic change, which increases integration of world markets and expands wealth. However, the additional wealth that it creates could, in principle, be distributed in a way that reduces in-country inequality, or that leaves it unaffected.

The sharp rise in income differences that has accompanied globalization is, to a large extent, the result of the economic and social policies that governments have adopted during this period. In the West, in particular, the redistributive mechanisms of progressive income tax and the social programmes of the welfare state have been pared down. Advocates of these 'supply side' policies justify them on the grounds that tax and spending cuts create growth and increase employment, while avoiding inflation. They reason that the resulting inequality is the price of economic expansion, which trickles down to the lower income groups. In fact, the available evidence strongly indicates that the main assumptions of this view are false. In a study of eighteen Organisation for Economic Co-operation and Development (OECD) countries, for the years 1965–2015, Hope and Limberg (2020) show that tax cuts on the highest income brackets produce significant inequality, but they have no measurable impact on GDP or employment. Hope and Limberg demonstrate that these effects are robust, at least through the medium term from the point in time when the tax cuts are made.

Although globalization, in itself, cannot be regarded as the agent of inequality, it has been accompanied by wrenching economic and social dislocation among large numbers of people who have not benefitted from the growth that it has yielded. This is particularly true of the pressed middle and lower classes in developed economies, and the rural poor, both in the West and in the developing world. That many governments have not managed these transitions in a way that ameliorates their effects has created a deep sense of abandonment and helplessness among those who have lost out in the new economy that emerged after the postwar era.

Many of these people associate globalization with the dispossession that they have experienced. They have come to regard the educated urban beneficiaries of this economy as manipulators of a system that has cast them aside. While the roots of their discontent may be economic and class based, they are increasingly prone to express their frustrations in cultural and ethnic terms. This has led to cultural warfare, in which ethno-nationalist politicians have mobilized working-class and rural people for a campaign against cosmopolitan elites. They portray the beneficiaries of the globalized economy as agents of exploitation and as a malign foreign influence. On the opposing side of this clash, much of the left has become gentrified, and it has lost touch with large swaths of the disadvantaged classes it once represented. Its supporters now view them with fear and contempt.

The three forms of extremism that dominate current radical political activism have all defined themselves as responses to what they take to be the effects of globalization. In fact, the main driver of this response appears to be the growing concentration of wealth upwards in a diminishing sector of the income scale. This effect is largely the result of economic policy choices, which are neither wise nor inevitable. However, globalization has helped to generate the disruption of traditional social patterns, through outsourcing of manufacturing, an influx of immigrants and changing demographic profiles. Alongside rising inequality, these changes have produced a growing sense of acute disaffection among those who are disproportionately affected by them.

These movements are, then, anti-globalist reactions to growing inequality combined with rapid economic and social change. The 'populist' character of anti-globalist movements derives from their view that the beneficiaries of the new economy are members of an international elite. They see this elite as orchestrating the world economic and political order for the purpose of enriching themselves at the expense of those who have been left behind by rapid change.[13]

The advent of social media has catalysed the formation of radical anti-globalism by giving extreme voices access to instant publication, with universal accessibility. Mainstream news media have increasingly lost traction in this environment, where many people have come to rely on X (formerly Twitter), Facebook, Instagram, YouTube and Tik Tok for their news and their understanding of events. The tech companies that host these platforms frequently amplify extreme views and disinformation campaigns, to maximize the advertising revenue that they generate.[14]

Social media are a product of the digital revolution that has facilitated the second wave of globalization. They did not create the extremist movements that use them to propagate their views. Such movements have taken over societies in the past, without the benefit of digital technology. However, these media have greatly promoted the dissemination and entrenchment of extremism across the world. They allow one to broadcast one's thoughts to millions of followers through posts typed or videoed on a mobile phone, without filter or intermediary. The power of mass communication is now available, at minimal cost, to anyone who cares to use it, for whatever purpose they wish to pursue. Radical purveyors of disinformation and conspiracy theories have made strikingly effective use of this inexpensive route to influence. The result is that very large numbers of social media users are exposed to ideas and information from a very limited set of highly partisan sources. They are not forced to contend with alternative news or opinions that run counter to the extreme attitudes that they are consuming. This creates a closed propaganda loop designed to reinforce ungrounded and dangerous attitudes.

1.4 Jews and Conspiracies: The Origins of Political Antisemitism

The first period of globalization in the nineteenth century was marked by rapid growth through industrialization in Europe and North America. Figure 6 shows the increase in the GDP of different regions from 1820 to 1913. European output increased from 30 per cent of World GDP to 46 per cent in this time. Much of this growth was concentrated in Western Europe. It produced major changes in the economic and social structure of the continent. Large sections of the peasant and rural population were displaced. Urbanization increased rapidly. Traditional craftspeople lost their livelihoods to manufacturing. A growing industrial working class filled the cities, experiencing comparatively low wages and poor living conditions. The professional and commercial middle classes expanded in size and political influence. As we saw in Figures 2 and 3, there was a significant rise in both between-country and in-country inequality during this century, and Europe was part of this pattern.

These economic and social changes were accompanied by political conflicts. The nineteenth century saw the rise of nationalism in Europe, with cultural and linguistic communities demanding independence from multinational empires and the aristocratic regimes that ruled them. The initial wave of revolutionary uprisings in 1848 was both nationalist and democratic in character. These uprisings demanded sovereignty and free political institutions. They did not, however, succeed in displacing the empires and the aristocracies at which they were directed. In the latter half of the century the movements for nationalism and democracy tended to diverge.

Many nationalist groups took on an exclusionary ethno-centric focus. Revolutionary socialists and anarchists pursued the struggle for democracy. Extreme ideologies and conflict became increasingly dominant elements of European public life. Xenophobia and antisemitism developed into organized political forces. These movements were, at least in part, fuelled by a reaction against rapid industrialization, and the social changes that it created.

Until the nineteenth century, hostility to Jews was expressed primarily in religious terms. In most European countries, Jews were the only substantial non-Christian minority. In the second half of that century, with the rise of nationalism, political antisemitism emerged as a powerful force.[15] It traded on the view of Jews as a foreign presence. Willhelm Marr published his pamphlet *Der Weg zum Siege des Germanenthums über das Judenthum* (The Way to Victory of Germanism over Judaism) in 1879, and in the same year he organized the Antisemiten-Liga (League of Antisemites) in Germany. Marr had started his political career as a left-wing democrat in the revolutions of 1848. With the failure of these uprisings he moved from liberal nationalism to ethnocentric pan-Germanism, placing a notion of racial purity at its core. He stressed that he was entirely uninterested in the religious beliefs of Judaism, and that he had no sympathy for religiously based anti-Jewish prejudice. He misappropriated the linguistic category *Semitic*, which denotes a class of phylogenetically related languages of the Middle East and East Africa, to describe Jews as a racial group. This provided the terminology for anti-Jewish racism formulated as a political programme.

Marr promoted a racialized view of Jews as a perverse Middle Eastern tribe that had infiltrated Europe, and that was destroying it through subversion. He painted a lurid image of an existential contest between the integrity of German culture and the Jewish attempt to dominate and corrupt it. Marr maintained that the Jews sought to use emancipation in

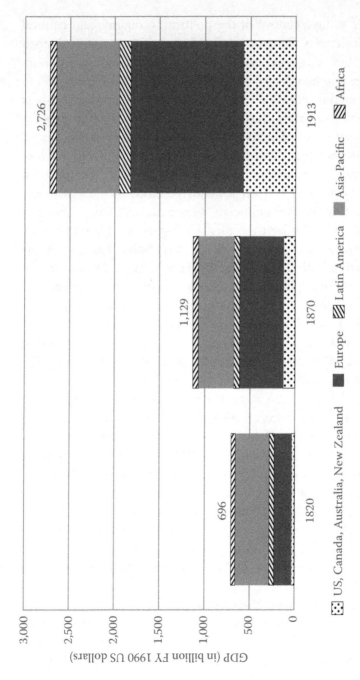

Figure 6: Growth in regional GDP by continent in 1990 US dollars. From Berend (2006), published online by Statista.

order to take control of the political, economic and cultural institutions of Germany, and of Europe in general. He claimed that they sought to destroy the integrity of German culture in order to achieve absolute power in a society where they would remain the only viable cultural presence. He portrayed this as a form of warfare through stealth. He identified progressive democratic movements, particularly social democratic parties, as an instrument that Jews used to pursue their campaign of conquest. He attributed the subterfuge and manipulation through which Jews gain power to their intrinsic racial features.

The Viennese politician Georg Ritter von Schönerer displayed a similar trajectory. He began as a liberal German nationalist and worked with Victor Adler, founder of the Austrian Social Democratic Workers Party (and from a Jewish family), on the Linz programme for Austrian German national independence. By the 1880s, he had moved to a far-right racist view of pan-Germanism. He conducted polemics against an international Jewish conspiracy to pervert Aryan German society. He agitated for a ban on Jewish refugees fleeing large-scale pogroms in Eastern Europe and Russia.

Karl Lueger also started out as a liberal, but then gravitated to a right wing anti-Jewish Catholic politics. He became the leader of the Christian Social Party and served as mayor of Vienna from 1897 to 1910 (his last two years in office overlapping with Hitler's time in Vienna). During this period, he pursued a programme that combined the expansion of social welfare and public building with anti-Jewish incitement. The Nazis used the racialized German nationalism of Marr and von Schönerer as the basis for their ideology, and the welfare antisemitism of Lueger's civic administration as a model for their social regime.

Pseudo-scientific theories of race purporting to show the superiority of White Europeans had been proposed at least since the eighteenth century (taking different forms preceding and following the publication of Darwin's *On the Origin of*

Species in 1859). They were routinely invoked to justify slavery and colonialism. So, for example, Thomas Jefferson (1785) describes Black people as inherently inferior to Whites in physical properties and cognitive abilities. Menard (2001–2) traces the process by which Louis Agassiz, a nineteenth-century Swiss American biologist at Harvard, came to adopt polygenism under the influence of Samuel George Morton, a Harvard anthropologist. This doctrine holds that different races have distinct biological origins as separate species. Both men regarded Black Africans as a lower species than Caucasians.

Racialized antisemitism not only takes Jews to be inferior, but also to be inherently treacherous and malicious in their psychological nature. It claims that Jews are predisposed to seek to dominate Western civilization through devious methods. Unlike other ostensibly inferior racial groups, they are not merely an object of disdain. They are a powerful foreign threat to be feared. They cannot be effectively controlled. Therefore, they must be expelled or annihilated.

The British German thinker Houston Stewart Chamberlain formulated this racialized antisemitism in his two-volume work *Die Grundlagen des neunzehnten Jahrhunderts* (The Foundations of the Nineteenth Century), published in 1899. He accused the Jews of causing all major wars, through financial manipulation, and of being responsible for what he regarded as destructive movements, such as Catholicism and democracy. In his view these movements were designed to destroy Aryian society. Like Marr and von Schönerer, Chamberlain was initially a liberal (in Britain). He became infatuated with Richard Wagner, a violently anti-Jewish cultural figure, and he moved to Germany, as well as spending time in Vienna. He enlisted pseudo-scientific racial theories to promote his claim that Jews constitute the primary danger to the survival and vitality of Aryan Europe. The Nazis adopted Chamberlain's race theories as the basis of their world view.

The German-speaking world did not enjoy a monopoly on political antisemitism in the nineteenth century. The French journalist and politician Édouard Drumont set up the Antisemitic League of France in 1889. He founded the newspaper *La Libre Parole* (Free Speech) to promote his views, and he was a leading figure in the campaign against Alfred Dreyfus. He was a major influence on Charles Maurras, the theorist of the Action Française, an extreme right-wing organization that supported the Vichy government during the Second World War.

Perhaps the most influential text of political antisemitism is *The Protocols of the Elders of Zion*, published in Czarist Russia in 1903. It purports to be the minutes of a meeting of Jewish leaders plotting to take over the press and other instruments of power, in order to achieve world domination for the benefit of Jewish bankers. They plan to do this through the systematic corruption of their host societies. In a series of articles that appeared in *The Times of London* in 1921, the Anglo-Irish journalist Philip Graves exposed *The Protocols* as a forgery plagiarized from earlier texts, most notably a fictional dialogue in hell between Machiavelli and Montesquieu. The pamphlet was used as a standard propaganda tract in Nazi Germany. Unlike the earlier writings of nineteenth-century political antisemites, *The Protocols* continued to circulate widely around the world after the Second World War. It was republished throughout the Middle East, where it was (and continues to be) regularly cited by several Arab nationalist and Islamist leaders in their polemics against Israel.[16]

The conspiracy theory that nineteenth-century antisemitism trades in is a paradigm of replacement theory. It portrays the Jews as the managers of a global plan to take over European civilization and replace its Aryan culture with a degraded Jewish alternative. This is a first-order notion of replacement, where the Jews themselves are the foreign invaders. The contemporary variants of this conspiracy theory that far-right movements promote in Europe and America tend to invoke a second-order notion of replacement. They describe Jews as importing immigrants from developing countries to overwhelm White European society, and to take control of it. In this version it is the immigrants who replace Europeans, with the Jews exploiting them to infiltrate and undermine a White social order.

The replacement claims of political antisemitism invert those of traditional religious hostility to Jews rooted in Christian and Muslim texts. In the latter Christianity and Islam replace the Jewish covenant by divine sanction, superseding its prophetic tradition. Common to both forms of antisemitism is the view that the Jews are an illicit people whose continued existence is an anomaly. They had a place in the ancient world, but they are problematic in the modern era. They are regarded as an obstacle to the realization of a grand historical project, either construed religiously as the fulfilment of a messianic promise, or in secular terms, as the revival of ethnic national greatness.

It is important to recognize that political antisemitism was not exclusive to the far-right ethno-nationalists of nineteenth-century Europe. It also frequently emerged on the left. The French anarcho-socialist Pierre-Joseph Proudhon, for example, advocated a rabidly racist view of Jews. In a diary entry for December 1847 he wrote:

Jews – make a provision against this race which poisons everything by meddling everywhere without ever merging with any other people – Demand its expulsion from France, except for individuals married to French women. – Abolish the synagogues; don't allow them to enter any kind of employment; finally proceed with the abolition of this religion. It is not for nothing that the Christians called them deicides. The Jew is the enemy of mankind. One must send this race back to Asia or exterminate it.[17]

The Russian anarchist Mikhail Bakunin held similar views. He regarded the Jews as a foreign presence, bent on exploiting the poor and working classes through usury, financial manipulation and control of the press. He stated these views in detail in his *Letter to the Comrades of Jura Federation* of 1872.[18]

More benignly, socialists like Karl Marx and Otto Bauer (a leader of the Austrian Social Democratic Workers Party) saw Jewish survival as a peculiarity of the economic roles that they had been forced to occupy in the Middle Ages, and the subsequent distortions of capitalism. They anticipated that Jews would disappear as a distinct ethnic group through assimilation, after the general emancipation that the coming socialist revolution would afford. Interestingly, Bauer did not envisage the disappearance of other ethnic groups in the post-revolutionary order. In a text on the future of nationalities in a socialist society Bauer (1924) proposes a multicultural federative model of socialism in which all national groups enjoy linguistic, educational and cultural autonomy. He excludes Jews from a collective presence in this federation, because he regards them as a deformed national group in Eastern Europe, and a post-national relic in the West. Both the revolutionary socialists of Eastern Europe and the social democrats of Western Europe rejected the Bund, a secular Jewish socialist party, as separatist. They refused to accept its programme for Jewish cultural autonomy within a socialist society.[19]

Many social democratic parties in Western Europe, while officially opposed to religious and ethnic discrimination, refrained from openly condemning antisemitism in their own countries, for fear of alienating workers attracted to its anti-capitalist message. So, for example, the Austrian Social Democrats declared themselves neutral on the issue. They were concerned that, by committing themselves to a struggle against anti-Jewish racism in the Austro-Hungarian Empire, they would weaken their appeal to Lueger's Social Christian base, from whom they were seeking to recruit support.[20]

In general, the European left, like the right, regarded the continued existence of a Jewish collectivity as acutely problematic. For the left it was an anomaly that constituted an obstacle to its realization of the revolutionary project of a fully egalitarian society. This is a further instance of replacement cast in secular terms. The socialist revolution is a non-religious version of the Jewish messianic vision of a redeemed age of universal peace and justice. It supplants that vision, and so the continued historical presence of the people who originally proposed it renders the fulfilment of its successor incomplete.[21]

The First World War destroyed the large empires, most of them multicultural, that had dominated vast sections of Europe and the Middle East. The Austro-Hungarian Empire and the German imperial regime gave way to a set of relatively weak nation states, while the Soviet Union replaced Czarist Russia. The Ottoman Empire was carved up into Balkan countries, a Turkish Republic and a network of European colonial mandates in the Middle East. Political antisemitism turned lethal in Europe in the interwar period, in the hands of Nazi Germany and its fascist allies. Stalinism in the Soviet Union incorporated the anti-Jewish racism of some of its left-wing revolutionary antecedents, as well as Russia's Czarist past.

From this brief summary of political antisemitism in Europe we see its development from a reaction to the economic and social upheaval that produced both nationalism and left-wing revolutionary movements in the nineteenth century into the engine of the Nazi genocide in the twentieth. History rarely if ever repeats itself. It is unwise to interpret current events as a replay of the past. However, there are obvious and disturbing points of comparison between some of the extremist movements in nineteenth-century Europe and those that have come to dominate political life across the world in recent years. In both cases the social dislocation generated by massive economic change has nourished these movements.

I am not suggesting that political patterns in general, and extremist movements in particular, can be reduced to economic factors. However, when these factors cause large-scale displacement and a sense of crisis, people seek security in theories that purport to relieve their anxieties through simple, if drastic, explanations. It is in such an environment of fear and uncertainty that themes deeply embedded in the history of a culture can be transformed into the vehicle for a toxic programme of action.

In the following chapters I will explore how the three dominant forms of anti-globalist reaction that I have identified update versions of anti-Jewish conspiracy theories that drive contemporary political antisemitism. Chapter 2 gives some historical background. It studies the historical roots of antisemitism in Western and Middle Eastern culture over millennia. Chapters 3, 4 and 5 look, in turn, at anti-Jewish ideas in the far right, the far left and radical Islamism. In Chapter 6 I take up the way in which the Israeli–Palestinian dispute has been mobilized as an element of this response. I attempt to disentangle the dispute from the concerns that anti-globalists are dealing with, and to return it to its historical context. I also argue that Israeli politics actually exhibits many of the patterns that we are observing in other countries experiencing anti-globalist extremism. Chapter 7 examines Jewish reactions to the rise in antisemitism. We will see that most of these reactions are backward looking, in that they rely heavily on strategies that were applied to anti-Jewish racism in previous historical periods. These strategies are not well suited to the present crisis. Finally, in Chapter 8 I briefly suggest some possible directions for developing a new progressive politics with which to combat the current extremist threat. These suggestions involve addressing problems of inequality and democracy from an integrated international perspective, rather than as issues that can be effectively handled by individual countries.

2

The Roots of Antisemitism
in Western Culture

The leading idea of this book is that anti-globalization movements share a common focus on identity politics and a sharply anti-elitist rejection of established political institutions. This leads them to adopt conspiracy theories of global power and manipulation. These myths frequently target ethnic minorities and immigrants as the agents or the instruments of this power. While extremist ideas of this kind are always present in different societies, in normal times they are confined to the margins of public discourse. In periods of prolonged economic turmoil they enter the mainstream, as the consensus that sustains the social order gives way to polarizing conflict. In Chapter 1 we saw that the high level of inequality in the within-country distribution of income that has accompanied the two main eras of globalization in the nineteenth and the second half of the twentieth century correlate with the rise of extremist anti-globalist reactions in different parts of the world.

The particular forms of anti-globalist extremism that emerge in a country depend largely on its cultural and social history. Throughout the West and the Islamic world antisemitism is a powerful element in the three types of anti-globalist reaction that I will discuss in Chapters 3–5. It is striking that similar conspiracy theories converging on the same anti-Jewish attitudes are shared across the boundaries dividing ideologically disparate groups, pursuing incompatible agendas. This indicates that these prejudices are expressions of themes that are deeply embedded in a shared cultural history, or, in the case of political Islamism, that are imported from it. It is important to understand how these themes took root in Western culture.

2.1 Hostility to Jews in the Pre-Christian Ancient World

It is often assumed that anti-Jewish polemics first emerged with Christianity. In fact they predate it by several centuries in the Greco-Roman world. A variety of Greek, Egyptian and Roman authors portrayed Jews in a strongly negative light. Most of these commentaries described Jewish religious and cultural practices as unnatural and designed to discourage contact with non-Jews. They regarded Jewish monotheism as incomprehensibly abstract, and as disrespectful of other nations' deities and traditions.[1]

Some of the most hostile of these polemics came from several Hellenized Egyptian thinkers in Alexandria, who promoted an alternative to the biblical account of the Exodus from Egypt. On this 'pro-Egyptian' version, the Jews were a foreign group of subversive shepherds led by Moses, a rebellious Egyptian. They were expelled from Egypt, wandered in the Sinai desert and conquered Israel. Here they set up an outlaw kingdom with its Temple in Jerusalem. The Jews are described as a malevolent, vagabond people, who practise bloody and barbaric religious rites. They are held up as enemies of civilized society. The Jewish historian Flavius Josephus (first century CE) identifies the third-century BCE

Hellenized Egyptian priest Manetho of Alexandria as the source of this narrative. He attributes its development and propagation to Apion, a Hellenized Egyptian commentator who lived in Alexandria in the first century. Josephus defends the Jews against these charges in his work *Against Apion*. The Roman historian Tacitus picked up many of these anti-Jewish claims and recycled them at length in his *Histories*, written at the beginning of the second century CE.[2]

Greek and Roman Alexandria hosted a large Jewish community, which had problematic relations with the Greek and Egyptian populations of the city. These tensions appear to have been caused largely by economic and political competition. They flared into a large-scale anti-Jewish riot by Alexandrian Greeks in 38 CE, with numerous Jewish casualties and destruction of property. The anti-Jewish propaganda that Josephus was responding to may well have been a significant factor in igniting the violence. Greek and Jewish representations (embassies) were sent to Rome to meet with the emperor Caligula to press their respective complaints. The Jewish philosopher Philo led the Jewish embassy, while Apion headed the Greek delegation.

Anti-Jewish prejudice in the classical pre-Christian world was not formulated as a systematic ideology. It had neither the theological grounding of Christianity nor the pseudo-scientific notion of race that drives far-right antisemitism. It generally arose due to competition with other cultural groups, as in Alexandria, or in the context of Jewish resistance to foreign imperial rule. The successful Maccabean revolt against the Seleucid Empire (167–160 BCE), and the failed revolts against Rome in 66–70 CE and in 132–6 CE, were primary instances of such resistance. The occupying Greek and Roman powers had to contend with a fiercely independent people strongly attached to its religious culture. The Jews' refusal to integrate pagan cultural influences into their core religious and social practice seemed perverse and incomprehensible to their foreign rulers.

However, it is worth noting that some of the elements that became central to medieval and modern anti-Jewish attitudes were already on prominent display in the Alexandrian myths and polemics. The notion that Jews are malefactors who exclude non-Jews and are loyal only to their own people has remained a robustly core feature of anti-Jewish conspiracy theories throughout the history of antisemitism. Similarly, variants of the absurd claim that Jews engage in human sacrifice, first raised in the Alexandrian counter-Exodus narrative, has survived as the blood libel, which continues to be directed against Jews even in modern forms. Finally, the view that Jews seek to corrupt their host societies in order to control them has been a mainstay of religious and political antisemitism over many centuries. It too has its origins in the classical pre-Christian polemics. There is, then, a clear historical lineage connecting these prejudices to later traditions of antisemitism that emerged in the medieval and the modern world.

2.2 Anti-Jewish Themes in Christian Theology

The basic elements of Christian theological anti-Judaism are articulated in the New Testament, particularly in the writings of Paul, which make up a significant portion of the book.[3] The most significant of these elements is the charge of deicide. In the New Testament narrative the Jews were directly responsible for the crucifixion of Jesus, whose death they demanded from Pontius Pilate. The latter reluctantly handed Jesus over to the angry mob for execution. The Jews willingly took on collective historical responsibility for this crime for future generations.

The second charge that the New Testament brings against the Jews is their wilful blindness in refusing to accept Jesus as the Messiah and the Son of God. This results in replacement or *supersession*. By rejecting Jesus the Jews lose their status as the chosen people. Their covenant with God passes to the Christian Church, which inherits God's divine mission, and they become a people living in sin and error.

The source of Jewish blindness and the crime of deicide are attributed to the evil nature of those Jews who refuse to accept Jesus as the saviour. This property is presented as intrinsic to at least the Pharisees, who are portrayed as stubborn, legalistic and obtuse to the Christian message of salvation through love and faith in Jesus.

The New Testament view of Jews was developed into a central component of systematic theologies by the early Church Fathers from the second to the fifth centuries.[4] It constituted a body of polemical writing described as *Adversus Judaeos*. The second–third-century Christian thinker Tertullian provided one of the first set of such treatises. Much of this polemic was presented in the context of arguments with non-Orthodox Christians and gnostics. Fredrikson and Irshai (2022) observe that it was part of an effort to distinguish Orthodox Christianity from competing religious groups, among them Jews, and Christian Jewish sects. Jews, Christians, gnostics and pagans coexisted in large metropolitan centres throughout the Greco-Roman world in the Mediterranean region. They frequently interacted socially, and they shared in each other's social and religious events. This posed a clear threat to the emerging Orthodox Church, which sought ideological hegemony.

Tertullian, for example, was concerned to argue against the Christian gnostic Marcion, who sought to de-Judaize Christianity entirely. This led Marcion to postulate two distinct deities, a lesser Jewish deity who created the physical world, as the process is described in the Old Testament, and the higher Christian deity of abstract faith, presented in the New Testament. Tertullian rejects this duality, and he affirms the unity of the Jewish and Christian God. He deals with the Church's replacement of the Jewish covenant by claiming that the Jews systematically misunderstand their own texts. Old Testament laws and practices are intended to be interpreted allegorically, as spiritual commitments rather than physical actions. This argument extends Paul's exemption of Gentile converts to Christianity from the requirements of circumcision and other aspects of Jewish law.

Saint Augustine (the fourth–fifth-century Bishop of Hippo in Roman North Africa) proposes a particularly original theological view of Jews. He maintains that even after the coming of Jesus the Jews have an important role to play in the spread of Christianity. Their continued existence in conditions of oppression and dispersal testifies to their divine punishment for rejecting Christ, and it vindicates the Orthodox Church's doctrines. Augustine compares the Jews to Cain, who was destined to wander the earth as an outcast, protected from obliteration by the mark of Cain. Augustine suggests that Jews must be tolerated and allowed to practise their religious traditions, precisely so that they can bear witness to the consequences of non-belief in Jesus. They are to be permanently ostracized, but they must be permitted to exist. They are, then, a showcase criminal community whose continued presence serves to educate humanity on the necessity of Christian belief. For Augustine, like other advocates of anti-Jewish polemics, the only escape from the Jewish predicament was conversion to Orthodox Christianity.

The anti-Jewish polemics of the Church Fathers established a theology of hostility to Judaism. However, in the Roman Empire, Judaism was recognized as a legal (licit) religion. Jewish communities living within the empire enjoyed protection of religious freedom, and exemption from pagan practices that violated their traditions. Therefore, the theology of the Church did not translate directly into public policy. In 312 CE the emperor Constantine converted to Christianity, and in 380 CE Theodosius I established Orthodox Christianity as the official religion of the empire. This development empowered the bishops of the Church with the authority of state officials. Roman law continued to protect Jewish communities until the empire was officially divided into western and Byzantine components in the fourth century, and the western empire began to dissolve through invasions from northern Gothic tribes in the fifth century.

At this point, legal exclusions and restrictions were imposed on Jews that provided the templates for persecutions in medieval Christian empires and domains. Jews were not permitted to own land. They were excluded from a large variety of professions, and the guilds that controlled them. Many were forced into financial and tax-collecting roles, where they needed royal protection, and they were required to fund the monarch's ventures. A series of mass expulsions forced Jews out of West European countries. Edward 1 expelled the entire Jewish population of approximately 16,000 people from England in 1290, after a century of pogroms in the country, which featured the massacre (mass suicide as an alternative to forced conversion) of York in 1190. Waves of Crusades slaughtered Jews throughout Europe, particularly in the Rhineland, from 1195 until the mid-thirteenth century. They also killed large numbers of Eastern Christians in Byzantium, and Jews and Muslims in the Middle East. In 1246 Jews were expelled from Upper Bavaria, and from the twelfth to the fourteenth century they were periodically ejected from France. In 1253 they were forced to leave Vienna, and in 1288 they were thrown out of Naples.

After an extended period of persecution at the hands of the Spanish Inquisition, 100,000–200,000 Jews were expelled from Spain and Sicily, and in 1496 they were ejected from Portugal. Most of the Spanish and Portuguese Jews found sanctuary in the Ottoman Empire, with others going to the Netherlands and to Eastern Europe. This pattern of periodic mass expulsion continued in the eighteenth century, affecting much of Central and Eastern Europe. While many Spanish and Portuguese

Jews converted to Catholicism, the Inquisition continued to pursue these Conversos, on the suspicion that they were living as *anusim* (Jews who conceal their Jewish identity through outward conversion). The Inquisition extended into Latin America, particularly Brazil and Mexico, where it remained active until 1834.

In addition to expulsions, legal restrictions on profession and pogroms, Jews throughout Europe were confined to ghettos in many areas in which they lived. In the Czarist Empire Jews were restricted to the Pale of Settlement, which included sections of Poland, the Baltics and Ukraine. They were not permitted to live in most of Russia proper. The Pale remained in force until the Bolshevik revolution of 1917. The ghettos were not abolished until emancipation in Central and Southern Europe in the nineteenth century.

A significant trigger for anti-Jewish violence in Europe was the blood libel.[5] This myth held that Jews used the blood of young Christian boys to bake Passover matzah. That Jewish dietary laws strictly forbid the consumption of blood of any kind did not undermine the popularity of the fantasy. The libel originated in England with William of Norwich in 1144. It was followed by a series of similar accusations throughout England, including Hugh of Lincoln. These provoked the pogroms in London and York that preceded the expulsion from England. While the blood libel started in the Middle Ages, it continued to provoke violence and false legal charges well into the modern age. In fact it appears to have been a factor in the notorious postwar Kielce pogrom of 4 July 1946, in which forty-two Jews returning from the camps, and from Russia, were murdered, and forty were injured, by a Polish mob, while the police and the army looked on. Interestingly, the blood libel is a clear instance in which millennia of clerical anti-Jewish polemic generated a species of popular mythology that the Church authorities disapproved of. Popes issued papal bulls condemning the libel over many centuries. This did little to inhibit its spread. It appears to be a clear derivative of the original charge of deicide that the New Testament and the Church Fathers levelled against the Jews. The young Christian boys who are martyred in the myth represent Jesus.

One might have expected that the Protestant Reformation, with its emphasis on returning to the original Hebrew sources of the Old Testament, and removing the iconography, as well as much of the complex theology, of Catholicism, would ameliorate the anti-Jewish content of Christian doctrine and practice. In fact, this did not happen. Martin Luther, the founder of the Reformation in the sixteenth century, initially courted Jewish support, in the expectation that his innovations would attract them to mass conversion. When Jews did not respond as Luther had hoped, he became acutely hostile to Jews as a people.[6] In his book *The Jews and Their Lies*, written in 1543, he calls for (among other actions) the burning of synagogues, the destruction of Jewish religious texts, particularly the Talmud, the suppression of Rabbinic teaching, the banning of Jewish homes among Christians and the removal of protection from Jews on public highways. He described Jews as an evil and corrupt people who threaten the integrity of Christian society. He commissioned demonic images of Jews with pigs (*Judensau*) on churches. Luther's inflammatory rhetoric inspired a series of anti-Jewish measures in Protestant domains in Europe throughout the early modern period. In the twentieth century the Nazis used this rhetoric to lend religious legitimacy to their campaign of genocide. They displayed *The Jews and Their Lies* at the Nuremberg rallies.

In the post-Holocaust era both the Catholic Church and many Protestant denominations have sought to confront their histories of anti-Jewish incitement. Beginning with Vatican II, convened by Pope John XXIII, large sections of the Catholic Church have attempted to redefine their relationship to Jews and Judaism in positive terms. Many Protestant theologians and thinkers have rejected Luther's anti-Jewish views and adopted a conciliatory perspective on Jewish–Christian relations. Welcome as their efforts are, these are recent developments that run counter to a long history of systematic defamation formulated in theological terms and implemented as legal measures.

This history has created a reservoir of images and references concerning Jews that remain deeply entrenched within the fabric of Western culture. They inform a sequence of canonical works of English and American literature that include, among many others, Chaucer's *The Prioress's Tale*, Shakespeare's *The Merchant of Venice*, Christopher Marlowe's *The Jew of Malta*, Charles Dickens' *Oliver Twist*, T. S. Eliot's *Burbank with a Baedeker: Bleistein with a Cigar*, F. Scott Fitzgerald's *The Great Gatsby* and Ernest Hemingway's *The Sun also Rises*. These are not crude pieces of propaganda, but great literary achievements that also feature strongly negative portraits of Jewish characters, shaped by longstanding racist stereotypes. Similar patterns exist in other European literatures. They indicate less about the personal attitudes of their authors to Jews than the role assigned to Jews in the cultural traditions on which these writers draw in shaping their art.

2.3 The Absence of an Anti-Jewish Theology in Traditional Islam

In contrast to Christianity, traditional Islam does not have an anti-Jewish (or anti-Christian) theology. The Muslim Prophet Muhammad initially regarded the Jews as allies in his religious mission, given their common monotheistic commitment. Islamic sources present his prophecy as the completion and perfection of the Jewish and Christian prophetic lineages. Muhammad encountered three Jewish tribes in Medina when he moved to the city from Mecca. These were the Banu Nadir, the Banu Qaynuqa and the Banu Qurayza. They were integrated into the tribal network of Medina. Disappointment and conflict emerged when the Jews did not accept his teaching. The dispute centred on the charge that the Jewish tribes violated treaty commitments that they had made to Muhammad and his army to support him against his adversaries. According to Islamic sources, Muhammad's army slaughtered the adult males of the Banu Qurayza, enslaved the women and expelled the Banu Nadir and the Banu Qaynuqa from Arabia. The nature of the dispute appears to have been political rather than religious.

Subsequently Muhammad formulated the Constitution of Medina, defining the role of Jews and Christians under Islamic rule. This later evolved into the Pact of Umar, which specified the rights and obligations of dhimmi.[7] In general Islam regarded Jews and Christians as fellow believers who had received valid revelations. However, their texts had been corrupted, and they had misinterpreted them, failing to recognize that they anticipated Muhammad's prophetic mission. The Quran, as revealed to Muhammad, had restored the integrity of these earlier prophecies and completed their purpose. The oral legal tradition that follows from this revelation, Sharia law, defines the requirements of a life devoted to God, lived in the light of this prophecy. Dhimmi are protected minorities. They are permitted to follow their earlier religious practises, on condition that they accept Islamic rule, and the subordinate role that it assigns to them. As we will see in Chapter 5, the level of tolerance and generosity involved in the implementation of this arrangement, with respect to Jews, varied greatly across historical periods and Islamic empires.

While replacement (supersession) is a central feature of the Islamic view of Judaism, as it is in Christianity, deicide is not an issue. The notion of Jesus, or any other person, as the human incarnation of a deity makes as little sense within Islam as it does in Judaism. The Trinity is as alien to Muslims' strictly monotheistic belief system as it is to Jewish religious ideas.

Similarly, the traditional Christian view of Jews as agents of evil and the murderous enemies of God's plan for human redemption is not present in mainstream Islamic religious texts and traditions. Jews are regarded as genuine believers who cling to an outmoded and misguided understanding of their own sources. They have been defeated and subordinated by the followers of the authentic prophetic line.

Although a theology that demonizes Jews is foreign to traditional Islamic religious culture, such views began to be imported into political Islamist movements at the end of the nineteenth century and the beginning of the twentieth. As we will see in Chapter 5, Christian-style anti-Judaism and Western ethno-nationalist antisemitism were incorporated into Islamist responses to the collapse of the Ottoman Empire and the rise of nationalism in the Middle East. Jews were identified as the agents of corruption that brought about the abolition of the Ottoman Caliphate, and as the source of Western ideas destroying traditional Islamic societies. This process started prior to the rise of Zionism and the creation of Israel. In recent years anti-Jewish religious themes have become central elements of radical Islamist movements. The result is that the Israeli–Palestinian conflict has been transposed from a clash of national movements over territory into a cosmic religious contest between the defenders of the faith and demonic forces threatening a redemptive religious movement. This has rendered the conflict all but intractable, and it has excluded compromise solutions intended to accommodate the needs of both sides.

On the Israeli side right-wing religious nationalists have increasingly cast the dispute in messianic terms, and so theologized it from a Jewish perspective. In the early history of Zionism, religious Zionists were moderate and pragmatic. They generally aligned themselves with the Labour movement and supported partition plans for Israel Palestine. With the rise of the settler movement in the occupied territories since the 1967 war, a radical strain of mystical historicism has come to dominate the religious Zionist movement. This group regards expansion of settlements in the territories as part of a process of redemption that will hasten the coming of the Messiah. They view their Palestinian adversaries as modern incarnations of biblical enemies of Israel. The more extreme members of this group have adopted obscure Kabbalistic notions of historical events affecting higher cosmic processes that can bring about the salvation of Israel.[8]

To the extent that both Islamists and Jewish messianists have seized control of the dispute between Israelis and Palestinians, the politics of the conflict has left the realm of rational discussion and entered the domain of the mythic. The acceleration of this process over the past two decades has increasingly coloured the international perception of Israel's place in the Middle East. This has had deeply problematic consequences for Jews both in the Diaspora and in Israel, as well as for Palestinians.

2.4 Replacement in Secular Political Movements: The Jews as an Illicit People

As we saw in Chapter 1, nineteenth-century racist antisemites, like Marr, von Schönerer and Chamberlain, regarded Jews as both inferior and threatening. They attributed to them properties of dishonesty and corruption, as well as the intent to control Western civilization. They claimed not to have any interest in the content of Judaism, and to be free of Christian anti-Jewish prejudice. They situated the negative qualities that they assigned to Jews in their biological nature, rather than in their religious beliefs. For the right-wing ethno-nationalists who adopted their ideas conversion to Christianity offers no escape. Only expulsion or physical annihilation of the Jews will suffice. This was the ideological basis for the Nazi genocide in the twentieth century.

While racist antisemitism is clearly distinct from Christian anti-Judaism, it embodies some of its central elements. Specifically, it inherits the traditional Christian view of the Jews as an evil and degenerate people, who stand against the enlightened values of a decent society. It also adopts the Christian idea that in order to achieve full redemption Jews must cease to exist as a presence in the social order. For ethno-nationalist antisemites redemption consists in a national renaissance free of the corruption that Jews have introduced into public life. Racist antisemitism is not disconnected from Christian hostility to Jews. It provides a secularized mode of expression for a particularly virulent strain of this hostility.

What about left-wing political movements? Let's consider the dispute between Bruno Bauer, the left Hegelian, and Karl Marx over the issue of Jewish emancipation.[9] Bauer initially wrote and taught Christian theology and biblical criticism. He developed into a militantly secular Hegelian, advocating a non-religious civil state. His political model extends and articulates the radical republicanism of Clermont-Tonnerre, which we will return to in Chapter 3. In his book *Die Judenfrage* (The Jewish Question), published in 1843, Bauer argued that a democratic state must be entirely free of religious influence, and it must embody the universal consciousness of political enlightenment.

He argued that while the civil state would discard all religion, Christianity represents a superior stage of development relative to Judaism, as it replaces the Jewish covenant of laws with a doctrine of individual faith and salvation. Therefore Christians could more easily integrate themselves into the civic state. By contrast, Jews are part of a community that defines itself through a tradition of religious legal practice. They are members of a collective that runs counter to the ethics of an enlightened society. Granting them political rights would not resolve this conflict, and so Bauer opposed the emancipation of Jews. Neither transferring orthodox Jewish practice to the private domain nor adopting Reform Judaism were viable options, as they did not reconcile the public, communal dimension of Jewish life with the demands of citizenship. The only way in which Jews could join the state as free citizens was to give up their identity as Jews entirely, and to subordinate themselves to the state's laws. Interestingly, while Christians were also required to abandon their public religious commitments in this arrangement, their cultural identity, as characterized by language, social custom and national affiliation, remains intact.

Bauer identifies the Jews as theologically and culturally incompatible with a radical liberal political order. They must disappear as Jews to gain the right of entry to this order, as transformed individuals. This is, in effect, a secularized version of the Christian insistence on Jewish conversion as a condition for salvation. It drives both supersessionist and dispensationalist Christian views of the role of the Jews in the redemption of humanity.

Marx wrote 'Zur Judenfrage' (On the Jewish Question) in 1843 as a reply to Bauer. It was published in the *Deutsch–Französische Jahrbücher* (German–French Yearbook), in Paris, in 1844. The essay consists of two main components. The first is a critique of Bauer's notion of the civil state. Marx argues that while this model grants political rights to its citizens, it does not solve the problem of human alienation, and so it does not ensure genuine liberation from the forces that oppress humanity. This is due to the fact that it is a bourgeois structure that sustains private property and the market relations that commodify human existence. Marx observes that a democratic bourgeois state guarantees freedom of religion to all its members, and so Bauer cannot consistently deny these rights to Jews. In this way he defends the political emancipation of Jews against Bauer's discriminatory claims.

In the second, shorter part of the essay Marx identifies Jews and Judaism with capitalism. He sees them as embodying the essence of the commercial and financial activities that define a market economy. Marx concludes that human liberation will be achieved only when a different kind of community is created that transcends the exploitative structures of capitalism. As Jews are defined by the economic roles that they perform, they will cease to exist in such a liberated society. Humanity's emancipation will consist in the disappearance of the economic patterns that Jews exemplify. The final paragraph of his essay is as follows.[10]

> As soon as society succeeds in abolishing the empirical essence of Judaism, i.e. haggling and its presuppositions, the Jew will become impossible, because his consciousness will no longer have an object, because the subjective basis of Judaism, practical need, will be humanised, because the conflict of individual sensuous existence with the species-existence of man will be superseded.
>
> The social emancipation of the Jew is the emancipation of society from Judaism.

While Marx's political analysis of an enlightened society diverges significantly from Bauer's liberal state, his view on the role of Jews in such a society is not substantially different. They are slated to disappear by virtue of the fact that the economic relations that sustain them, and that constitute their primary reason for existing as a community, will be superseded. This will be achieved not through coercion or denial of rights, but through social transformation. This account anticipates Marx's later view of revolution through class struggle, where a universal socialist society replaces the bourgeois state. Jews will disappear in this society as their economic functions fall way.

For both Bauer and Marx there is no place for Jews as a distinct cultural minority in a rational social order. Unlike other cultures, they are required to dissolve into the fabric of a progressive universal society. In Chapter 1 I mentioned the Austrian social democratic leader Otto Bauer's vision of a socialist federation of nations, in which Jews also have no communal place. It is an additional instance of such an approach. This is, then, the secular version of Christian replacement. Jewish disappearance through conversion is a necessary condition for the historical redemption of humanity.

The hostility of sections of ostensibly progressive opinion to Jewish collective existence, formulated as opposition to 'Jewish particularism', has remained an active current of Western thought throughout the postwar era into the present. The British historian Arnold Toynbee provides a striking example. He regards the Jews as a fossilized relic of an ancient Middle Eastern civilization that has no reason for persisting in the modern world. He finds their continued presence as a people to be deeply problematic and undesirable. Toynbee (1961) states:

This is a great spiritual treasure which the Jews have to give to all peoples. But one cannot give a treasure and at the same time keep it to oneself. If the giving of this treasure is the Jews' mission, as it surely is, then this mission requires them, now at last, to make that their paramount aim in place of the incompatible aim that they have always put first, so far, ever since their experience of the Babylonish Captivity. They will have to give up the national form of the Jewish community's distinctive identity in order to become, without reservations, the missionaries of a universal church that will be open, on an equal footing, to anyone, Jew or Gentile, who gives his allegiance to Deutro-Isaiah's God and seeks to do His will. In our time the Zionist movement has been travelling in just the opposite direction to this. It has not only clung to, and accentuated, the national form of Jewish communal life. It has also put it back on to a territorial basis.[11]

. . .

The Jewish religion is meant for all mankind. So far from its being 'unthinkable' without the 'Chosen People', it cannot fulfil its destiny of becoming a universal religion unless and until the Jews renounce the national form of their distinctive communal identity for the sake of their universal religious mission.[12]

Toynbee expresses his insistence on an end to Jewish collective existence in religious terms that come directly from classical Christian theology. For a historian, his rejection of Zionism is remarkably ahistorical. It takes no account of the Holocaust, which had occurred sixteen years prior to the publication of his book. Nor does he consider the fact that Britain, along with other Western democracies, had systematically denied entry to most Jewish refugees seeking sanctuary from the Nazis, as well as to earlier immigrants fleeing East European pogroms.[13] Like Bruno Bauer, he considers 'the Jewish problem' in theological rather than historical terms, and he comes up with a version of a traditional Christian response.

Toynbee (1969) anticipates the contemporary charge that Israel is the embodiment of colonialist oppression:

Israeli colonialism since the establishment of the state of Israel is one of the two blackest cases in the whole history of colonialism in the modern age; and its blackness is thrown into relief by its date. The East European Zionists have been practising colonialism in Palestine in the extreme form of evicting and robbing the native Arab inhabitants at the very time when the West European peoples have been renouncing their temporary rule over non-European peoples. The other outstanding black case is the eviction of five agricultural Amerindian peoples – the Chickasaw, Choctaw, Creeks, Cherokees and Seminoles – from their ancestral homes in what are now the states of Georgia, Alabama, Mississippi and Tennessee to 'reservations' in what is now the state of

Oklahoma . . . This nineteenth-century American colonialism was a crime; the Israeli colonialism, which was being carried out at the time when I was writing, was a crime that was also a moral anachronism.[14]

The comment is rich in unintended irony. In other writings Toynbee had criticized Western imperialism. Here he ignores the fact that the slaughter and dispossession of indigenous North American peoples was an integral feature of the British colonial enterprise centuries before the creation of the United States, and it continued well into the nineteenth century in Canada. The comment sets aside Britain's history of colonialism in the Caribbean, Asia, Australia, New Zealand and Africa through the second half of the twentieth century. It overlooks Britain's role as one of the leading agents of the North Atlantic slave trade for more than 150 years. Toynbee portrays the Zionists as European colonialists, without considering the history of mass violence and persecution that caused them to seek a national home as a place of sanctuary. He ignores the expulsion of Middle Eastern and North African Jewry. He passes over the fact that Britain ruled Palestine during much of the formative period of the modern Yishuv (the Jewish community of Palestine), in the period of 1918–48, and that it made conflicting promises of national independence to its Jewish and Arab residents.

His primary objection to Zionism and to Israel's existence appears to be motivated less by Israel's actions than by the view that Jews have no right to a collective existence, as indicated by his remarks in the extended quote above from Toynbee (1961). Presumably he would not withdraw the right to sovereignty from Arab (or other) peoples because of atrocities that they had committed in their struggles for independence. His view is an unmodulated forerunner of the extreme anti-Zionist attitudes expressed by some of the anti-globalist activists of today.

In the postwar period liberal multiculturalism began to replace an assimilationist model of civil society in many Western democracies, most clearly in Canada and the United States. On this view distinct cultural groups retain their collective identities without stigma, while integrating into a more federalized common space. The continued presence of minority groups defined by language, religion and custom came to be seen as an enriching factor rather than as an impediment to social cohesion. In this framework Jews were able to find a comfortable social place to inhabit as just one among many immigrant-based cultural minorities.

In the current social turmoil and political polarization multiculturalism is under threat. Right-wing ethno-nationalists regard it as an acute danger to the integrity of their nation. They see it as a concession to immigrants, whom they regard as intent on replacing the nativists as the dominant demographic group. Parts of the postmodernist left use the well-motivated policy of promoting diversity to pursue political agendas in which ethnic and gender identity become the basis for determining virtue and status.[15] Radical Islamists embrace the conspiracy theories of both right and left. Jews do not do well in this environment. They are identified as subversive agents of corruption by the far right, and they are treated as beneficiaries of White privilege by elements of the postmodernist left. For both they are vilified as members of an elite who manipulate instruments of financial and state power to advance nefarious interests. Radical Islamists cultivate and promote this view among their target audiences.

The notion of the Jews as an illicit people has resurfaced with increasing prominence in this context. The fact that it is derived from centuries of European religious incitement, easily transposed into secular terms, allows it to resonate widely. As we have seen, this notion has its origins in a theology that assigns a cosmic role to Jews as a primary obstacle to human redemption. Their disappearance as a people is posited as a necessary condition for achieving this redemption. Secular movements have reformatted this theology in historical terms. It becomes dangerous when it achieves mainstream credibility in an era of intensifying instability, where moderating constraints on public discourse give way to the rhetoric of extremist political movements.

3

The View from the Right

As we have observed, one of the three dominant forms of
extremism that has been sweeping through many countries
over the past several decades is aggressive ethno-nationalism.
These movements are targeting immigrants and minorities,
often through violent persecution. While there is a clear
similarity in the structural patterns that they display across
distinct environments, the cultural context in which they
emerge determines their agendas. Such movements often
unseat established traditions of secular, pluralistic political
life. They come to power by portraying themselves as answers
to an existential threat that minorities present.

Where Jews have not been a significant part of the history
of the society in which ethno-nationalism arises, antisemitism
is generally not an issue. So, for example, the Hindu nationalist
Bharatiya Janata Party (BJP) of India, founded in 1980, is focused
largely on the country's Muslim minority, which constitutes 15
per cent of the population. The Indian Jewish communities
were historically very small (never more than 30,000 in total),
and the majority of Indian Jews have immigrated to Israel
since 1948. Neither religious nor political antisemitism has
ever had a presence in India. By contrast, Hindu–Muslim

conflict has been a central element of the country's history for centuries. Since Modi became prime minister in May 2014, his government has sought to replace the secular democracy that the Congress Party of Gandhi and Nehru established in 1948 with a Hindu nationalist order. His government has presided over a rising tide of anti-Muslim violence. It has pursued a campaign of discriminatory legislation and practice against Indian Muslims.[1]

Jews have had a substantial historical presence in Europe, America and the Middle East. They have played a prominent cultural role in Christian and Islamic societies in these regions. It is here that the ethno-nationalist reaction to globalization correlates strongly with antisemitism. It is worth noting that this correlation frequently manifests itself even in places where the Jewish community has long since disappeared, through either annihilation or emigration (often by means of expulsion). In these cases, it is a cultural reflex, lacking a local Jewish target. This phenomenon holds for some East European countries, as well as in Spain and Portugal.

It is clearly in those parts of the diaspora that sustain sizeable Jewish communities that the sharp increase in ethno-nationalist anti-Jewish racism poses a serious danger. We will consider several of them in this chapter.

3.1 America: The Alt Right and the Quest for a New Confederacy

Since Jews first arrived in the United States in significant numbers in the nineteenth century and early twentieth, they have enjoyed a level of acceptance and integration unknown throughout their history in other parts of the Diaspora. In Europe they had been subject to religious and then racial exclusion, often enforced through violent persecution. Even during periods of relative tolerance in Islamic countries, they occupied a subordinate social role. Both persecution and marginalization fell away with immigration to America. Even in the segregated South, where their situation was occasionally precarious, Jews escaped the racial hierarchy. They were effectively classed as 'honorary Whites', analogous to the position that they had held in apartheid South Africa. For the most part Jews were treated as another (largely) White ethnic immigrant community.

There were, in fact, serious expressions of antisemitism in America, particularly at the beginning of the last century. Between 1890 and 1920, approximately 2 million Jews came to the US, primarily from Eastern Europe, fleeing pogroms and discrimination. A nativist reaction against large-scale immigration from Eastern and Southern Europe and Asia led to the passage of the Immigration Act of 1924 (Johnson–Reed Act), which sharply restricted entry from these places.[2] Part of this reaction was motivated by the desire to curtail Jewish arrivals. Throughout the late 1930s and early 1940s, isolationists and pro-German propagandists agitated against America's entry into the Second World War, portraying Jews as war profiteers seeking to gain from the conflict. Jews faced quotas at many elite universities and social venues through the 1950s.[3]

But in general, in the postwar era, American Jews enjoyed unprecedented freedom and success. They became the first post-exile Diaspora community in Jewish history. They increasingly saw themselves as outside of this history, which they observed from the safety of a secure environment in which they had become part of the fabric of the society that they live in. They came to relate to other Jewish communities, and to Israel, largely as benefactors and philanthropists.

This deep sense of security was seriously undermined in the wake of Trump's election in 2016. For the first time American Jews were confronted with a president whose electoral base included large numbers of White supremacists and far-right extremists for whom antisemitism is an integral part of their world view. Throughout his time in office, Trump made a point of not distancing himself from these groups. Since losing to Biden in 2020 he has been even more explicit in embracing this wing of his coalition. White supremacists are prominent at Trump's rallies, as they were during the violent assault on the Capitol on 6 January 2021. He has repeatedly made hostile statements about Jews, and he has entertained neo-Nazis at his home in Mar-a-Lago. While insisting that he is neither a racist nor an antisemite, he has welcomed far-right ethno-nationalist racism and antisemitism into the mainstream of American politics. Large swaths of the Republican Party have been either silent on Trump's conduct, or actively followed his lead.[4]

An important vehicle of the antisemitism that has accompanied Trump's political rise is the second-order replacement conspiracy theory that I noted in Chapter 1. It holds that Jews are organizing large-scale immigration of 'non-White' people to America in order to replace the resident White majority. This view combines hostility to immigrants with the myth of malicious Jewish power. In the terrorist attack on the Tree of Life Synagogue in Pittsburgh on 27 October 2018 eleven people were killed. Shortly before the assault, the person convicted of the crime posted online texts claiming that HIAS (the Hebrew Immigrant Aid Society) was importing foreigners to destroy White America. At the time Trump had been portraying a caravan of Central American refugees heading for the US–Mexican border as a dire threat to national security. This threat disappeared from his rhetoric after the midterm elections in November 2018.

One of the most potent conspiracy cults to arise within the Trump orbit is QAnon, which first emerged online in October 2017.[5] It holds that the world is run by a cabal of satanist paedophiles, who control the 'deep state'. The cult identifies the leadership of the Democratic Party, as well as a host of senior government and public figures, as agents of the conspiracy. It also regards George Soros and the Rothschild family as integral to the cabal. The QAnon myth presents Trump as the leader of an eschatological battle against the cabal, anointed to save civilization from its predations. Its followers have been active in his campaign, and some were involved in the 6 January riot. Others have committed acts of violence against QAnon targets. The cult has spread to Europe and Japan. It appears to have been a factor in the far-right terrorist group plotting to overthrow the German government and restore an imperial regime. While not specifically aimed at Jews, QAnon incorporates strongly antisemitic themes. Its main fantasy bears a striking resemblance to the one presented in the *Protocols of the Elders of Zion,* and it draws in people receptive to anti-Jewish conspiracy theories. It has become an active and influential part of the Trump wing of the Republican Party.

Trump's success has turned on his ability to galvanize far-right ethno-nationalists into a powerful coalition that has colonized the core of one of America's two major political parties. It is important to recognize that this is not a passing phenomenon. The attitudes that excite this 'base' to action are deep rooted and existed prior to Trump. Mason et al. (2021) show that independently sampled racist attitudes are a strong predictor of support for Trump. They demonstrate these results by analysing survey data tracking respondents from 2011, prior to Trump's appearance on the national political stage, through to 2017, after they had voted in the 2016 election. Levin et al. (2022) show a correlation between antisemitic prejudice and support for both QAnon and Trump. It is certainly not the case that everyone who voted for Trump is a racist or an antisemite, nor do all Republican politicians hold these prejudices. But as Trump's influence within the party expanded, its more moderate, non-racist elements have been marginalized or driven out. Others have fallen into line behind him for fear of losing favour with his supporters.

There is a tendency to see Trump as a radical break from the traditional Republican Party. The brazenness of his explicit appeal to xenophobic impulse is novel, and his chaotic style of government unprecedented in the modern era. But the themes out of which he has fashioned his political career have been gaining momentum within the party for decades. Pat Buchanan anticipated most of Trump's policies. He came up through the ranks as an assistant to Nixon, and then to Reagan. He ran in the 1992 and 1996 Republican presidential primaries. He was a presidential candidate for the Reform Party in 2000. Buchanan advanced a nativist anti-immigration stance, and he was hostile to ethnic minorities, specifically to Jews and African Americans. He was strongly isolationist, opposing foreign military engagements, or American leadership of international alliances. He advocated protectionist tariffs to support American industry. Although he failed to win office, the views that he promoted remained influential within the Republican Party.

The Tea Party, which emerged as an anti-establishment rebellion within the Republican Party in 2009, was ostensibly focused on a right-wing 'libertarian' programme of low taxes, fiscal restraint and small government. In fact it channelled far-right, anti-elitist frustrations into a campaign of vilifying Barack Obama and the Democrats generally, while obstructing any form of bipartisan cooperation in Congress. It invoked the idea of reclaiming America from an urban elite that had misappropriated it from the 'ordinary Americans' who are its rightful custodians. Part of the movement was strongly anti-immigrant and racist. Its supporters were fierce defenders of gun rights and opponents of government social programmes. After it disbanded, the insurgency that it had energized provided the momentum for Trump's Make America Great Again (MAGA) movement.[6] It is certainly the case that the MAGA movement departs from the traditional conservatism of Republican leaders like the Bushes. However, it did evolve from elements that have long been influential among Republicans. There is a clear line of political descent from Buchanan through the Tea Party to Trump.

Trump suffered a serious setback in the midterm elections of 2022, with many of his endorsed candidates going down to defeat. Support for the myth of 2020 voting fraud, which he used to incite the 6 January Capitol riot, proved to be a disadvantage in many midterm contests. However, even if Trump should withdraw from the political scene entirely, the coalition that he has activated is unlikely to dissipate in the near future. More efficient authoritarian leaders may well lay claim to it. Such a figure could operate with greater respect for the appearances of propriety, while continuing to exploit the bigotry that Trump has used as his primary recruiting tool. They might rely on subtler encodings of Trump's message, but they would pursue a similar agenda. Several possible claimants to this mantle have already appeared on the horizon.

Some of Trump's former close officials, as well as members of his family, are Jewish. Similarly, several of his enthusiastic supporters and members of his previous administration are African Americans. He is happy to accept fealty from any source, regardless of background. This in no way alters his profile as the leader of a far-right authoritarian movement animated by the desire to establish a neo-Confederate order in which nativist, White nationalist and fundamentalist Christian norms prevail. The presence of a few individuals from targeted ethnic minorities in his entourage provides decorative cover for a movement that sees these minorities as a major cause of its frustrations.

America is home to approximately 6 million Jews. This is the second-largest Jewish community in the world, surpassed only by the Jews of Israel (slightly over 7 million), and it makes up 39 per cent of the world's 15.3 million Jews.[7] Throughout most of its history, and certainly during the postwar era, they have lived in the glow of American exceptionalism, the idea that the United States is a uniquely secure, welcoming liberal democracy, free of the persecution they had suffered in the places that they or their ancestors had come from. America is now at a crossroads where the long-term viability of its democracy is being tested.

The forces that Trump has unleashed within the mainstream of American politics constitute an existential threat to this democracy. Jews were largely exempt from the racist oppression that the old Confederacy and its Jim Crow successor institutionalized. It is not at all clear that they would be insulated from the racism of the neo-Confederacy that the hard core of MAGA seeks to construct. Such a social order would be universal in its aspirations, rather than regional. Its outlines are clearly visible in the recent rulings of the Supreme Court that roll back voting rights, abortion rights and affirmative action programmes. These rulings bear more than a passing resemblance to the attack on civil rights that the Supreme Court launched at the end of the nineteenth century, as part of a campaign to dismantle the achievements of Reconstruction.[8] The assault by far-right activists on the teaching of America's history of racial injustice in schools, their attempt to censure 'controversial' books in school libraries and their efforts to introduce Christian religious observance in public institutions have transformed the educational culture of the country. The continuing political crisis in the US has overturned many of the myths of American exceptionalism. In doing so, it has also cast doubt on the durability of American Jewish exceptionalism.

3.2 Neo-Fascism in Europe

Parallel far-right movements have been moving into the mainstream throughout Europe over the last two decades. In Western Europe many of these parties have historical roots in traditional fascist and pro-Nazi organizations, but they have sought to modernize themselves. They have purged the more extreme expressions of overt racism and antisemitism with which they started out, in order to cultivate an image of democratic respectability. Their focus is on opposing immigration, and cultural pluralism. They target Muslims as a threat to the native cultures of their respective countries. While insisting that they are not antisemites, they frequently promote revisionist accounts of the Second World War and downplay the significance of the Holocaust. They are hostile to the European Union as an encroachment on national sovereignty, even if they recognize the practical necessity of a single European market. These parties seek protectionist tariffs to shield local industry and agriculture from global competition. They are also distrustful of military and political alliances like the North Atlantic Treaty Organization (NATO). In many places they have largely displaced the centre right conservative parties that were once dominant forces of both opposition and government. They have also made significant inroads into the working-class constituencies of social democratic parties.

The European far-right parties resemble Trump's MAGA coalition in harnessing ethno-nationalist grievance as their primary source of energy, and they embrace many of the same policy positions. However, there are two important points of divergence worth noting. First, while the MAGA insurgency has been dragging the Republican Party to an ever more extreme right-wing posture, its European counterparts have sought to project the appearance of relative moderation for the sake of electability, even while retaining much of the substance of their earlier extremist incarnations. Second, Trump's wing of the Republican Party continues the Tea Party's 'libertarian' hostility to social programmes and government involvement in the economy. Despite insisting that he would defend the interests of his economically disadvantaged voters, Trump followed longstanding Republican precedent by enacting a massive tax cut for the wealthy and the corporate sector. By contrast, the European far right sustains the 'welfare fascism' of its historical antecedents. It advocates expanded government support for the native working class and rural poor, while seeking to exclude immigrants and other 'undeserving' minorities from most of these benefits.

The French National Rally is a paradigm of the current wave of West European far-right parties. Until 2018 it was known as the National Front, founded by Jean-Marie Le Pen in 1972. Le Pen engaged in inflammatory anti-Muslim and anti-Jewish rhetoric, as well as dismissing the importance of the Holocaust. He was an apologist for Pétain and the collaborationist Vichy government. His daughter Marine Le Pen took over the leadership of the National Front in 2011 and set about reconstructing its image as a party that officially eschews racism. She expelled her father in 2015 as part of this process. The National Front/National Rally has frequently come second in presidential elections since 2002, and it increased its representation in the French parliament during this period. In the second-round run-off of the presidential election of 2022 Le Pen received 41.5 per cent of the vote to Emmanuel Macron's 58.4 per cent. Jordan Bardella took over as leader of the party in November 2022, while Le Pen remains in charge of the National Rally's parliamentary group.

The French journalist and television commentator Éric Zemmour ran to the right of Le Pen in 2022. He is even more stridently anti-immigrant and hostile to Muslims than the National Rally. Although he is the son of Jewish immigrants from Algeria, he has sought to exculpate the Vichy regime from responsibility for the deportation of Jews from France to Auschwitz, and he has expressed doubt about the innocence of Alfred Dreyfus. Zemmour shares the National Rally's hostility to multiculturalism. He insists on the complete assimilation of all minorities into native French culture.[9] The National Rally is a blend of militantly conservative French republicanism and a Pétain-coloured revanchist view of French history. Zemmour takes these currents to even greater extremes. Although he generated considerable excitement on the far right in the 2022 election, he did not achieve electoral success.

Although the National Rally does not target Jews directly, the nativist ethno-nationalism that it promotes constitutes a serious threat to organized Jewish life. It attracts support from neo-fascist antisemites for whom Jews remain irredeemably foreign in France, and in Europe generally. This hostility to Jewish collectivity has strong roots in traditional French republicanism of the sort that both the National Rally and Zemmour purport to promote.

In his 'Speech on Religious Minorities and Questionable Professions', delivered to the National Assembly on 23 December 1789, Count Stanislas Marie Adélaïde de Clermont-Tonnerre expressed the classical French republican view of the place of Jews in a civic society.

> We must refuse everything to the Jews as a nation and accord everything to Jews as individuals. We must withdraw recognition from their judges; they should only have our judges. We must refuse legal protection to the maintenance of the so-called laws of their Judaic organization; they should not be allowed to form in the state either a political body or an order. They must be citizens individually. But, some will say to me, they do not want to be citizens. Well then! If they do not want to be citizens, they should say so, and then, we should banish them. It is repugnant to have in the state an association of non-citizens, and a nation within the nation.

This variety of republicanism rejects the sort of pluralism that is integral to a liberal democracy, insisting, instead, on cultural uniformity as the price of civic rights and equality. Interestingly, militant secularism (*laïcité*) was traditionally a cause of the French and, more generally, the European left. As we discussed in Chapter 2, Bruno Bauer, the left Hegelian philosopher, disagreed with Marx on Jewish emancipation. Marx endorsed emancipation, and he held that Jews would disappear as a people with the demise of capitalism through the workers' revolution. Bauer argued that Jews should be denied political and civic rights unless they abandoned Jewish religious practise and communal affiliations. It is important to observe that neither saw any positive value in Jewish culture, history or communal life. Both envisaged the absorption of the Jews into a non-Jewish European mainstream as a necessary condition for achieving an enlightened social order. The far right in France now invokes radical secular republicanism as a core element in its campaign against immigrants and multiculturalism.

There are 440,000 Jews in France today, the third largest community in the world. Many of them are descended from North African Jewish refugees, who were expelled in the 1950s and 1960s, after their ancestors lived in these countries for millennia. It is a vibrant community whose members have enjoyed considerable success in France. They are now caught between a serious threat from the far right, deadly attacks from Islamist extremists and hostility from the far left. This has produced a rising tide of anti-Jewish violence, which has caused an increasing number of French Jews to leave the country, many of them immigrating to Israel.

The trajectory of the Sweden Democrats (SD) resembles that of the National Rally. Originally a party with neo-Nazi roots, Jimmie Åkesson, its leader since 2005, has transformed it into a mainstream party of the far right, officially rejecting racism and antisemitism. However, it continues to attract large numbers of both racists and antisemites, who are frequently purged from the party when they make ill-judged statements that reveal their true sympathies. SD policies align with those of the National Rally. They are anti-immigrant, hostile to Muslims and staunchly nativist in outlook. They subscribe to the protectionist, nativist welfare views that characterize other far-right European parties. The SD has steadily increased its parliamentary representation over the past twenty years, and in the 2022 Swedish election they became the second-largest party, with 20.5 per cent of the vote. Their support (from outside the government) keeps the conservative coalition, led by the Moderate Party, in power. The Jewish community in Sweden is small (15,000–20,000). The rise of the SD, together with increasing radical Islamist violence and extreme far-left anti-Israel sentiment, has placed them under the same three-pronged threat that challenges other Jewish communities in Europe and America.

In Italy, Giorgia Meloni, leader of the Brothers of Italy (Fratelli d'Italia (FdI)), was elected prime minister in 2022. The FdI is derived from the National Alliance, which emerged from the neo-fascist Italian Social Movement (Movimento Sociale Italiano (MSI)). Like other radical right leaders in Europe, Meloni has sanitized her party to eliminate explicit expressions of racism or fascism. Traditional Italian fascism was not initially anti-Jewish, but it went on to adopt Nazi race laws in 1938, in part under pressure from the Germans. The FdI's core policies converge on those of the National Rally and the SD. It constitutes a clear threat to cultural pluralism and to liberal democracy. To the extent that it succeeds in promoting ethno-nationalist nativism, it will intensify the difficulties that Italy's 27,000 Jews contend with.

While right-wing ethno-nationalist politics poses a serious threat to liberal democracies throughout Western Europe, it is in Eastern Europe that it has achieved a particularly far-reaching impact, most spectacularly in Russia. In the course of the two decades since he came to power, Vladimir Putin has systematically dismantled the weak institutions of post-Soviet democracy that he inherited from Boris Yeltsin. He has constructed a deeply repressive authoritarian state that rules through his security agencies and the oligarchs whom he has favoured with influence. Putin has replaced independent media with a government-run propaganda machine that completely dominates the flow of information into the country. He has imprisoned or eliminated his most vocal critics. He pursued bloody wars in Chechnya in 1999–2000 and in Georgia in 2008. He annexed Crimea in 2014, and he initiated conflict with Ukraine by using Russian separatists to seize the eastern Donbas region. In February 2022, he launched a full-scale invasion of Ukraine. His campaign there has been distinguished both by the repeated failure of his military operations and the extreme brutality of his relentless assaults on civilian targets.

Putin justifies his military adventures by claiming that the territories that he demands contain ethnic Russian populations, and they are an integral part of the extended Russian homeland. This is a revival of a traditional imperial vision of a Greater Russia, incorporating the countries that had achieved independence after the dissolution of the Soviet Union. It is reminiscent of the pretext that Hitler invoked for the annexation of Austria, Czechoslovakia and Poland. The pan-Slavic Russian nationalism that Putin promotes has its roots in a reactionary neo-Czarist ideology that is deeply hostile to liberal values. It sees the West as an existential threat to Russia's interests, and the repository of decadent forces that threaten the civilization he seeks to protect. Snyder (2018) shows that Putin draws inspiration from the Russian fascist thinker Ivan Ilyan, who admired Mussolini and Hitler. Ilyan was expelled from the Soviet Union in 1922 for anti-Communist activities. He took up residence in Germany and worked for several Nazi agencies, until he was forced to move to Switzerland in 1940.

Aleksandr Dugin is one of Putin's influential propagandists. He is a purveyor of the current ultra-nationalist pan-Slavism that Putin adheres to. Like West European far-right parties, both Putin and Dugin insist that they reject racism and antisemitism. However, as Stanley and Stern (2022) observe, they identify their adversaries through qualities that have often been used to vilify Jews. Specifically, they regard cosmopolitans, modernists and liberals as destroyers of society. They are conducting an ongoing campaign against advocates of civil society, democratic reform and the lesbian, gay, bisexual, transgender and queer (LGBTQ) community. Putin is waging his war on Ukraine under the bizarre claim that the country is run by drug-addled Nazis. Russia's Foreign Minister, Sergei Lavrov, was asked how this assertion could be reconciled with the fact that Ukraine's president, Volodymyr Zelenskyy, is openly Jewish, and part of his family was murdered in the Holocaust. He replied by suggesting that Hitler had Jewish ancestry and stating that many of the worst antisemites were Jews. The clear purpose of this inversion is to deprive the charge of Nazism of its usual meaning, allowing it to be applied as a weapon against any arbitrarily chosen target, Jews prominently among them.

Far-right parties in the West have generally been supportive of Putin. They recognize in him an ideological ally pursuing an agenda similar to their own. Trump has been consistently friendly towards him, both during his presidency and in recent years. Fox News has provided sympathetic coverage of the Russian version of events in Ukraine, with Tucker Carlson acting as a Putin cheerleader. The Trump wing of the Republican Party has been unenthusiastic about the extensive level of military and economic support that the Biden administration is providing for the Ukrainian war effort. Viktor Orbán is a loyal Putin advocate, attempting to obstruct European Union sanctions and NATO military aid.[10] Even when leaders of some of the far-right parties condemn Putin's invasion of Ukraine, they refrain from supporting the Ukrainian people's courageous defence of their country. As we will see in the next chapter, much of the far left has adopted a similarly ambivalent position, effectively providing apologetics for Putin's war of aggression. For his part Putin has been promoting far-right movements abroad for many years, both because of ideological concurrence, and as instruments for destabilizing Western democracies.

The war in Ukraine has obscured the difference between liberal and illiberal regimes in at least one interesting case. Poland's Law and Justice Party, founded in 2001, is a right-wing nationalist movement with a reactionary, Catholic orientation. It has exhibited hostility to Jewish concerns, particularly in connection with the historiography of Polish–Jewish relations under German occupation during the Second World War. Law and Justice has been in power since 2015, and during this time it has systematically weakened liberal democratic institutions. It has subordinated the judiciary to political control, and it has curtailed the independence of parts of the media. The government that it leads has strengthened the role of the Church in public life and restricted women's rights and LGBTQ liberties. It rejects non-European immigration, and it upholds a strongly nativist brand of conservatism. But unlike Hungary, Poland is staunchly opposed to Putin's military adventures, recognizing the acute threat that they pose to Polish independence. Poland has been a stalwart ally of Ukraine, and a generous host to many of its refugees.

In Poland's recent parliamentary election on 15 October 2023, the Law and Justice Party appears to have lost its ability to form a governing coalition. Donald Tusk's liberal centrist Civic Platform Party seems to be in a position to take over as the main component of the country's next government.

Putin's war against the Ukraine is inflicting appalling devastation on the Ukrainian people. His attacks on civilian targets and infrastructure reprise the tactics that he used in Syria to support the Assad regime. Putin is also visiting carnage on his own army, whose soldiers he uses as disposable pawns in his imperial campaign. The war has put Russia's 145,000 remaining Jews in an untenable position. In addition to the hardship that the war is imposing on all Russians, the Jews face a particular threat. As Putin's military efforts flounder and he resorts to increasingly desperate methods to sustain domestic support, his need to deflect frustration to suitable targets of blame is becoming more pressing. Facing a steadfast Jewish president in Ukraine, who presents a heroic figure of national resistance, and with several Jews prominently visible in positions of economic power in Russia, the danger of Putin's supernationalist zeal turning toxic for the country's Jews, as well as for other minorities, is quite clear.

Putin's alliance with Iran, on which he has become dependent for weapons supplies, has caused him to take an increasingly hostile attitude to Israel. Many Russian Jews recognize the threat that he poses to them, and they are leaving in growing numbers. If this pattern continues, a community that had thrived in the post-Soviet era may be emptied out, with many going to Israel, to join the very large number of former Soviet residents already there.

3.3 Pro-Israel Antisemitism

The traditional far right has, for the most part, been strongly anti-Zionist and anti-Israel as an extension of its hostility to Jews. Pat Buchanan, for example, claimed that the 'Jewish Lobby' controlled American foreign policy through Jewish financial influence. He attributed American support for Israel, and its intervention in Iraq to the pressures that Israel and the lobby exerted on the US government. He regarded American Jews as disloyal to America's vital interests abroad.[11]

Chiarini (2008) describes the anti-Israel stand of the neo-fascist Italian Social Movement (MSI) in the postwar period, and its gradual replacement by a pro-Israel position in later years, under pressure of electoral pragmatism. Birnbaum (2007) observes that the French radical right initially endorsed Zionism in the late nineteenth century and early twentieth as a means of preventing the integration of Jews into French society. He documents its transition to a militantly anti-Israel policy in the wake of the Algerian war of independence. As in the case of the MSI, the traditional French far right regarded Israel as an outpost of Western democratic power that constituted an obstacle to the nationalist renaissance that the movement aspired to. Both groups envisaged an alliance between Arab nationalism and European neo-fascism. Bland (2019) shows how the British National Front and the British National Party used Holocaust inversion – the claim that Israel's treatment of the Palestinians was comparable to (or exceeded) Nazi barbarism towards the Jews – as an attempt to deflect the stain that the Nazi genocide left on Oswald Mosley's British fascist legacy. They also employed it to forge alliances with some far-left groups, and to recruit support from them. As we will see in the next chapter, parts of the left have, in fact, taken up Holocaust inversion as one of their propaganda tools. It has gained increasing traction in current discussions of the Israeli–Palestinian conflict.

In marked contrast to their historical antecedents, most current Alt Right movements and governments have adopted a pro-Israel stand, while retaining their antisemitic attitude to Jews. Perhaps the clearest instance of this pattern is Trump's support of the annexationist policies of Benjamin Netanyahu's government during Trump's presidency. This support was expressed in his decision to move the US embassy to Jerusalem, and his recognition of Israeli sovereignty over the Golan Heights, which Israel captured in the 1967 war. It seems clear that this policy was not primarily conditioned by commitment to Israel's security or an identification with Jewish concerns. Instead, it appears to have been driven by his desire to appease the evangelical Christians who constitute a significant constituency within his MAGA coalition. An indication of this motive is provided by the fact that he arranged for two evangelical pastors, Robert Jeffress and John Hagee, to lead the prayers at the opening of the Jerusalem embassy. Both pastors have a history of making inflammatory anti-Jewish, anti-Muslim and anti-LGBTQ statements (Haag, 2018).

Israel's former prime minister Menachem Begin began to cultivate the support of American evangelicals when he met Jerry Falwell in September 1981. Since that time, they have become vocal advocates of Israel, generally endorsing the maximalist policies of right-wing Israeli parties, rather than the peacemaking efforts of moderate Israeli governments and organizations.

The evangelicals involved in this alliance generally subscribe to a variant of Protestant dispensationalist theology.[12] This is a millenarian doctrine that holds that the restoration of the Jewish people to Israel is a precursor to the second coming of Jesus, and the final judgement. Part of this prophecy involves most Jews accepting Jesus as the Messiah and the Son of God. This is hardly a philosemitic perspective. It does not turn on a recognition of the Jewish need for a secure sanctuary after millennia of Christian persecution followed by the Holocaust. It assigns a mechanistic role to Jews in the historical process required to achieve the fulfilment of a Christian eschatological vision. As LeTourneau (2019) remarks, this is a 'twisted form of antisemitism'. Inbari et al. (2021) conducted a survey on a large sample of self-identified American evangelicals. They report that belief in the restoration of the Jews to Israel as a necessary condition for the second coming is a particularly strong predictor of support for Israel. By contrast, neither concern with the historical persecution of Jews under Christianity nor the Holocaust display a statistically significant correlation with a pro-Israel position. Interestingly, they also identified a marked decline in support for Israel among younger evangelicals, which confirms the results of earlier independent studies. The dispensationalist evangelicals remain a powerful element of Trump's base.

Another factor in Trump's pro-Israel stance was his transactional relationship with Benjamin Netanyahu. In exchange for Trump's backing, Netanyahu provided him with political support in the American context. Netanyahu also gave him cover by remaining silent over the role of Trump's rhetoric in generating the hysteria that produced the attack on the Tree of Life Synagogue in 2018. When Netanyahu recognized Biden's election victory in 2020, Trump turned on him as disloyal and rejected him. Trump's lack of interest in Israel is reflected in his response to Hamas' 7 October terrorist attack, which was conditioned by his sense of personal betrayal. He issued a sharp criticism of Netanyahu, and praised Hezbollah as 'very smart', rather than expressing any concern with the mass slaughter of Israeli civilians.[13]

A similar, if less personal, sort of transactional exchange seems to be at work with contemporary European far-right parties, most of which have also taken pro-Israel positions. This sanitizes the anti-Jewish bigotry that remains deeply embedded in their constituency, even if this bigotry is officially denied. For his part, Netanyahu does not call out their antisemitism. Orbán continues to portray Soros and liberal 'cosmopolitans' as a major threat to Hungary while being staunchly supportive of Israel. The Law and Justice Party of Poland passed legislation making it a criminal offence to suggest Polish collaboration with the Nazis in the Holocaust, and it instituted a law that makes it virtually impossible for Jewish refugees from the Nazis, and the Communist regime, to reclaim lost property. It remained a reliable ally of Israel, with Netanyahu not criticizing its domestic actions. Interestingly, this situation changed under the centrist Israeli government of Naftali Bennett and Yair Lapid, which was in power between June 2021 and December 2022. During his tenure as foreign minister, Lapid was sharply critical of some of the legislation that the Polish government has adopted on issues relevant to Jews. This gave rise to a serious diplomatic controversy.

Despite the acutely xenophobic nature of Putin's regime, with its strongly neo-fascist orientation, he had, until recently, remained reasonably friendly to Israel. This has now changed due to the pressures of his war in Ukraine. Israel has refrained from participating in sanctions against Russia, or providing military assistance to the Ukrainian army, for fear of incurring complications with Russian forces operating in Syria. It has, however, been unequivocal in its condemnation of Putin's aggression, with large demonstrations outside the Russian embassy in Tel Aviv expressing widespread popular opposition to the war. More significantly, Putin's increasing dependence on Iranian weapons is realigning Russia in the Middle East in a way that deeply threatens Israel's security interests. Putin's announcement that the Jewish Agency for Israel is a foreign organization, and so it would no longer be permitted to operate within Russia, indicates a sharp turn away from good relations. It also poses a serious obstacle to Jewish immigration from the country. Putin has recently supported Hamas and refused to condemn the mass terroist attack that it committed on 7 October 2023. This is part of his cultivation of an anti-Western alliance, which includes his embrace of Iran. Open hostility to Israel and to Jews is now an increasingly prominent element of his regime.

An obvious reason that many far-right parties have come to support Israel is that they see it as a bulwark against Arab and Islamic power, which they regard as feeding the immigrant threat in their own countries. An additional factor is the existence of points of ideological similarity between these parties and the sorts of governments that Netanyahu has presided over in the course of his fifteen years in power. This is even more clearly the case with the new regime that he assembled at the end of 2022. Netanyahu's new government has been pursuing many of the same policies that other Alt Right regimes have implemented. These include the subordination of the judiciary to political control, restriction of the press, rabid incitement against its critics and the deflection of working-class economic discontent through ethnic and racial politics.

3.4 The Alt Right in Israel

From his first period as prime minister during 1996–9 through his continuous tenure in power from 2009 to 2021 Netanyahu has consistently pursued a strongly ethno-nationalist programme that departs from the original principles of liberal democratic Zionism that most earlier governments had officially maintained. While previous governments had adhered to the principle that the Jewish character of the state would depend on sustaining a large demographic Jewish majority, rather than on coercive legislation, Netanyahu's coalition passed the Nation State Law in July 2018. The first three clauses of the Law specify:

A. The land of Israel is the historical homeland of the Jewish people, in which the state of Israel was established.
B. The state of Israel is the national home of the Jewish people, in which it fulfils its natural, cultural, religious and historical right to self-determination.
C. The right to exercise national self-determination in the state of Israel is unique to the Jewish people.

Section 4 reduces the status of Arabic from an official to a 'special language', with the caveat, 'This clause does not harm the status given to the Arabic language before this law came into effect.'[14]

This legislation was passed as a Basic Law, which forms part of a set of quasi-constitutional statutes that the Israeli Supreme Court can rely on to override other laws that the Knesset may pass. Proponents of the Nation State Law claim that it does not overturn guarantees of equal rights for minorities, and commitments to non-discrimination enshrined in Israel's Declaration of Independence, which the Supreme Court also uses to as a basis for some of its decisions. In fact this argument is disingenuous. Given its status as a Basic Law, the Nation State Law could well be invoked to justify discriminatory practices in a variety of areas of public and private life. Interestingly, this law is similar to ethnically and religiously exclusionary principles contained in the constitutions of several Arab States. So Articles 1 and 2 of the Jordanian constitution are as follows:

Article 1
The Hashemite Kingdom of Jordan is an independent sovereign Arab State. It is indivisible and no part of it may be ceded. The Jordanian people is a part of the Arab Nation, and its ruling regime is parliamentary with a hereditary monarchy.

Article 2
Islam is the religion of the State and Arabic is its official language. (http://www.kinghussein. gov.jo/const_ch1-3.html)

The 2014 constitution of Egypt states:

Article 1. Nature of the Republic
The Arab Republic of Egypt is a sovereign state, united and indivisible, where nothing is dispensable, and its system is a democratic republic based on citizenship and the rule of law. Egypt is part of the Arab nation and enhances its integration and unity. It is part of the Muslim world, belongs to the African continent, is proud of its Asian dimension and contributes to building human civilization.

Article 2. Islam, Principles of Islamic Sharia
Islam is the religion of the state and Arabic is its official language. The principles of Islamic Sharia are the principal source of legislation.
(https://www.constituteproject.org/constitution/Egypt_2019.pdf?lang=en)

Both these constitutional clauses and the Nation State Law are accompanied by assurances of equal rights for minorities. These rights are granted within the context of a legal definition of the state as solely belonging to a particular majority group. By adopting the Nation State Law Netanyahu's government moved away from a liberal democratic understanding of the state, bringing Israel closer to the ethno-religious states in the area.

Throughout his period as prime minister, Netanyahu has sought to weaken the judiciary, specifically the Supreme Court, by rendering it subordinate to the Knesset. With his current coalition of extreme right-wing and Ultra-Orthodox partners, he has partially realized this objective by discarding the Reasonableness Doctrine as a constraint on laws that the Knesset passes. He is also preparing the ground for a host of laws legalizing discrimination on grounds of religious, ethnic, gender and sexual identity. This places him firmly in the league of other Alt Right leaders, like Hungary's President Viktor Orbán and Poland's Law and Justice Chair Jarosław Kaczyński, both of whom organized legislative campaigns to undermine the independence of the judiciaries in their respective countries. One of his primary objectives in this attack on the legal system is his desire to avoid conviction on several fraud and corruption charges that are pending against him. By overriding the authority of the Supreme Court he is able to grant himself legal immunity. Like other Alt Right politicians, Netanyahu has waged an ongoing assault on the independent news media, dismissing critical reports as 'fake news' designed to discredit him. He has branded his critics 'leftists' and 'enemies of Israel', whom he accuses of mounting a conspiracy to depose him.

A central element of this appeal to voters is his manipulation of ethnic divisions. He has frequently portrayed Israeli Arabs as a fifth column. He warns the Ultra-Orthodox community that his opponents on the centre and the moderate left will deprive it of religious autonomy and force its Yeshiva students to do army service. He skilfully exploits the cultural resentments and economic disadvantages of many Jewish Israelis from Middle Eastern and North African origin. In this respect he follows the longstanding electoral techniques of conservative American Republicans, who use poor and working-class White grievance to deflect attention from economic policies that intensify their disadvantage. Trump perfected this strategy, but Netanyahu is one of its original master practitioners. Like his Alt Right counterparts, Netanyahu portrays the liberal left as an urban elite devoted to the dispossession of his constituency. Despite the fact that he has held power for more than fifteen years, his diversions continue to succeed. This is, in no small measure, due to the fact that the liberal left in Israel, as in most other countries, is now largely gentrified, economically well established and concentrated in urban centres.

There are a variety of causes for Israel's continuous move to the right over the past twenty-five years. The collapse of the Oslo peace process and the violence of the second Intifada of the early 2000s helped to undermine the credibility of the Israeli peace movement working toward a two-state solution. Hamas' seizure of power in Gaza after Israel's withdrawal in 2005, followed by several Gaza wars, further aggravated this process. The 2006 Lebanon war and the failure of Ehud Olmert's peace offer to the Palestinian Authority in 2008 largely disabled the centre left as a credible force in Israeli politics. Netanyahu was then able to pursue settlement expansion and an annexationist agenda without domestic political constraint. During Trump's presidency, American restrictions were also largely removed.

While these causes are specific to the Israeli scene, there is another factor that is more general in nature. In the first thirty years following its independence Israel was governed by Labour-led coalitions that pursued social democratic economic policies. It had powerful unions, a large government sector that controlled public services and a relatively generous welfare system. Income distribution was comparatively egalitarian, despite regional and ethnic differences. From 1980 onwards, right-wing and centrist governments instituted large-scale privatization of services and liberalization of the economy, that greatly reduced income equality. Private quasi-monopolies became increasingly dominant in large sectors of activity, and the price of housing rose sharply. The emergence of a robust high-tech sector and a financial services industry, both with internationally competitive salaries, contributed to the importance of university education as a driver of economic success.

Chancel et al. (2022) provide data showing that from 1980 to the present Israel has sustained high income and GDP, together with an unusually sharp degree of income inequality, comparable to that which prevails in the US and the UK. This ratio of inequality has remained fairly stable over the past forty years. As we observed in Chapter 1, the rise of inequality from 1980 onwards has shown a correlation with the emergence of political extremism and instability. Israel strongly conforms to this paradigm. Clearly, the behaviour of Netanyahu's Alt Right ethno-nationalist movement is, in part, conditioned by factors unique to Israel. But from a broader historical perspective the connection between Israel's political evolution and its economic development indicate that it patterns like a 'normal' country.

It is worth keeping this in mind when thinking further about Israeli politics. Israel's exceptionalism is frequently emphasized, while its parallels with other countries are ignored. This can, and often does, lead to an inaccurate and unbalanced view of its political life and its historical development.

The drastic failure of Netanyahu's government, the intelligence services and the army to anticipate the 7 October Hamas terrorist attack, or to respond effectively to it, has resulted in a massive loss of confidence in his leadership, and in his policies, throughout the Israeli electorate. These events are likely to transform the Israeli political scene for generations to come. The impact upon it may well be at least as profound as that of the 1973 war, which ultimately led to the loss of the Labour Party's extended hegemony in government and the rise of the Likud as a ruling party. It is unclear precisely what direction this upheaval will take, but it is difficult to see how the current coalition, and much of the country's higher military leadership, can remain in power after the war ends. The reckoning that brings about this process will reconfigure many of the assumptions that have determined Israeli political life over recent decades.

4

The View from the Left

Jews have always presented a problem for the European left. They do not fit comfortably into the traditional European categories of religion, ethnic culture or nation, although they clearly combine elements of all three. Their integrative understanding of themselves and their role in history does not conform to the usual classifiers of Western political traditions, and it marks them as both foreign and familiar at the same time.

From its genesis in the enlightenment and the revolutions in the eighteenth century the left has always regarded itself as the engine of progressive change and human liberation. It championed the extension of human rights to all classes and groups of people, national self-determination and the abolition of social privilege. The left placed itself in the forefront of the fight against economic exploitation and social exclusion. This led it to take up, initially, the cause of the disenfranchised middle classes in eighteenth-century Europe, then moving to the European working class in the nineteenth. It opposed slavery and indentured labour. In the twentieth century, it adopted the campaign for women's rights, racial justice and, in the latter part of the century, anti-colonialism.

Jewish history in both Europe and the Middle East was replete with persecution. A large part of the Jewish population in Eastern Europe was impoverished, and it had become part of the new industrial working class. But the anti-Jewish exclusions of the Middle Ages had forced some Jews into financial and entrepreneurial roles that were regarded as exploitive. Jewish communities in Europe and the Middle East had frequently relied on royal or aristocratic protection for survival, for which they performed stigmatized services (tax and rent collection, and money lending to finance royal activities) in exchange. As a result, the Jews did not constitute a natural constituency for the left, even as many of them flocked to it as a vehicle for emancipation.

Unable to slot Jews into a clearly defined role within their political agenda, most of the left tended historically to regard them with considerable ambivalence, and, in some cases, intense hostility. While supporting universal human rights, the left never saw opposing antisemitism as a primary concern. Instead, it was a secondary issue (if an issue at all) that would be resolved as a side effect of the general social liberation that the left was pursuing. Intrinsic to this approach is the view that Jewish particularity is, in itself, a defect to be remedied through assimilation and disappearance. The most that could be tolerated in an enlightened social order would be a safely constrained religious denominational afterglow, or a carefully sanitized nostalgic folk memory, preserved in curated (and ideologically policed) communal organizations. Any attempt by Jews to make the struggle against antisemitism into a separate problem deserving of the same passion devoted to other progressive causes was rejected as a diversion from the main issues that animate the left. The demand for recognition as a cultural and/or national minority on a par with other groups was vigorously dismissed as reactionary separatism. These attitudes have re-emerged with particular force in the contemporary radical left. They have also spread to parts of the liberal left.

4.1 From Class Struggle to Critical Theory and Identity Politics

In the nineteenth century and first part of the twentieth the radical European left was not particularly interested in colonialism. It was focused on class struggle and socialist revolution in advanced industrial countries. Marx devotes only a brief ten-page chapter to colonialism in the three volumes of *Capital*. It appears at the end of Volume 1, and in it Marx is exclusively concerned with the way in which British landowners in America and Australia turned colonist free labour into hired wage earners. He does not address the dispossession of indigenous peoples, and his discussion of slavery is brief. He regards slavery as the historical precursor of capitalist exploitation of labour. In the colonial context, he sees it as an extreme form of such exploitation.

In Marx's description of British rule in India in his reports for the *New-York Daily Tribune* he characterizes colonialism as brutal and self-interested, but he argues that its economic and social effects are ultimately progressive. It destroys traditional reactionary forms of society, replacing them with more advanced industrialized economies. In his article for the paper on 25 June 1853 he says:

> England, it is true, in causing a social revolution in Hindostan, was actuated only by the vilest interests, and was stupid in her manner of enforcing them. But that is not the question. The question is, can mankind fulfil its destiny without a fundamental revolution in the social state of Asia? If not, whatever may have been the crimes of England she was the unconscious tool of history in bringing about that revolution.

Marx regarded colonialism as an instrument of capitalism in transforming primitive non-Western societies into more advanced economies. While colonialism was destructive and violent, it prepared the way for an eventual socialist transformation of non-Western countries. Like most of his contemporaries in the European left, he saw no intrinsic value in the traditional cultures of colonized countries. He considered them to be underdeveloped and despotic.

In fact history took a different course than the one that Marx had envisaged. In the first half of the twentieth century Communist revolutions occurred not in the advanced industrialized West, but in Russia and China, both economically underdeveloped, with large rural populations and agricultural economies. The Western capitalist countries accommodated reform through welfare states that social democratic and liberal governments constructed in the postwar era. The working classes of these countries were highly unionized and supportive of progressive reform. Their standard of living rose significantly during this period, and they generally avoided revolutionary political movements. Seeking an alternative to the proletariat as the engine of revolution, the radical left turned increasingly to the anti-colonialist movements of the developing world. In the 1960s, the New Left identified these movements as the primary agents of transformational change. The focus of the radical left shifted from class struggle to anti-colonialism and cultural issues. It moved from political economy to identity politics.[1]

Increasingly the radical left, particularly in America, has come to rely on postmodernist ideas and critical theory as the tools for formulating its agenda. It has embraced an updated version of Antonio Gramsci's view that established cultural institutions and received knowledge constitute oppressive devices of social control, which must be deconstructed through critical scrutiny. While for Gramsci social control served the interests of capitalism, for the postmodernist left it sustains the historical legacy of colonialism. The categories of race, gender and ethnic identity have come to replace class as determining the way in which the world is divided into progressive and reactionary forces. From postmodernism it has taken the idea that the demand for objectivity in science and other disciplines is, in itself, an oppressive and ungrounded aspiration, which supports established privilege. Science, and rational enquiry in general, is a social construct that exists within a particular culture and serves clear interests, often suspect.

If the nineteenth-century left was Eurocentric in its rationalist and other cultural commitments, the contemporary postmodernist left is no less so, but in a strangely inverted mode. It takes oppression, racism and colonialism to be exclusively Western diseases. The fact that non-Western empires committed similar atrocities is dismissed as an irrelevance, or simply read out of the record. So, for example, the large-scale colonization of territory, ethnic cleansing and genocide committed by the Ottoman Empire, the latter during the early twentieth century, do not figure in the critical anti-colonialist studies of the current left. The existence of an Arab slave trade in East Africa and Europe that shipped African and East European slaves throughout the Middle East, centuries before the European slave trade to the Americas, is generally not discussed in the context of the radical left's concern with the effects of slavery. None of these facts detract from the horrors of European colonialism and the European slave trade. They do, however, indicate quite clearly that these are not uniquely Western crimes. This is not something that one would learn from the writings of most theorists and activists of the current radical left.

The traditional Marxist left classified social groups as 'objectively' progressive or reactionary in terms of their roles in the class struggle. The working class was designated as on the right side of history, while the bourgeoisie and capital-owning classes were construed as destined to be displaced in the coming revolution. On this view, even bigoted members of the working class were historically progressive, while socially enlightened capitalists were not, unless they actively supported the workers' struggle. This perspective led some left-wing revolutionaries to endorse peasant and working-class antisemitism as a primitive form of class awakening. As we have seen, it also led Austrian Social Democrats to refrain from taking an active stand on Karl Lueger's antisemitic incitement, for fear of alienating his working-class supporters. By contrast, other members of the left correctly identified antisemitism as the 'socialism of fools'.

The current postmodernist left has inherited the notion that social entities are objectively agents of progressive or oppressive politics, but it has replaced class with ethnic and gender identity. Groups that have been victimized by racism, slavery, colonialism, patriarchal control or gender exclusion have taken over the role previously reserved for the working class, as protagonists of positive social change. White Europeans and their descendants are bearers of privilege, even if poor, exploited or ethnically stigmatized. This has given rise to a peculiar notion of intrinsic virtue and original sin that has turned much political discourse on this part of the left into a latterday medieval morality play. It has also produced some rather striking intellectual contortions in which movements that pursue deeply reactionary agendas are glorified as progressive, by virtue of the ethnic identity of their protagonists.

So, for example, the Berkeley literary critical theorist Judith Butler is quoted as saying,

> Similarly, I think: Yes, understanding Hamas, Hezbollah as social movements that are progressive, that are on the Left, that are part of a global Left, is extremely important. That does not stop us from being critical of certain dimensions of both movements. It doesn't stop those of us who are interested

in non-violent politics from raising the question of whether there are other options besides violence. So again, a critical, important engagement. I mean, I certainly think it should be entered into the conversation on the Left. I similarly think boycotts and divestment procedures are, again, an essential component of any resistance movement.[2]

To the extent that this quote accurately reflects Butler's views on Hamas and Hezbollah, these views appear to include the conclusion that the misogyny, hostility to LGBTQ people, theocratic fundamentalism and antisemitism of these two organizations in no way undermines their status as progressive movements of the left.

As we have noted, the postmodernist left tends to restrict its concern with colonialism and racism to the crimes committed by the West, specifically Europe and the United States, against the peoples of Africa and the indigenous populations of Western colonies. Acts of colonial aggression, genocide and mass murder which take place outside this sphere of concern are generally dismissed as irrelevant. In many cases, they are traced indirectly to Western influence, even when the primary actors are not Western, and run into conflict with Western interests. The response of a significant part of the radical left to Putin's invasion of Ukraine is a striking case in point. On 26 February 2022, the Democratic Socialists of America (DSA) released a statement condemning Russia's invasion, but also holding the US and NATO responsible for 'setting the stage' for the conflict. The DSA calls for a diplomatic solution to the conflict and opposes arms being sent to the Ukraine (https://www.dsausa.org/statements/on-russias-invasion-of -ukraine/). The UK Stop the War Coalition, of which Jeremy Corbyn is a leading member, has adopted more or less the same view. It organized a demonstration on 25 February 2022 in which it called for both the withdrawal of Russian troops from the Ukraine and an end to NATO. It also rejects arms

shipments to Ukraine (https://www.stopwar.org.uk/article
/tanks-tanks-and-more-tanks/). Both these groups, and other
members of the radical left, have made it clear that they regard
NATO's expansion into Eastern Europe as a provocation
that triggered Putin's war. They strongly oppose supporting
Ukraine's effort to defend itself against Russian aggression.
Instead they call for a 'diplomatic solution'.

This is a peculiar form of anti-colonialism. When the US
or other Western powers invade countries in Asia, Latin
America, the Middle East or Africa the radical left urges
resistance by any means necessary. They cite the right of a
people to self-determination, and they place the full responsibility for the conflict where it belongs, on the Western
aggressor. These principles are suspended when the invader
is anti-Western, as is Putin. At this point a facile pacifism in
the face of war crimes replaces revolutionary support. There is
a clear historical precedent for this conduct. When Stalin was
allied with the Nazis in a non-aggression pact, the pro-Soviet
left strongly opposed American entry into the war, which it
described as a conflict among rival imperialist forces. After
the Germans invaded the Soviet Union in 1941, this part of
the left reversed its policy and enthusiastically endorsed the
Allied war effort. In both cases the response was conditioned
by narrow ideological concerns. In the current situation we
see not a consistent commitment to anti-colonialism, but
an overriding hostility to the West as the dominant factor in
conditioning this part of the left's response to events.

The current anti-colonialist left's focus on identity rather
than class politics is in large part a reaction against globalization. It sees the neo-liberal corporate economic policies that
have been driving the integration of global markets as a new
form of imperialism that reinforces the oppressive structures
of racism, patriarchy and gender autocracy. In this respect it is
responding with analogous strategies to the same social dislocations that have activated the far right. It also occasionally

arrives at similar policy positions, as in the case of its relative tolerance of Russian aggression against Ukraine. As we will see, like its far-right counterpart, it also frequently resorts to conspiracy theories to explain complex events.

4.2 Jews as Bearers of White Privilege

Jews do not fare well in the ethnic classifier system of the postmodernist left. They are stigmatized as bearers of White privilege, and they are folded in with other Europeans who are marked as benefiting from the legacy of slavery and colonial oppression. The fact that the overwhelming majority of Jews in North America and Europe are descended from refugees who fled pogroms, or who were survivors of the Holocaust, is not counted as a serious objection to this narrative. Increasingly the 'progressive' take on antisemitism in general, and the Nazi genocide in particular, is that while these are terrible crimes, they cannot be meaningfully compared to slavery, or the racial exclusion endured by people of colour and indigenous populations. They were injustices inflicted by one White European group on another, and so they constitute an internal European problem, rather than a genuine case of racism.[3] Moreover, a part of the far left has become increasingly vocal in insisting that the Jews have misused the Holocaust and European antisemitism in order to further a narrow particularist agenda, in a way that detracts from the recognition of other instances of genocide and oppression. This has led to calls for Holocaust education to focus less on the Jewish aspect of the Nazi genocide and more on racism inflicted on all groups that have suffered violence.

The move to bleach Holocaust memory of its Jewish content is not new. It has a well-established precedent in Soviet historiography of the Second World War. Of the 6 million Jews murdered in the Nazi genocide, more than 2 million were shot by Einsatzgruppen in Soviet territory, often with the support of some of the local populations. Soviet historians portrayed the War as a great patriotic struggle against fascism, and its Jewish victims were subsumed under the generic category of Soviet citizens. Memorials that made reference to the Jewish identity of those killed by the Nazis were generally proscribed. Stalin banned the publication of Ilya Ehrenburg and Vasily Grossman's *Black Book of Soviet Jewry*, originally compiled in 1944, because it documented the annihilation of Jews as the prime target of the genocide. The purging of the Jewish aspect of the Holocaust was enforced throughout the Soviet sphere of influence in Eastern and Central Europe. This policy changed only after the fall of these regimes in the late 1980s. Zeldin (2022) gives a vivid description of the experience of growing up in a Soviet Jewish family where he encountered two versions of the history of the war. The official narrative taught in the schools made no mention of the Jewish dimension of the catastrophe. From his family he learned the facts of how his relatives were exterminated. He connects this two-track view of Jewish history with Zelensky's understanding of his own family's experience in Ukraine.

It is important to recognize that the Soviet suppression of Jewish references in official accounts of the Holocaust is an extreme expression of a significant current in the left's attitude to Jews. The longstanding inability of large parts of the left to see in the Jews a legitimate collectivity has led to distrust of Jewish particularism. It has also generated a strong sense among many on the left that antisemitism is a secondary issue, which will disappear on its own in the context of a progressive revolution. Focusing on it as a primary concern deflects resources from those struggles that constitute the left's true calling.

These attitudes have re-emerged with particular robustness in large parts of the postmodernist anti-colonialist left. If Jews enjoy White privilege and are prime beneficiaries of the globalized economy, then antisemitism cannot be a serious problem. Victims of racism, misogyny and gender exclusion must be respectfully listened to and allowed to shape their own historical narratives after generations of repression. Their lived experience takes precedence over documented historical research in determining the validity of their views. By contrast, Jewish charges of antisemitism are received with scepticism as neither credible nor pressing, particularly if directed against members of the left. As Jews are an interested party in such disputes, and they enjoy power, their own reports on issues of anti-Jewish racism are to be distrusted as the complaints of the powerful. Again, there is a clear historical precedent for this attitude. As I noted in Chapter 1, some elements of the nineteenth-century left in Europe regarded the Jews as agents of capitalism. These members of the left were tolerant of certain kinds of antisemitism as expressions of class consciousness, and they were unwilling to take a clear role in resisting antisemitism. In some cases, they actively trafficked in it.

The notion of Jewish privilege has given rise to a number of potent conspiracy theories on the left. One of the most extreme is the claim that Jews played a leading role in financing and operating the transatlantic slave trade. In 1991, the Nation of Islam published an anonymous historical pamphlet entitled *The Secret Relation between Blacks and Jews*, which purports to show that Jews effectively ran the slave market. It comes replete with footnotes and lists of Jewish slave traders and African slaves. A number of mainstream historians have studied these claims in light of the available evidence, and they have thoroughly debunked them. Davis (1994) and Faber (2000), for example, demonstrate that while there certainly were Jewish slave traders and slave owners, they played a minimal role in the overall slave economy. In no sense can Jews be regarded as having had a large-scale presence in this market. However, Louis Farrakhan, the leader of the Nation of Islam, continues to promote the charge, and it has gained a certain amount of traction among people sympathetic to the just cause of black liberation. It is, in fact, a contemporary version of the sort of conspiracy theory peddled in the *Protocols.*

The extent to which the notion of Jewish privilege and the Farrakhan libel have gained currency in the postmodernist left is exhibited in the recent Netflix film *You People* (January 2023), co-written by Kenya Barris and Jonah Hill. The film is a romantic comedy that trades in a variety of demeaning stereotypes concerning Black and Jewish life in America. It features derisive 'jokes' about the Holocaust and constant apologies from a Jewish family burdened by guilt over its privileged economic and social position. The Black family are converts to the Nation of Islam and followers of Farrakhan. At one point the mother of Hill's prospective fiancée asks indignantly, 'Are you comparing slavery to the Holocaust?' The question goes unanswered. In another segment of the same scene the charge of Jewish responsibility for the slave trade is raised. It too is allowed to stand without a reply. The film received a large number of negative reviews pointing out that it is awkwardly unfunny. However, several reputable critics (writing in *The New York Times* and *The Washington Post*) praised the film for raising difficult issues of race and power in a courageous manner. The film has become a major success on Netflix. That serious critics are hailing an embarrassment of this kind as important social commentary indicates the extent to which the bizarre historical misrepresentations of the postmodernist left have been allowed to colonize parts of the American entertainment industry.

Integral to the critical theory that guides much of the postmodernist left is the notion of intersectionality. Kimberlé Crenshaw, an African American legal scholar, introduced the term in a number of seminal papers in the late 1980s and early 1990s. Crenshaw (1991) provides a detailed presentation of the intersectional perspective. Contrary to right-wing hysteria over critical race theory, the core assertions of Kimberle's hypothesis are entirely reasonable. She observes that many groups encounter oppression across several interconnecting dimensions. So, for example, women of colour are frequently subjected both to male violence and to racism. It is only by addressing the nexus of factors that generate this condition that one can effectively seek to alleviate the persecution of the relevant group. This is a valuable insight that has led to fruitful legal and social discussion. However, it has also been misapplied to produce some acutely problematic consequences.

One of these is the emergence of a wholistic view of oppression focused on ethnic and gender identity. Specifically, part of the postmodernist left is of the view that in order to challenge any form of social injustice it is necessary to take on the entire network of oppression that sustains it. Such a view works against the creation of large, diverse, single-issue coalitions that have been so effective in achieving reform in the past.

A second result is the calcification of a rigidly integrated set of moral and political commitments into an inflexible, totalizing ideology for social and political action. If one is not prepared to sign on to resisting the entire package of forces identified as generating intersectional oppression, then one is not a progressive. Therefore, in order to establish one's credentials as an anti-racist, one must also oppose Zionism in Israel-Palestine and Western military support for Ukraine.

A third consequence of the intersectional perspective in critical theory is the subordination of issues of class to identity politics. This plays directly into the hands of the far right, who use it to incite disaffected White working-class and rural voters to adopt ethnonationalist xenophobia as a reaction to the historical guilt that many postmodernist leftists seek to impose on them. This prevents the formation of working-class solidarity across ethnic lines.

Finally, for Jews the intersectionality programme has had a particularly toxic impact. Combined with the notion of Jewish privilege, it causes Jews to be identified with the network of oppression that constitutes the legacy of colonialism and racism in America and abroad. The only avenue available to Jews who wish to participate in the progressive movement is to reject the mainstream Jewish communities of which they are a part, and to declare their active hostility to Israel as a country, rather than simply to oppose the policies of its government. Those who refuse to engage in such collective self-denial are subjected to severe censure and rejection. Again, the historical parallel with the way in which the Soviet Union sought to dismantle organized collective Jewish life in Eastern Europe is clear. The important difference, of course, is that the postmodernist left works without the apparatus of state control, using social sanction instead.

Depicting Jews as agents of White privilege is a clear attempt to project the dynamics of American racial relations onto a people whose history and culture cannot be properly accommodated in these categories. While the overwhelming majority of North American Jews are of European Ashkenazi background, this is certainly not true of Jews in general. More than half of Israel's Jewish population comes from the Middle East, North Africa and Central Asia. There are upwards of 160,000 Ethiopian Jews in Israel, many now second and third generation. A large part of French Jewry is of North African origin. Many of these non-European people would be classed as 'of colour' on the peculiar metrics of the American racial coding system. Jews are, and have always been, a multiracial people (to the extent that the notion of race has any clear content at all in this context, which is highly doubtful). To cast them in the role of inheritors of White European colonial privilege is absurd, given their diversity, and in light of their experience in Europe as a severely persecuted minority.

Many far-left anti-Israel activists seek to diminish the significance of non-European Jews in Israel for their claim that Jews enjoy White privilege. They insist that these 'non-White' Jews are, like the Palestinians, victims of Zionist colonialism. They describe them as 'Arab Jews' who were forced to leave their homelands by Zionist agents recruiting immigrants and provoking conflict with their host societies. While a small number of Middle Eastern and North African Jews may accept this view of themselves, the overwhelming majority reject it out of hand. It is, in fact, at striking variance with the historical record. Prior to the emergence of nationalism in the Arab world at the end of the nineteenth century, people in these territories identified themselves primarily in terms of language and/or religion. The Jews always saw themselves as a distinct connected historical cultural community, and they were regarded as such by the Muslims, Christians and other groups, among whom they lived.[4]

With the break-up of the Ottoman Empire and the rise of Arab (as well as Turkish) nationalism, the position of non-Arab minorities became increasingly precarious throughout the Middle East and North Africa. Large-scale violence against Jewish communities in these countries began during and immediately after the Second World War. Following the collapse of Rashid Ali al-Gaylani's pro-Nazi government in Iraq in June 1941, 180 Jews were killed in the Farhud, a pogrom launched in Bagdhad during 1–2 June 1941. This violence undermined the security of Iraqi Jewry, and it facilitated the emigration of Jews in the government-orchestrated expulsion of the community to Israel in 1951–2. Pogroms throughout North Africa in the 1940s and 1950s created an environment in which the Jews of these countries began to leave. By the mid-1960s, virtually the entire population of 850,000–900,000 Jews in Arab countries had been expelled or had left. Most came to Israel, with a smaller number of wealthier families taking up residence in Europe, or in North and South America.[5]

Some left-wing anti-Zionists see the expulsion of Middle Eastern and North African Jews as a regrettable but understandable Arab nationalist response to the 1948 war and the Palestinian tragedy. Even if this view were historically accurate (which it is not), it is, at best, misguided. If the forced exodus of Palestinian refugees from territory in Israel is unacceptable, how can the expulsion of Jews from Arab countries be dismissively regarded as 'understandable'?

We will return to these issues in later chapters. They are difficult and complex. At this point it should be clear that the attempt by the postmodernist left to construe Jews in general as beneficiaries of White European privilege is a gross misrepresentation of the facts.

4.3 Zionism as Colonialism

As part of its determination to view all situations in terms of American and European historical paradigms the radical left construes Israeli Jews as White colonialists who have disinherited indigenous Palestinian Arabs of colour. They have freighted the Israeli–Palestinian conflict with the full substance of the anti-colonialist narrative, turning the conflict into the embodiment of the struggle for liberation from White colonial aggression. In the case of Israel-Palestine, this narrative has become largely detached from the historical facts of the dispute, and it has entered the realm of the mythic. In fact the postmodernist left has inherited and updated the traditional anti-Zionism of the twentieth-century Marxist left. The latter regarded Zionism as a reactionary expression of Jewish separatism. Even when Stalin supported the creation of Israel in 1948, he conducted bloody purges and show trials against Jewish intellectual and political figures, whom he labelled Zionist agents of subversion and rootless cosmopolitans. These actions were part of his broader campaign of terror and repression. The crude anti-Zionism of the Soviet regime and its satellites outlasted Stalin into the 1970s. So, for example, Poland's Communist government launched an 'anti-Zionist' campaign in 1968 to deflect attention from an emerging student and worker protest movement. In the course of this campaign 20,000–25,000 Polish Jews lost their jobs and were forced out of the country, leaving a residue population of 5,000–10,000.[6]

Another far-left inheritance of Soviet anti-Zionism is the constant comparison of Israel to Nazi Germany. This move serves two purposes. First, it seeks to transform Israel from one of many countries committing serious human rights abuses into the embodiment of absolute evil. Second it is intended to diminish the significance of the Nazi genocide against the Jews by casting the Jews as the new Nazis.

London's former mayor Ken Livingstone has promoted the claims that Hitler supported Zionism, and that the Zionists collaborated with the Nazis. He bases these assertions on Lenny Brenner's *Zionism in the Age of the Dictators* (London: Croom Helm, 1983). Jim Allen recycled Brenner's arguments in his 1987 play *Perdition*. Neo-Nazi groups have also cited Brenner's book as part of their Holocaust denial campaign. These claims have been systematically exposed as untrue and misleading by a variety of historians (Bogdanor, 2016; Frazer, 2016). Interestingly, a number of Arab nationalists did actively collaborate with Germany during the Second World War, in exchange for promises of support for their national movements. Haj Amin al-Husseini, the British-appointed Grand Mufti of Palestine, and Rashid Ali al-Gaylani, prime minister of Iraq in the early 1940s, both worked closely with the Nazi regime (see Herf, 2014 on the role of the Mufti). These sorts of facts are rarely, if ever, allowed to complicate the far left's anti-Zionist narrative.

As we have observed, more than half of Israel's Jewish population is descended from refugees forced out of Arab and other Muslim countries. Its European Jews are derived from people who fled East European pogroms and the Nazis, or from Holocaust survivors. Colonialists come to a country in the service of a colonial mother country. They enrich this mother country by exporting natural resources back to it, and they provide a captive market for its manufactured goods. The Jews of Israel did not come to serve a colonial mother country. They arrived to escape violent persecution in their host societies. There is also the fact that, unlike the European colonists of these countries, the Jews had a longstanding historical and cultural connection with Israel-Palestine, and a small but constant presence in it, of fluctuating size, throughout the millennia since their departure from the territory. In the period of Muslim empires this connection was recognized by the resident Arab Muslim population and its leaders, as specified in their own religious sources.

If considered in any detail, the analogy between Israel and genuine colonial settler states like the US, Canada, Australia or Argentina breaks down quickly. The settler populations of these colonial states were sent as agents of the European countries that took possession of them. They imposed the language and culture of their home societies on the territories that they expropriated, and they dispossessed the indigenous populations in order to enrich themselves, and the colonial powers on whose behalf they operated. Even after they achieved independence from their colonial sponsors, either through revolution or political agreement, they continued to sustain the imported culture and institutions of their European homelands. Interestingly, the legitimacy of these postcolonial states is never questioned by the anti-colonialist left, even as the brutality of their histories is rightly exposed. No one seriously suggests dismantling these countries and handing their territories back to the remnant indigenous populations.

The Jewish settlers in Palestine were, for the most part, fleeing their host countries, not coming as their agents. Their political agenda was directed not to serving the economic or geopolitical interests of these countries. It sought the establishment of a place of refuge where they could achieve independence from the violent exclusion that they had suffered in their Diaspora homes. The language and culture that they cultivated in Israel-Palestine was not that of a colonial regime, but a revival of their own. The dispossession of the Arab population that this venture generated was the result of a conflict of competing national movements, both determined to maintain dominance in the same territory, rather than a programme of expropriation on behalf of a non-resident colonial power. It is certainly the case that the Palestinian Arabs were displaced by the creation of Israel, and they suffered a serious injustice in this process. It is not helpful to misrepresent these events as an instance of Western colonialist dispossession when they clearly cannot be accurately integrated into such a paradigm. I will be taking up the Israeli–Palestinian conflict in Chapter 6. At this point it will be useful to briefly review the history of Zionism as a political movement, in order to better understand it in its natural context, apart from the demonic role that the radical left has assigned it.

The nineteenth century was a period of political and cultural ferment for European Jewry, as it contended with the effects of the industrial revolution and the attendant rapid social changes of this period. A plethora of secular Jewish political movements emerged in the second half of the nineteenth century, which attempted to develop strategies for negotiating the increasingly complex and volatile world in which the Jewish communities of both Western and Eastern Europe found themselves. These included liberalism, socialism, Communism, anarchism, assimilationism, folkist autonomism (a movement that sought to create culturally autonomous Jewish communities within the Diaspora), Zionism and territorialism (a programme for a Jewish state in a geographic area other than Israel-Palestine). A lively debate among these approaches ensued, drawing in an increasing number of ordinary people, who moved beyond the traditional religious structures that had dominated Jewish life until then. Zionism remained a minority option in this debate until the cataclysms of the twentieth century drastically altered the landscape of Jewish life in Europe.

Theodor Herzl's *Judenstaadt*, published in Vienna in 1896, laid out the first detailed proposal for a Zionist programme. However, the development of Zionism as a popular movement with mass support was already taking shape in Russia several decades prior to the publication of Herzl's book, and the first congress of the Zionist Organization in Basel in August 1897. The *Hovevei Tzion* (Lovers of Zion) was founded in Russia in 1881, in response to the sequence of pogroms taking place in the Czarist empire. It consisted of young East European Jews who were immigrating to Palestine (then under Ottoman rule) to set up agricultural settlements on land that they had purchased, in what became known as the first *Aliya* (first immigration).

Leon Pinsker was one of the leaders of *Hovevei Tzion*, and its main theoretician. Pinsker was a physician who had previously advocated liberal assimilation into Russian society. The pogroms persuaded him of the futility of this approach. His pamphlet *Auto-Emancipation* appeared in 1881. It argued that the Jewish condition of powerlessness as an excluded minority without a homeland perpetuated the persecution to which Jews were subject throughout the Diaspora. He suggested that only by establishing a renewed national life in a territory where they enjoyed self-determination could this pattern be discarded. In many ways *Auto-Emancipation* anticipates the ideas of twentieth-century liberation politics.

In the first part of the twentieth century the Zionist movement split into a set of competing factions. The largest of these was a block of socialist-Zionist parties that controlled the leadership of the Yishuv, the Jewish community in Palestine.

They were responsible for establishing the Histadrut Labour Federation, and networks of Kibbutzim and moshavim (collective and cooperative agricultural settlements). Right-wing and religious Zionists competed with the labour parties for power and influence.[7] Given the dominant role that the far right has played in Israeli politics over the past two decades, the fact that the country emerged out of labour and socialist roots is difficult to imagine for people unfamiliar with its history.

One of the largest Jewish political organizations in Europe was the General Jewish Labour Bund, a Jewish socialist party founded in Vilna in 1897.[8] The Bund was anti-Zionist, arguing for Jewish participation in a general socialist revolution in Eastern Europe. It promoted Yiddish as the language of Jewish culture, and it came to embrace Jewish cultural autonomy within a federated socialist order. It competed with the Labour Zionist parties, whose economic and social programmes overlapped with Bundist ideological commitments. After the Soviet revolution part of the Bund disbanded and joined the *Yevsektsiya*, the Jewish wing of the Soviet Communist Party (1918–29). Another section remained allied with the Mensheviks, who were social democrats opposed to the Bolsheviks. The Yevsektsiya was dissolved in 1929, when it had completed its assigned task of suppressing independent Jewish communal activity in the Soviet Union. Its members and those of the remnant Bund were persecuted and, in many cases, eliminated in Stalin's purges. In Poland the Bund continued to operate as an independent Jewish political and cultural organization through the 1930s. It played an active role in organizing Jewish resistance to Polish antisemitism in the interwar years, and to the Nazi genocide in the 1940s. It ceased to exist in Poland after the war, but its supporters and publications continued to function in America during the postwar years.

The disappearance of the plethora of Jewish alternatives to Zionism, and specifically of the Bund, was the direct result of the Nazi's destruction of European Jewry, and of the

Soviet Union's systematic repression of independent Jewish community life within its domain of control. The expulsion of Middle Eastern and North African Jewry in the second part of the twentieth century completed the set of cataclysms that turned Israel into the only option available to most of the refugees from these events. Western countries remained closed to most of them. This fact is frequently omitted in the radical left's anti-Zionist polemics. The role of their own political antecedents in closing their respective countries to Jewish refugees, particularly those attempting to escape the Nazis onslaught, is rarely, if ever, addressed. This is particularly true of the British labour movement, part of whose leadership strongly supported the Conservative government's policy of drastically restricting Jewish immigration to the UK in the 1930s, for economic reasons. When in government in the late 1940s, Labour's foreign secretary, Ernest Bevin, blocked access to the survivors, while encouraging non-Jewish immigrants to fill a labour shortage.[9]

Jewish politics in the nineteenth and twentieth centuries exhibits an interesting dialect between integrationist and separatist forces. The relationship between the Bund and the Zionists, particularly the Labour Zionists, illustrate this dynamic. A similar pattern is apparent in African American political movements of the same period. W. E. B. Du Bois, an advocate of African diaspora socialist reform, represents the integrationist wing of the dialectic, while Marcus Garvey, the leader of the Back to Africa movement, is the counterpart of a Zionist leader. Martin Luther King and Malcolm X continued this dialectic, with important modifications, in the postwar era. Historical circumstances both in America and in Africa rendered the separatist alternative unrealistic for the majority of African Americans. By contrast, the history of Europe, the Middle East and North Africa excluded the integrationist option for most Jews in these areas, and it left the separatist project as their only route to survival.

In the hands of the postmodernist left the historical context in which Zionism emerged and Israel came into being has become largely opaque. It is promoting an anachronistic view on which Israel, in its current situation as a powerful state occupying a large Palestinian population in the West Bank, is projected back into the origins of the conflict at the beginning of the twentieth century. It portrays the Yishuv as the creation of colonialist settlers who came to the country with the express purpose of dispossessing the Arab population of its land.

This part of the left has also transformed Zionism from a political ideology that was formulated as an attempt to solve the problem of severe racist persecution in the Diaspora into an international conspiracy that manipulates governments and agencies through a network of powerful lobbies. This view flourished in sections of the British Labour Party during the years of Jeremy Corbyn's leadership between 2015 and 2020. It produced a series of high-profile conflicts concerning the way in which the party was responding to claims of antisemitism among some of its officials, and it led to the departure of large numbers of Jewish members and MPs from Labour. The normally staid leadership of the Jewish community organized a demonstration outside Labour headquarters in March 2018. Corbyn's defenders insisted that he and his associates were being smeared by Zionists because of their criticism of Israel.

Johnson (2019) compiled a detailed report on the rise of antisemitism in the Labour Party under Corbyn's leadership. It describes the abuse directed by Corbyn supporters against Jewish MPs and members of the party who objected to the hostile environment that they experienced. Many of them eventually left the party. On 29 October 2020 the UK's Equality and Human Rights Commission published its report on the Labour Party's handling of charges of antisemitism (available at https://www.equalityhumanrights.com /en/publication-download/investigation-antisemitism-labour -party). The report found that there had indeed been cases of illegal anti-Jewish harassment within the party, and these had not been properly addressed. It specified a set of demands for correcting the procedures through which such behaviour is to be dealt with. Corbyn rejected the major findings of the report, insisting that they had been 'dramatically overstated for political reasons' (Walker and Elgot, 2020). This led to Corbyn's successor, Keir Starmer, withdrawing the whip from him, thus effectively ejecting him from the Parliamentary Labour Party. Corbyn's allies continue to insist that he is the victim of a Zionist smear campaign.

That one of Britian's two major political parties was rocked by this controversy for five years indicates the extent to which the conspiracy theory of an international Zionist lobby has moved from the margins of public discourse into the mainstream. It has also become a fixture of academic life in Europe and America. The case of David Miller, a lecturer in sociology at the University of Bristol, illustrates this phenomenon with particular clarity.[10] Miller claims to be an anti-racist who supports progressive anti-colonial causes. During his classes he presented diagrams of the organizations of the British Jewish community, purporting to show their coordinated activity as elements of the Zionist lobby. When the University of Bristol Jewish Society and the British Union of Jewish Students complained that he was promoting anti-Jewish conspiracy theories, he targeted these organizations, claiming that they are 'Islamophobic' and acting as agents for the Israeli government. The university administration initially refused to intervene. After many months of scandal in the press, they terminated Miller's contract, on the grounds that his conduct was inappropriate. He is challenging the decision, claiming that he has been victimized by the Zionist lobby, which manipulates institutions in Britain. His dismissal led to a petition and statements of support by large numbers of British academics. They charge that the university's action violates the principles of free speech and academic freedom.

One wonders how they would have responded if another ethnic or gender minority had been the object of Miller's relentless assault.

Unfortunately Miller's conduct is not unique. Comparable cases are increasingly frequent at British, American and European universities. The entry of Zionist conspiracy theories into the political and academic mainstream is generating an increasingly toxic environment for Jews in the broader public domain. They and their communities are portrayed as the locus of a criminal cabal seeking to manipulate the machinery of state and the agencies of information through nefarious influence and financial pressure. This is the classic anti-Jewish racism of the far right, parading in anti-colonialist garb. It has little if anything to do with the Israeli–Palestinian conflict.

The extreme anti-Zionist agitation of the far left creates a strange paradox. This agitation is purportedly directed at Israel, rather than Jews. However, as it becomes increasingly widespread, the environment for Diaspora Jews turns more hostile. This in turn creates a deep sense of insecurity that encourages immigration to Israel, thus achieving the opposite effect of the campaign's stated objective. It is revealing that the far left never seeks to create an open and accepting environment for Jews in their host countries as a way of pursuing their anti-Zionist commitment. At no point do extreme anti-Zionists promote the idea that Jews in general have an integral and valued role in their host societies. This status is reserved for the 'good Jews' who explicitly align themselves with the far left's anti-Zionist campaign. Instead, they aim to criminalize Jews who refuse to disavow any connection with Israel, even if this connection is critical or non-political in nature. The latter group constitutes the overwhelming majority of the Jewish population. To the extent that the left's strident anti-Zionism becomes an influential mainstream attitude, it serves to undermine the sense of these Jews that they have a natural place in their host societies.

The acute danger that the far left's extreme hatred of Israel poses to Jews in the Diaspora was thrown into sharp relief in its reaction to the 7 October Hamas terrorist attack. Student organizations at leading American universities such as Harvard, Stanford and the University of Pennsylvania, as well as the Democratic Socialists of America, issued statements celebrating the attack, or justifying it, as a heroic act of anti-colonial resistance. Large pro-Palestinian demonstrations in New York, London and other major cities around the world featured the now common slogans of 'Free Palestine' and 'From the river to the sea, Palestine will be free', which, once again, flooded social media. The speakers at these demonstrations refused to condemn the mass murder of Israeli civilians that Hamas had committed. Anti-Jewish hate crime spiked throughout the UK, Europe and America, with Jewish schools, synagogues and communal institutions targeted.[11]

Significant parts of the left have now acted as cheerleaders for the commission of gruesome acts of mass murder, mutilation, rape and kidnapping inflicted on Israeli civilians, many of them infants and children. Senior university administrators responded to these events with evasive and equivocal pronouncements regretting violence on all sides. While government leaders expressed their horror at the attack, many public figures simply remained silent. Much of the hostility to Israel as a country has spilled over to Diaspora Jewish communities. This has generated the deepest sense of vulnerability and isolation among Jews in both Israel and the Diaspora. The attack and the widespread support for it have reactivated the sense of trauma attaching to previous pogroms and the Nazi genocide. It has confirmed the strong suspicion of many Jews that much of the anti-Zionist left has no hesitation in endorsing Hamas' programme for the elimination of most or all of the Jewish population in Israel, either by genocide or expulsion. It makes a mockery of the notion that the anti-Zionist left's goal is the creation of an egalitarian country in which Jews and Arabs enjoy equal rights, a state for all its citizens. The observed reaction suggests that 'Free Palestine' means a Palestine free of Jews (*Judenrein*). It exposes the absurdity of the Boycott, Divestment and Sanctions (BDS) movement's claim that it is pursuing an African National Congress (ANC) model of struggle for a multi-ethnic democracy. As the impact of the atrocity is absorbed, the far left's initial enthusiastic embrace of the assault may have far-reaching implications for its credibility. It will also have a serious long-term effect on the way in which many Jews in the Diaspora understand their relationship to their host societies, particularly on university campuses and in other environments in which the anti-Zionist left wields substantial influence.

The alacrity with which much of the postmodernist left endorsed the Hamas terrorist attack of 7 October as 'anti-colonial resistance' may well produce a far-right backlash, which focuses on the absurdities of 'woke' identity politics and the dangers of radical Islamism as rallying points for an extreme nativist reaction. Jewish communities in the Diaspora will find themselves caught directly in the middle of this clash.

The postmodernist left places considerable emphasis on studying the history of Western colonialism and the slave trade in order to better understand the centrality of these atrocities in shaping current institutions and social arrangements. This is a reasonable concern. To combat injustice effectively, it is necessary to document its history accurately. Interestingly, this preoccupation with the history of racism does not extend to the persecution of the Jews. In particular, the role of the radical Marxist left in inflicting this evil on the Jews of Europe is largely passed over in silence. As we have seen, one of the reasons for this lack of interest in the history of antisemitism is the fact that it cannot be easily assimilated to American models of racial oppression. A second is the conviction that Jews enjoy White privilege, and so they are a legitimate target of disapprobation. A third is an obsession with Zionist conspiracy theories that criminalize Jews as agents of an Israel-centred colonialist venture. Finally, much of the current radical left regards itself as the historically appointed instrument of progressive change. Therefore it is definitionally incapable of racism or bigotry. It embodies the very essence of anti-racist politics. Hence the hostility of large parts of this movement to Jews cannot be anything other than the expression of a progressive stance.

5

The View from Radical
Political Islamism

5.1 Jews in Traditional Islamic Societies

Jews lived throughout the Middle East and North Africa for millennia, often preceding the arrival of Islam and Arabic culture in these places. Their presence in this area dates from the ancient Jewish Diaspora, part of which started before the Roman oppression that followed the destruction of the Second Temple (70 CE) and the Bar Kochva rebellion (132–6 CE). When considering the nature of Jewish life under Islamic rule it is important to avoid two distorting myths, which are occasionally invoked to describe their situation. As Lewis (1987) observes, they experienced neither equality in a multicultural paradise (the 'Golden Age' of Islamic Spain), nor unrelenting oppression. As Dhimmi (a protected group of believers, which originally included Jews and Christians) they occupied the subordinated role of a tolerated religious minority. Within rigidly specified restrictions they enjoyed religious freedom and communal autonomy. For the most part, they avoided the systematic expulsions, mass violence and severe exclusion to which Jews in medieval Christian Europe were subjected.

There were periods of relatively liberal rule during which cultural exchange flourished between Jews and Muslims. Many of the great medieval Jewish philosophers, like Saadya Gaon, Solomon Ibn Gabirol and Moses Maimonides, played a significant role in the philosophical discussions that shaped Islamic philosophical thought in the Middle Ages. They were, in turn influenced by leading Islamic thinkers of their respective times, such as al-Kindi, al-Farabi, Ibn Sina and Ibn Rushd. Both Jewish and Muslim philosophers were involved in a common attempt to reconcile classical Greek philosophy and science with traditional monotheistic religious belief. This sort of interaction was unknown in the Christian world. In addition to scientific encounters, some Jews held prominent political and military positions in Muslim administrations. However, there were also recurrent incidents of violent perse-cution that punctuated long periods of relative symbiosis. It is worth briefly considering several examples of these to get a sense of the nature and the extent of this aspect of the Jewish experience in the Islamic world.

The Spanish Jewish leader Shmuel HaNagid rose to the position of vizier and general of the Muslim army in Granada in the eleventh century. When Shmuel's son Joseph succeeded him, Joseph was killed in a popular revolt, which destroyed the Granada Jewish community through a bloody massacre in 1066.

In 1148 the Almohads, a religiously extreme group of Berber Muslims from Morocco, conquered Cordoba. They cancelled the Dhimmi status of Jews and Christians, requiring them to convert or to leave. As a result, at the age of thirteen Maimonides and his family fled their native city. They wandered through Spain, North Africa and Israel-Palestine, before Maimonides settled in Fustad (Old Cairo) in Egypt, in approximately 1168. Here he became physician to the sultan (Salahadin) and religious leader of the Jewish community in Egypt. The Almohad Caliphate ruled parts of North Africa and expanded into much of Muslim Iberia during the twelfth century. As a result of its religious persecutions many Jews had to flee the area, while others lived as *anusim* (forced converts), outwardly feigning Islamic practice.

Yemenite Jewry endured an extended history of harassment at the hands of Shiite rulers. Some of this history is described in Maimonides' *Iggeret Teiman* (Epistle to Yemen, 1173–4). It is addressed to Yemen's Jews in response to an appeal from the community's leaders for guidance on how to respond to the oppression that they were dealing with. This persecution reached a climax with the Mawza exile of the seventeenth century. Yemenite Jews had steadfastly resisted demands that they abandon Judaism for Islam. In 1679 the king, Imām al-Mahdi Ahmad, issued a decree requiring the Jews of the capital city, Sana'a, and the surrounding highlands, either to convert or to be uprooted from their homes and forced to walk to Mawza, an arid coastal plain near the Red Sea.[1] The motivation for this action appears to be both religious and political. The king sought to extend the ban on non-Muslims within the Arabian holy land to Yemen. He also apparently feared Jewish support for the emerging Ottoman Empire. Contemporary accounts of the expulsion indicate that thousands of people died enroute to Mawza due to heat exposure, hunger and thirst, with many more succumbing after arrival there. After a year the survivors were permitted to return to Sana'a and other highland towns. This was due, in part, to the intervention of tribesmen who relied on the farm implements and other instruments that Jewish craftsmen produced. When the Jews came back to their homes in Sana'a they found them occupied by Muslim residents. They were forced to move outside the walls of the city and construct new adobe dwellings, as well as synagogues and other facilities. The events of the Mawza expulsion constituted a major trauma for the Yemenite Jewish community. Those who experienced it provided detailed accounts in their historical and literary writings.

In 1839, Shiite Muslims committed a pogrom against the Jews of Mashhad in Iran in which thirty to forty people were murdered and homes were looted. The rioters threatened the rest of the community with large-scale violence. To avoid further bloodshed the leaders of the community agreed to the mass conversion of its members. Some accounts of the attack claim that it was sparked by a perceived insult against Shiite Islam by a Jewish woman. The entire community lived as *anusim* for eighty-six years, posing as Muslims while sustaining Jewish practice in the secrecy of their homes. They re-emerged as openly Jewish only in 1925, when the comparatively liberal Pahlavi dynasty assumed power. Many Jews left Iran during this time for more secure environments.

Jewish life under traditional Islamic rule was very much a mixed affair. It involved periods of tolerance and stability, followed by significant incidents of violent oppression. It clearly differed from the more systematic record of deep persecution that Jews encountered in Christian Europe. It was not, however, the model of egalitarian acceptance that some more Panglossian accounts have suggested.

5.2 The Rise of Arab Nationalism

Large Islamic empires, in particular the Ottoman Empire, consisted of networks of communities identified on the basis of language or religion. One's position in the social order was largely determined by the particular community to which one belonged. National identity was not a category in these empires and emirates. Non-Arabic- and non-Turkish-speaking Muslim groups, like Berbers, and some Kurds, were culturally distinct elements of the Muslim majority. Jews who spoke dialects of Judeo-Arabic and Arabic-speaking Christians were subordinated minorities outside of this majority.

In the late nineteenth century notions of nationhood, based on common language, territory and ethnic identity, started to enter political and intellectual discourse in the Middle East, from Europe. As the Ottoman Empire began to unravel, both Turkish and Arab nationalist movements emerged as political forces in the area. The Ottoman Empire came to an end on 29 October 1923, when Mustafa Kemal Atatürk established the first Turkish Republic. The Ottoman Caliphate was abolished shortly after, on 3 March 1924. Atatürk's republic was designed to be rigorously secular and Western in its orientation. Religion was banished from the public domain, and the Latin alphabet replaced the Arabic script for Turkish, as part of this turn to the West.

Initially, Arab nationalist leaders sought sponsorship from European colonial powers to break free of Turkish rule. During the First World War, Britain enlisted the help of Ibn Saud, a tribal leader in Arabia, to fight the Ottomans. In return Britain pledged support for a pan-Arab state to replace Ottoman rule in the Middle East. Instead, Britain and France established a set of colonial protectorates in Iraq, Syria, Lebanon, Palestine and Jordan after the war. Saudi Arabia became an independent kingdom in 1932. Following the Second World War, Libya became independent from Italy in 1947. Arab nationalists launched anti-colonial campaigns and established republics in Syria, Iraq and Egypt in the early 1950s. National liberation movements achieved independence from France in Tunisia and Morocco in 1956, and in Algeria in 1962.[2]

When the Middle East moved from large, multi-ethnic empires to ethnocentric nation states the situation of non-Arab minorities (both Muslim and non-Muslim) became increasingly untenable. Kurds, Berbers and Christians were marginalized, and Jews were entirely forced out of Arab countries. Despite the ostensibly secular nature of some of these states, Arab and Islamic identities were inextricably connected. Even Jews who had actively participated in the political struggle for independence, or the cultural life of their country, found themselves unwelcome in their homelands. Two notable examples from North Africa are Albert Memmi and Enrico Macias.

Memmi was born in Tunis and he was active in the Tunisian independence movement. His book *The Colonizer and the Colonized* (Memmi, 2021), originally published in 1957, became a highly influential work in the literature of national liberation and anti-colonialism. Memmi retained a strong sense of Jewish identity, which he discussed publicly in his work. He also insisted on regarding Israel as a legitimate expression of national liberation for Jews, despite its imperfections and misdeeds. He argued that, just as other post-colonial countries are entitled to sovereignty, even when they behave badly, this right also applies to Israel. Memmi's prominent self-identification as a Jew, and his defence of Israel's right to exist, led the newly independent Tunisian government to insist that he leave. He continued to produce a stream of literary work and left-wing political comment in Paris for many decades.[3]

Enrico Macias (Gaston Ghrenassia) is an Algerian Jewish singer-songwriter and musician. His father was a violinist who played classical Andalusian Arab music. He left Algeria in 1961, during the war of independence, and settled in Paris, where he has had a distinguished career. Much of his music is heavily influenced by North African themes and melodies. Many of his songs express deep attachment to Algeria. Despite his popularity throughout North Africa and the Middle East, the Algerian government has prevented him from visiting the country or performing in it, largely due to his refusal to disavow his connection with Israel.

For the most part pan-Arab nationalists, who sought a unified Arab national movement, rather than a regional state-focused nationalism, were secular and anti-colonialist in their ideological orientation. The Baath Parties in Syria and Iraq are instances of this attitude. Secular pan-Arab nationalism reached its high point with Egyptian president Gamal Abdel Nasser in the 1950s and 1960s. It started its decline after Israel's victory in the 1967 war. Additional factors in the fall of Arab nationalism are its failure to promote significant economic development, and the highly repressive nature of the regimes that it produced. By the end of the postwar era (1980) secular nationalism was a force in retreat throughout much of the Arab world, and the wider Middle East. A range of Islamist movements filled the space that this left.

5.3 The Emergence of Political Islamism

Political Islamism developed in the late nineteenth century and early twentieth as a competitor to Arab and Turkish nationalism. Its advocates rejected the attempt of nationalists, liberal democrats and socialists to import European ideas into the Middle East. They saw these as a source of corruption that would lead to the dissolution of traditional Islamic societies. They regarded the creation of Arab national states, even those that claimed to be Islamic, as violations of the pan-Islamic mission. The Sunni current of this movement focused on the restoration of a unified Caliphate, that would embody the principles of early Islamic rule in the first generations of the Muslim conquest in the seventh century. It took the concept of the pan-Islamic Ummah (People) as being the primary social and political category of the Islamic world.

Muhammad Rashid Rida was a founding figure in the Sunni wing of the modern Islamist movement. He was a Salafist commentator from Ottoman Lebanon, born in 1865. He called for the renewal of Islam through a rigorously purified Muslim lifestyle, and the re-establishment of the Caliphate. Rida emigrated to Cairo in 1898, where he founded the periodical *al-Manar*, in which he expounded his ideas, and

presented religious commentary, until his death in 1935. He
published numerous pieces on Jews and Zionism.[4] While he
initially regarded Zionism as a humanitarian venture with
positive aspects, he quickly came to see it as a major threat
to Arab and Islamic interests. He described Jews as agents of
a global conspiracy determined to undermine and take over
the countries that they entered. He held Jews responsible for
the collapse of the Ottoman Caliphate, through manipulation
of the Young Turks revolution. He claimed that the Zionists
intended to take over the al-Aqsa Mosque in Jerusalem,
replacing it with a Third Temple. With this assertion he anticipated the call that the Grand Mufti Haj Amin al-Husseini used
to incite Palestinian riots in the 1920s and 1930s. Rida saw
Zionism as part of an international Jewish plot to take over
Palestine and expel its Arab residents.

Rida's writings were a major influence on a new generation
of Islamist thinkers who became active in the first half of
the twentieth century. One of these was Hassan al-Banna,
who founded the Muslim Brotherhood in Egypt in 1928.
Al-Banna saw both liberal democracy and Soviet Communism
as expressions of Western decadence. He urged a renewal of
Islamic society in the Arab world through comprehensive
jihad. He regarded this struggle as encompassing religious
renewal, charitable work among the poor and armed struggle
against occupying colonial powers. Al-Banna had close ties
with the Grand Mufti of Palestine, Haj Amin al-Husseini,
whom he welcomed as a hero on the latter's arrival in Egypt
in 1946. He came into conflict with the nationalist regime in
Egypt, and he was assassinated by the secret police in 1949.
The Muslim Brotherhood was pro-Nazi in the 1930s and
1940s. It disseminated Nazi propaganda and *The Protocols*
as part of its anti-Jewish campaign. It targeted the Egyptian
Jewish community, as well as the Zionists in Palestine.[5] The
Brotherhood sent a military contingent to fight in the 1948
war, alongside the Egyptian army.

One of the central figures in modern Islamist political thought is Sayyed Qutb, who was born in Egypt in 1906. He started out as a modernist, but increasingly came to reject Western culture as a corrupting influence. A two-year study trip to the United States during 1948–50 persuaded him that America was an entirely decadent society. After his return to Egypt he initially welcomed the Free Officers Movement coup that brought Nasser to power in 1952 as an anti-colonialist victory. However, he soon fell out with Nasser due to his strong opposition to secular pan-Arabist ideology. He was convicted of plotting Nasser's assassination, and he was executed in 1966. While in prison he wrote *Milestones* (Ma'alim fi'l-tareeq), a major work of jihadist politics, published in 1964. In this pamphlet he calls for a global jihad against the West to liberate the world from its corrupt, material social order. He envisages the creation of a universal caliphate that will rule by Sharia law alone, and that will be constructed in the image of the early Islamic period of the first four generations of Arab conquest. Qutb regards the empires and cultures that followed this era as degradations of the original Islamic vision. He dismisses centuries of high Muslim culture, as well as other civilizations, as entirely lacking in value. Qutb regarded modern Arab-Muslim states as products of Western colonialism, which artificially divide and weaken the Ummah.

An Islamist rendering of antisemitism is an integral part of Qutb's thought. In his essay *Our Battle Against the Jews* (Ma'rakatuna ma'a al-Yahud), written in the early 1950s, he expresses the view that Jews have been perfidious enemies of Islam from the genesis of the Islamic campaign in the seventh century. He imports classic European anti-Jewish conspiracy theories into this narrative, taking Jews to be agents of corruption that undermine civilization in their bid to control it. In Qutb's world view, defenders of authentic Islam are engaged in a cosmic conflict with a hostile West, and with the Jews, who manipulate it. Zionism and Israel are mere instances of this larger competition.[6]

Qutb's writings are pivotal to contemporary jihadist movements. Osama bin Laden and Al Qaeda were heavily influenced by his programme. The Ayatollah Khomeini and the Shiite current of Islamism venerated him as a martyr and a theorist of Islamist revolution. Hamas, the Palestinian wing of the Muslim Brotherhood, regard him as one of their prime ideological mentors.[7]

Secular Arab nationalism eclipsed Islamism throughout the 1950s and 1960s. The nationalists suppressed it in the states that they governed and portrayed it as a reactionary, anti-modernist trend. By contrast, they saw themselves as the vanguard of the anti-colonialist movement, and an integral part of the modernizing revolution of the developing world. By the end of the postwar era it had become clear that the nationalists had failed to achieve Arab unity. Their states had not provided the prosperity that they had promised, and their regimes were highly repressive. At this point Islamist groups rose to prominence as leading political actors throughout the Muslim world.

In 1979 Khomeini overthrew the Shah of Iran and established a Shiite Islamic Republic devoted to projecting power throughout the Middle East. As a result of the disastrous American war in Iraq in the early 2000s, Israel's occupation and departure from southern Lebanon and Russia's support of Assad's war against his opponents in Syria, Iran has been able to define an area of influence that stretches from its borders through to Lebanon. It is strategically aligned with the Shiite militia Hezbollah in Lebanon, and Hamas in Gaza, arming both. It threatens Saudi Arabia and the Gulf States through the Houthi rebel militias that it sponsors in Yemen.

One of Iran's overriding geopolitical objectives is the physical destruction of Israel, which it pursues as a religious imperative. In addition to its military programme of expansion through proxies that surround Israel, it is engaged in a relentless campaign of anti-Jewish propaganda. This has involved promoting Holocaust denial at staged conferences and 'art' exhibitions in Iran. It also targets Israeli and Jewish civilians outside of Israel, as does Hezbollah. On 18 July 1994, a suicide bomber blew up a Jewish community centre in Buenos Aires, killing eighty-five people and injuring more than 100. Iran and Hezbollah are widely suspected of having carried out the attack. The government of Argentinian president Cristina Fernández de Kirchner was accused of attempting to cover up the role of Iranian agents in the assault, but the legal case against her was dismissed in 2021.[8]

Al Qaeda and related Sunni jihadist groups have pursued mass terrorist attacks in the West, the most spectacular of them being the destruction of the twin World Trade Towers in Manhattan on 11 September 2001. While 9/11 was committed by Saudi and Egyptian operatives, the London transport bombing on 7 July 2005 was the work of British-born supporters of the jihadi movement. Islamist attacks on Jewish targets in Europe, particularly in France, have become increasingly common. This has led to Jewish communities in the Diaspora having to place their synagogues, schools and public institutions under extraordinarily heavy security protection. While these arrangements are largely unknown for other ethnic and religious communities, they are now standard procedure for Jews in much of Europe and North America.

Despite points of local cooperation there is a fierce rivalry between Shiite and Sunni jihadi movements. They represent distinct religious and political ideologies. The Shiite wing is more organized and hierarchical. It is focused on Iran. The Sunni Islamists tend to work in horizontal networks that pursue an international struggle. They see their domain as encompassing Muslim countries ruled by non-Islamist governments, and Western countries with sizeable Muslim immigrant populations. They are also active throughout sub-Saharan

Africa. Islamic State was able to take advantage of the chaos in Syria and Iraq to temporarily establish a territorial domain there in 2014–16, but it was eliminated by a variety of foreign and domestic forces. The Shiite Islamist strategy recalls Stalin's programme of building socialism in one country, extending its influence through territorial expansion and proxy influence. The Sunni jihadis bear a certain structural resemblance to Trotsky's project of a permanent international revolution. The Shiite Islamists are using the Islamic republic in Iran as the base from which to propagate a Shiite revolution, with the initial objective of securing hegemony throughout the Middle East. The Sunni jihadis are waging a campaign of insurrection around the world, in order to create a unified caliphate that will rule uncontested in all geopolitical domains.

Important strategic differences have emerged within Islamist Sunni movements concerning the timing of the caliphate. Islamic State seeks its immediate establishment. More politically oriented Islamists like the Muslim Brotherhood are committed to a lengthy period of preparation through non-violent revolution in Muslim-majority states, as the initial stage of a phased plan. Al Qaeda is interested in the establishment of a caliphate in the near-term future. But it has given priority to attacking both Arab-Islamic states and the West simultaneously.

A strain of Western opinion has suggested that radical Islamist violence against the West, and hostility to Jews, are direct consequences of the atrocities of Western, specifically American, imperialism in Muslim countries, and Western support of Israel's repression of the Palestinians. On this view, if the US were to end its military presence in these countries, and Israel was to withdraw from Palestinian land occupied since 1967, radical Islamist terror would cease. This is an absurd misrepresentation of jihadi politics. As we have seen, hatred of the West and antisemitism have been integral to political Islamist thought since its genesis, at the beginning of the twentieth century. These preceded both the emergence of Zionism as a significant political movement, and the creation of Israel.

Nor is it only the West that proponents of jihad find objectionable. Traditional Islamic empires of the later Middle Ages are also identified as corrupt. The great works of science, art, literature, music and philosophy that they produced are dismissed as the products of decadence. Contemporary non-Islamist governments in Muslim majority countries are pursued with the same intense hatred as Western regimes. Radical Islamism seeks to revive the glory of a mythic past in which a pure, ascetic form of Islamic life was in force, in the first few years of the religion's emergence in the Arabian Peninsula, in the seventh century. In this sense it resembles the European movements of the far right. These also seek a renaissance through rejection of decadent liberal institutions and a return to an imagined past glory, a past that, for the most part, has no basis in historical fact.

It is crucial to keep in mind that while highly influential, jihadi movements are in no sense the mainstream of most Muslim countries, nor do they enjoy majority support in Muslim communities in the West. To identify the majority of Muslims in general with radical Islamist politics and terror is to engage in group defamation, and to promote prejudice. This is one of the recruitment techniques of the ethno-nationalist far right.

5.4 The Alliance between Political Islamism and the Radical Left

An informal alliance between political Islamism and the far left has become increasingly influential in shaping what passes for progressive activism over the past twenty-five years. This alliance has generated some peculiar collaborations. As I noted in the previous chapter, Judith Butler described Hamas and Hezbollah as 'social movements that are progressive, that are on the Left, that are part of a global Left'. Some further examples of this alliance are as follows.

During his tenure as mayor of London from 2000 to 2008, Ken Livingstone, a far-left member of the Labour Party, embraced the Qatari-based Muslim Brotherhood cleric Yusuf al-Qaradawi as a 'leading progressive voice in the Muslim world'.[9] Qaradawi was known for endorsing suicide bombing against Israeli civilians, religious rejection of LGBTQ people and rigidly traditional views on the role of women in the family.

In 2009, Jeremy Corbyn invited representatives of Hezbollah and Hamas to Westminster and described them as 'friends'. He later claimed to regret using this term.[10] He did not express any misgivings over issuing the invitation.

Corbyn and other high-profile members of the British radical left have done paid political programming for Press TV, the Iranian regime's UK television station. Corbyn made five broadcasts for the station between 2009 and 2012.[11] Similarly, George Galloway, former leader of the UK Respect Party, hosted talk shows on Press TV. The British public broadcast regulator Ofcom criticized the shows for their lack of balance in coverage of Israel and the Middle East.[12] Respect was a coalition of far-left and Islamist groups. David Miller and Chris Williamson, a pro-Corbyn former Labour MP, produced programmes for the station, with anti-Israel and pro-Russian content.[13] Ofcom revoked Press TV's licence on 20 January 2012. Given the sharp ideological conflict between the postmodernist far left and political Islamist groups, this alliance appears paradoxical at first sight. It is tempting to try to explain it away as a tactical alignment of two movements that share common adversaries. In fact, the connection is deeper. As we observed in the previous chapter, in moving from class to identity politics the radical left has substituted anti-colonialism for class struggle as its main focus. The traditional Marxist notion of occupying an objectively progressive position in history was transferred from the working class to ethnic and gender groups that had suffered the oppression of White European colonial patriarchy. Islamist groups provide some of the most potent anti-colonialist forces available. The radical left has promoted them to a substitute for the working class in the struggle for revolutionary change.[14] The deeply reactionary theocratic objectives of Islamist politics are subordinated to its role as the vanguard of anti-colonialist resistance to Western hegemony.

The moral relativism of the postmodernist component of the radical left facilitates this bizarre alliance. This element of the left refuses to universalize its acutely Western commitments to personal liberation and freedom of lifestyle, which the Islamists regard as at the root of Western corruption, beyond its own cultural constituency. The foreign cultural practices of oppressed peoples are taken to be sacrosanct and exempt from criticism. To reject them on the basis of one's own values would constitute colonial patronage. Therefore, the Islamists are given a free pass on their theocratic and patriarchal ideology. Their antisemitism is accepted as an expression of anti-colonialism, very much as parts of the old left tolerated (and in some cases embraced) working-class and peasant antisemitism as a form of opposition to capitalism. The effect of this tortured view is a posture in which the radical left effectively infantilizes the agents of Islamism, depriving them of agency and autonomy. It is, in the end, a form of orientalism. It consists in a patronizing, neo-colonial refusal to relate to Islamists, and, in fact, to all groups whom they identify as victims of Western colonialism, as full equals, capable of rational decision making on the same grounds as those invoked by the progressives of the radical Western left.

Another consequence of this variety of anti-colonialism is that it abandons the victims of Islamist regimes to oppression without support. This part of the left expresses no solidarity with the feminists, human rights activists, LGBTQ people or labour organizers in Iran, Afghanistan, Gaza or other countries where they are relentlessly pursued by regimes hailed as standing up to Western imperialism. Similarly, Russian democrats who oppose Putin and his war against Ukraine, at great danger to themselves, are looked upon with indifference. The sense in which this can be described as a progressive political position remains, at best, unclear.

Aside from the conceptual and aesthetic difficulties raised by the radical left's alliance with Islamists, and other extremist opponents of the West, historical precedents for such arrangements indicate that they invariably end badly. The Tudeh Party (Iran's Communist movement) and other left-wing Iranian groups initially supported Khomeini's revolution. Once the Islamic Republic was established, they were brutally suppressed, with many of their members killed and others imprisoned or thrown out of their jobs. The Taliban have shown little tolerance for left-wing activists. Apparently Islamists are not constrained by the same ecumenical relativism that permits the postmodern left to overlook the incompatibility of their own ideology with that of their allies. Once in power they do no not regard a common opposition to colonialism as a sufficient condition for political acceptance.

The Islamist–far left alliance has generated a toxic environment for many Jewish communities in the Diaspora. The large demonstrations that members of this alliance hold to protest violence between Israel and the Palestinians frequently spill into attacks on Jewish targets. This happened in London, and throughout American cities, in the wake of fighting in Gaza, in May 2021. It was on particularly vivid display in the far left's support for the Hamas terrorist atrocity of 7 October 2023.

Other countries involved in violent ethnic conflicts, with deeply problematic human rights records, have substantial expatriate communities in the West. These communities are rarely, if ever, subjected to violence or harassment because of the events in which their countries of attachment are involved. Indians in Europe and America are not held accountable for Modi's assault on Muslims in India. Chinese students from the People's Republic studying at European and American universities are not shunned due to their government's persecution of its Uyghur Muslim population in the Xinjiang region. Russian expatriates in the West are not targeted as agents of Putin's aggression in the Ukraine. Second- and third-generation Turkish immigrants are not expected to apologize for Turkey's ongoing suppression of its Kurdish minority, or its continuing occupation of northern Cyprus.

Muslim communities in the West are indeed frequent victims of right-wing racist violence. The left, and enlightened opinion generally, expresses solidarity with them, and support for their struggle against these outrages. In the case of far-left, Islamist attacks on Jews, even when they are officially condemned, are invariably perceived as the unfortunate consequence of Israel's conduct.

Increasingly, Jews are expected to publicly disavow Israel as a condition for acceptance into widening areas of civilized society. This is particularly the case at universities in the West. Jewish students are frequently required to run a gauntlet of political legitimacy tests in order to participate in a variety of campus organizations. When responding to these sorts of discriminatory restrictions, university administrators' fear of offending 'progressive' opinion has significantly encouraged their spread. A recent illustration of this pattern is the decision in 2022 of nine student groups at the UC Berkeley Law School to ban speakers (on any topic) who hold 'Zionist' or pro-Israel views.[15] The Dean of the Law School criticized the bans, but he has refused to intervene on grounds of free speech. Similar controversies have rattled numerous American and British campuses over the past several years.

The Hamas attack of 7 October 2023 generated vocal support on American and European campuses, with too many university officials initially doing nothing to restrain advocacy of terrorism against Israeli or Jewish targets. Their administrations issued safely ceremonial condemnations of violence. They took minimal action to protect the Jewish students directly threatened by these hostile demonstrations, and often only after external criticism.

The general effect of the growing campaign of violence, harassment and intimidation is to raise the cost of involvement in organized Jewish life to the point that Diaspora Jews are increasingly forced to choose between coping with a barrage of public abuse and personal insecurity or the concealment of their Jewish identity (passing quietly under the radar). This is the contemporary version of a traditional mode of racist exclusion, which Jews and other ethnic minorities have dealt with in the past. The fact that political Islamists and large parts of the radical left have collaborated to generate this climate, which is actively reinforced by violence from the far right, creates a particularly challenging environment for Diaspora Jews to navigate.

6

The Israeli–Palestinian
Conflict Re-naturalized

Few disputes have been as extended in time and as intractable as the conflict between Israelis and Palestinians. Now into its second century, it remains stubbornly inaccessible to compromise. It has generated incompatible sets of historical narratives, and it has been endowed with iconic dimensions. The dispute is frequently portrayed as a struggle between the forces of good and evil. It has become the locus of conspiracy theories concerning the power of the 'international Jewish lobby'. It has also been used to vilify Palestinians, and the Arab world in general. To return the struggle to the realm of rational discussion, it is necessary to understand it as an ongoing collision between two nations thrown together in the same territory by a complex sequence of historical events. When viewed in its fuller historical context, points of similarity to other inter-ethnic national disputes emerge.

6.1 A Brief Historical Overview

Let's start with a brief sketch of the history of the conflict.[1] It is important to set aside two frequently repeated claims of traditional Israeli and Palestinian descriptions of the conflict. According to a once-common Israeli view, Palestine was a largely empty territory to which Jews returned after two millennia of exile. The Arab presence developed in tandem with Jewish immigration. The majority of Palestinian refugees generated by the 1948 war left of their own accord, as a result of Arab propaganda broadcasts that created fear of Jewish retaliation. On the other side, a dominant Palestinian narrative holds that a large Arab population inhabited Palestine prior to Zionist immigration. It had an articulated national identity and developed social institutions. When Jewish settlers arrived from Europe, they came to a country with which they had no previous connection. They arrived with the express purpose of dispossessing its indigenous Arab inhabitants, to establish a beach head of Western colonial power. Neither of these accounts is accurate. Each is a caricature of a complex history.

The population and the demography of Israel-Palestine has varied widely throughout the past 3,000 years.[2] Jews sustained a majority until the first century, when Roman and Christian residents started to become dominant. By the fifth century Byzantine Christians were a majority, but sizeable Jewish communities remained, particularly in the Galilee. After the Arab conquest in the seventh century the Muslims achieved majority status, with small Jewish and Christian communities. The entire population of Palestine declined from 225,000 to 150,000 in the fourteenth century, largely due to the plague. By the time that the Ottomans took control at the beginning of the sixteenth century there were 157,000 people in Western Palestine, 145,000 of them Muslim, 6,000 Christian and 5,000 Jewish. The population rose to 232,000 in 1690 (219,000 Muslims, 11,000 Christians and 2,000 Jews), and it remained stagnant at this level until the beginning of the nineteenth century. When large-scale Zionist immigration started at the end of the nineteenth century there were 532,000 people in Palestine. They included 432,000 Muslims, 57,000 Christians and 43,000 Jews (with a Jewish majority in Jerusalem).

Jewish immigration increased significantly after the Balfour Declaration in 1917 and the establishment of the British mandate in Palestine (1918–48). Most of the Jewish immigrants during the mandate were refugees from Europe escaping interwar anti-Jewish violence and the rise of Nazism. Immediately after the war they were refugees and survivors, many entering the country illegally due to a British ban on Jewish immigration. When the UN Partition Plan was announced on 29 November 1947, there were 1,970,000 residents of Palestine. They included 1,181,000 Muslims, 630,000 Jews and 143,000 Christians. The Jewish community (the Yishuv) had acquired 6 per cent of the land through a programme of land purchase.

It is clear that in the nineteenth century Israel-Palestine was neither empty nor densely populated. Jews were not foreign to the country, but had maintained a physical presence, as well as an ongoing religious, cultural and historical connection with it throughout the two millennia since the loss of Jewish sovereignty there. In fact, Muslim rulers permitted them back into Jerusalem in the seventh century, after the Romans had expelled them from the city in the wake of the rebellion of 66–70 CE. The Byzantines continued to enforce the ban on Jewish residence in Jerusalem. Salahadin invited Jews back to Jerusalem in 1187, after he recaptured the city from the Crusaders, who had expelled its Muslim and Jewish residents. However, the number of Jews in the country was small throughout most of the Middle Ages and during the centuries of Ottoman rule, until the Zionist immigration. There was a substantial and sustained Muslim Arab majority during these centuries. The country remained a largely under-developed periphery of the Ottoman Empire until the latter of half of the nineteenth century.

The Jews who came, first as Zionist settlers and then as refugees, were not colonialists looking to displace the Arab population. As I argued in Chapter 4, they were seeking a collective political solution to the racism and exclusion that they had encountered in their host countries over many centuries. However, they harboured naïve and misguided ideas of their future relations with the Arab residents of the country. Most early Jewish immigrants thought that the Arab population would welcome them, as their presence produced development and economic benefits for all. This was the view expressed in Theodor Herzl's novel *Altneuland* (Old–New Land), published in 1902. Many of the socialist Zionist immigrants of the Second Aliya (1904–14) initially envisaged a Jewish–Arab alliance that would build a joint workers' commonwealth. These notions took no account of the political and social realities of Arab society in Palestine. Large-scale Jewish immigration coincided with the rise of Arab nationalism during the decline of the Ottoman Empire. Palestinian Arabs quickly came to see the Zionist enterprise as an encroachment on their territory and a threat to their aspirations for independence.

Ahad Ha'am (Asher Ginsberg) was one of the few early Zionist leaders to recognize the danger of conflict between Jewish immigrants and Palestinian Arabs. He addresses this problem in Ahad Ha'am (1891), which presents a series of criticisms of the early Zionist settlement movement of the First Aliya. The piece does not frame the issue in terms of a clash between competing national movements. Instead Ahad Ha'am reprimands some of the immigrants for insensitive behaviour towards their Arab neighbours. He seems to suggest that conflict could be avoided if Jews treated the Arab residents of Palestine with respect, and guarded against encroaching on their interests. He does not indicate how encroachment could be avoided when the Arabs were quickly coming to see the Jews as national rivals whose influx impinged on what they saw as their exclusive domain. Jews could be accepted as a subordinated minority within a Muslim empire. When they sought to create a sovereign national presence in a territory that its Arab residents took to be the site of their own future nation state, they became a deeply threatening presence.

In 1917, Britain took control of Palestine from the Ottoman Empire during the First World War. On 2 November 1917 the British government issued the Balfour Declaration recognizing the right of Jews to establish a 'national home for the Jewish people' in Palestine. This was done as part of Britain's effort to gain international support for its war effort. They were convinced that Jews could influence Western countries, particularly the United States, to join the Allies. They also enlisted Arab assistance with the promise of support for Arab nationalist movements. This created a clash of expectations in Palestine. The British mandate for Palestine was established in 1920. The League of Nations recognized the mandate, with the Balfour Declaration as one of its principles, in July 1922. The British separated the eastern part of their mandate territory to create the Emirate of Transjordan for the Hashemites in 1921 in an effort to satisfy Arab nationalist demands. It became the Hashemite Kingdom of Jordan on 25 May 1946.

Communal conflict between Jews and Arabs soon followed the Balfour Declaration. It escalated throughout the 1920s, and it reached a climax in widespread Arab riots in 1929. These started with incidents around the Western Wall and the al-Aqsa Mosque. Haj Amin al-Husseini, the Mufti, incited unrest by claiming that the Jews were seeking to take over the Temple Mount. The violence spread throughout the country, affecting Jaffa, Safed, the coastal plain and the Galilee, as well as Jerusalem. The Jewish community of Hebron, numbering 600, which had lived in the city for centuries, was destroyed, with 65–68 people killed. In total 133 Jews were killed, and 339 were injured; 116 Arabs lost their lives, and approximately 232 were wounded, largely at the hands of British mandate police suppressing the riots. In response to these events the Yishuv organized armed militia to defend its civilian population centres.

In 1936 a large-scale Arab revolt erupted against British rule and the expansion of the Jewish presence in Palestine. It continued intermittently until 1939, with strikes and armed conflict. The uprising produced the Arab Higher Committee, led by the Mufti, as the political and military leadership body of the Arab population of Palestine. It demanded the formation of an Arab state, an end to Jewish immigration and a cessation of land sales to Jews. British military forces suppressed the revolt with considerable violence, resulting in several thousand Arab casualties and widespread destruction in Arab villages. The revolt ended in 1939.

The British established a royal commission, the Peel Commission, in 1936 to recommend a solution to the conflict. In 1937, it published a report proposing a partition plan in which a small Jewish state occupying roughly 20 per cent of western Palestine would be established in the coastal plane and the Galilee. Most of the remaining 80 per cent would make up an Arab state. The plan also called for a transfer of 225,000 Arabs to the Arab state, and 1,250 Jews to the Jewish state, on the model of the Greek–Turkish population exchange of 1923. This was the first of several partition plans suggested for Israel-Palestine. The right-wing Revisionist Zionist party under Ze'ev Jabotinsky opposed both partition and transfer, as did other Zionist parties. David Ben-Gurion, chair of the Jewish Agency in Palestine, and Chaim Weizmann, president of the World Zionist Organization, persuaded the organization to endorse the proposal, despite widespread reservations. Al-Husseini and the Arab Higher Committee rejected it.

The British attempted to arrest Al-Husseini because of his role in the Arab revolt, but he escaped to Iraq, where he supported Rashid Ali al-Gaylani, the pro-Nazi leader of Iraq. After the British took control of Iraq in 1941, Al-Husseini and al-Gaylani fled to Berlin. Al-Husseini spent the war years broadcasting pro-Nazi propaganda to Muslim countries and recruiting support for the German army. After the war he escaped from France to Egypt, where he remained until 1959, when he moved to Lebanon.

By the late 1930s, the British were deeply concerned by the prospect of Axis penetration of the Middle East through rising support of Germany and Italy among Arab nationalists opposed to British and French colonial rule. To accommodate Palestinian Arab interests, the British government adopted the White Paper of 1939, which drastically reduced Jewish immigration to Palestine. This came at a point when Jewish refugees from the Nazis had few, if any, options for sanctuary. Most were not permitted to enter Britain or other Western countries. The ban on Jewish immigration remained in effect until the end of the mandate in 1948. After the war British forces prevented survivors and other refugees from landing in the country, forcing them to return to DP camps in Europe, or interning them in detention facilities in Cyprus and East Africa.

After the war inter-communal violence resumed, and Jewish militias of both the left and the right attacked the British military in an attempt to end the mandate. Britain announced in February 1947 that it would withdraw from Palestine. The conflict was referred to the newly formed United Nations, where the United Nations Special Committee on Palestine (UNSCOP) produced another partition plan in 1947. It assigned 55 per cent of the territory to a Jewish state, and 45 per cent to an Arab state. It specified that Jerusalem would be an international zone, and it proposed that the two states would form an economic union. The Jewish state would include approximately 500,000 Jews and 400,000 Arabs, with the expectation that Jewish immigration would significantly increase the Jewish majority. The Arab state would have approximately 725,000 Arabs and 10,000 Jews. Population transfer was not part of this plan. The UN General

Assembly adopted the UNSCOP proposal as resolution 181 on 29 November 1947. Once again, the right-wing Revisionist Zionists opposed partition, as did the far-left Hashomer Hatzair. However, Ben-Gurion's Labour Party and most of its allies endorsed the UNSCOP plan, and so the Jewish Agency convinced the leadership of the Zionist movement to officially accept it. The Arab Higher Committee and all the states of the Arab League rejected it.

In the period following the UN partition resolution the British began to withdraw from Palestine in preparation for the end of the mandate. Palestinian irregulars, supported by foreign Arab volunteers of the Arab Liberation Army, attacked Jewish population centres in an effort to prevent the implementation of the resolution. Jewish forces responded with counter-attacks. These forces consisted of the Haganah, the main military organization of the Yishuv, which became the Israel Defence Force (IDF), and two right-wing militias, the Irgun and Lehi. On 14 May 1948, Ben-Gurion declared Israel's independence. The armies of Egypt, Transjordan, Syria and Iraq, with Lebanese support, attacked shortly after, transforming what had been a civil conflict into a regional war. The fighting lasted ten months until it effectively came to an end in January 1949 with the start of negotiations in Rhodes. Israel signed armistice agreements with each of the Arab countries involved in the war between February and July 1949.

In the course of the 1948 war approximately 700,000 Palestinian refugees were forced out of their homes. This happened due to both expulsion by Israeli military forces and the conditions of armed conflict in civilian areas. Shortly before Israel's declaration of independence and the outbreak of the regional war, the Hagana adopted Tochnit Dalet (Plan D) for the defence of the emerging Jewish state. Considerable controversy among historians surrounds the precise intent of this plan. On Palestinian accounts (endorsed by some more radical revisionist Israeli historians), Tochnit Dalet was a programme for the ethnic cleansing of Israel's Arab population. Morris (2004, 2009) argues, on the basis of extensive archival evidence, that, in fact, it was a military plan for securing control of the country's borders and strategic highways. He exposes a series of local expulsions and massacres of civilian Arabs, but he concludes that there was no overall plan for population transfer that drove these actions. Both sides committed atrocities. Morris estimates that 800–900 Arab civilians and prisoners of war (POWs) (perhaps slightly more) were killed in massacres by Jewish forces. One of the first incidents of the war took place in the Haifa oil refinery on 30 December 1947. The Irgun attacked Arab refinery workers, killing six and wounding forty-two. The Arabs responded with an assault on the Jewish refinery workers that left thirty-nine dead and forty-nine injured. The Jordanian Legion and Palestinian irregulars wiped out 129 residents of kibbutz Kfar Etzion near Jerusalem. Most were killed during the battle for the kibbutz, and some as prisoners after their surrender. Palestinian irregulars killed seventy-eight Jewish medical staff when they attacked a convoy headed to the Hadassah Hospital on Mount Scopus in Jerusalem. Jordanian forces expelled the Jewish residents of the Old City of Jerusalem. A total of approximately 6,000 Jews (close to 1 per cent of the population of the Yishuv) and 10,000 Palestinians Arabs were killed in the hostilities (combatants and civilians on each side). As a result of the 1948 war hundreds of Palestinian villages were destroyed (Palestinian sources put the number at about 400).

Israel increased its territory in the Negev, the Galilee and the coastal plain, relative to the UN partition plan. Jordan took over the West Bank, East Jerusalem and the Old City of Jerusalem. Israel incorporated West Jerusalem. Egypt controlled the Gaza Strip. The majority of Palestinian refugees fled to the West Bank, Jordan and Gaza. Out of a total pre-war population of close to a million Arab residents in the territory within Israel's 1949 ceasefire lines, 160,000 (15 per cent) remained in Israel at the end of the war. They became Israeli citizens, but they continued to live under military rule until 8 November 1966, when these restrictions were abolished. The war gave Israel independence, establishing a sovereign Jewish presence in Israel for the first time in more than two millennia. For Israelis it was the War of Independence. It also destroyed Palestinian Arab society in the territory, turning most Palestinians into refugees. For them it was the Nakba (catastrophe).

Immediately after the war, in 1949, Israel's foreign minister, Moshe Sharett, suggested the return of up to 100,000 refugees to Israel proper within the context of a peace agreement. The proposal became moot when the Arab League refused to consider a peace treaty. Sharett also wished to explore the possibility of negotiating a Palestinian state in the West Bank and Gaza. Ben-Gurion was not interested in talks with Palestinians.[3] He sought to deal with Jordan rather than an independent Palestinian leadership.

Between 1948 and 1967, Israel's population more than tripled, due largely to the influx of Jewish refugees from Europe, the Middle East and North Africa. The Arab League and the Palestinians maintained a policy of rejection, refusing to negotiate a permanent settlement of the conflict. In their view, Israel remained an illegitimate presence within Arab territory. During this period Palestinian fedayeen conducted raids against civilian targets in Israel, from Jordan and Gaza. Israel retaliated forcefully. The cycle of atrocities against civilian populations on both sides continued the pattern of earlier phases of the conflict. Ben-Gurion launched the Sinai Campaign against Egypt in 1956. He justified it as a response to Egypt's support for fedayeen activity against Israel, and the growing Egyptian military threat. The campaign was coordinated with a combined British and French invasion of the Suez Canal area. Nasser had recently nationalized the Suez Canal. Israel was subsequently forced to withdraw from the Sinai by an American ultimatum and UN peacekeeping troops were placed in the Sinai as part of a political settlement that specified that Egypt would refrain from placing its army in the peninsula.

The Palestine Liberation Organization (PLO) was established on 28 May 1964, including a range of Palestinian militias and political parties. Its charter ruled out recognition of Israel, and it classified all Jewish immigrants to Israel–Palestine after the Balfour Declaration as illegal. Yasser Arafat was elected chair of the PLO's executive committee in 1969. The PLO became the dominant political leadership, and the umbrella for guerrilla groups, representing most Palestinians living outside of Israel.

In May 1967, after false Soviet reports of Israeli troop movements towards the Syrian border, Nasser ordered the UN peacekeeping force out of the Sinai, massed his army on the border with the Negev and closed the Straits of Tiran to Israeli shipping. Jordan and Syria also mobilized their armies on their borders with Israel. The IDF's reserves were called up for a month, bringing the country's economy to a near standstill. On 5 June Israel launched a pre-emptive strike, knocking out most of the Egyptian air force on the ground. Its army quickly occupied Gaza and the Sinai. It then responded to Jordanian and Syrian attacks by capturing the West Bank and East Jerusalem, with the Old City, from Jordan, and the Golan Heights from Syria. At the end of the war on 10 June, the large Palestinian populations of Gaza, the West Bank and East Jerusalem, many of them refugees from 1948, were under Israeli rule. Israel announced its willingness to return territory in exchange for peace agreements with neighbouring Arab states. Negotiations with the Palestinians were not part of this policy. The Arab League rejected recognition or negotiations at its summit meeting in Khartoum on 1 September 1967. Nasser's pan-Arab nationalist project of unifying distinct Arab states in the area within a single country was effectively shattered by the

1967 war. He died in October 1970, and Anwar Sadat took over as his successor.

Egypt and Syria unleashed a coordinated surprise attack against Israel on 6 October 1973, making deep inroads into the Sinai and the Golan. After initial reversals Israel regained most of the lost territory by the time that the war ended on 25 October, crossing the Suez into the African part of Egypt. In subsequent disengagement agreements Israel withdrew from part of the Sinai and the easternmost section of the Golan Heights. The shock of Israel's lack of military preparedness in 1973 generated an electoral rebellion against Labour's uninterrupted control of government since 1948. It brought a right-wing coalition under Menachem Begin to power in the election of June 1977.

Israel's Labour government had begun to establish settlements in parts of the West Bank near the 1967 border, and in the Jordan Valley, shortly after June 1967. These were limited in number and population. They were presented as security outposts, or, in some cases, as the re-establishment of Jewish communities destroyed in the 1948 war (Hebron and Gush Etzion). Its official policy remained land in exchange for peace. Begin's Likud government greatly expanded the settlement enterprise with the intention of annexing the territories. Successive Israeli governments of the right, Labour and the centre have indulged the settler movement with expansion of construction and extensive military protection. This group has become a substantial political lobby with significant electoral influence. The current settler population in the West Bank stands at more than 500,000 people.

Begin negotiated a full peace agreement with Anwar Sadat at Camp David in September 1978, and it was signed in March 1979. The agreement established full diplomatic relations between Israel and Egypt and demilitarized the Sinai under a US-led multinational observer force, in exchange for full Israeli withdrawal. Gaza remained under Israeli control, as a

Palestinian territory. Islamists within Egypt strongly opposed the peace agreement and plotted to overthrow the regime. The plot was suppressed, but on 6 October 1981 an Islamist gunman assassinated Sadat as he observed a military parade in Cairo. His successor, Hosni Mubarak, continued to sustain the agreement.

Jordan moved to strategic alignment with Israel after King Hussein expelled the PLO from the country in 1970–71 for threatening his regime with Syrian support. Arafat and most of the PLO moved to Lebanon, where they established bases in the southern part of the country. They shelled and rocketed Israeli towns across the border and engaged in terror attacks from these bases, prompting large-scale Israeli responses, leading to the first Lebanon war in the summer of 1982. Jordan signed a peace treaty with Israel, normalizing relations, on 26 October 1994.

The withdrawal of Egypt and Jordan from the conflict, and the stable ceasefire with Syria, shifted the focus of the Israeli–Arab dispute from a military confrontation between states, as it had been since 1948, back to a clash with the Palestinians, as it was prior to 1948. However, the fact that most Palestinians were now under Israeli military occupation altered the nature of the conflict significantly.

In June 1982 Ariel Sharon, then minister of defence in Begin's government, invaded Lebanon, with the stated aim of dislodging the PLO from its bases in the south of the country. It quickly became apparent that he had planned a much larger operation when he moved the army up to Beirut and took the western part of the city. Arafat and the PLO were forced out of Lebanon, to Tunisia. One of Sharon's objectives had been to install Bashir Gemayel as the Maronite president of Lebanon, in the hope that he would make peace with Israel. Gemayel did take power on 23 August 1982, but he did not offer Israel a peace agreement. He was assassinated on 14 September 1982, possibly by a Syrian intelligence agent. In the aftermath of this event soldiers of the Christian Lebanese Forces murdered 800–2,000 Palestinian and Shiite civilians in the Sabra neighbourhood of Beirut, and the Shatila refugee camp next to it, during two days in September 1982. The IDF had permitted them to enter the areas on 16 September, and it intervened to stop the massacre only on 18 September. A large demonstration of more than 400,000 Israelis (close to 10 per cent of the population) took place in Tel Aviv to protest Israel's complicity in the atrocity. Sharon was forced to resign as defence minister in 1983, on the recommendation of the Kahan Commission enquiry into the events of the Sabra and Shatila massacre. The IDF withdrew to southern Lebanon. Hezbollah replaced the PLO as the dominant military force in the south, and its attacks on the IDF eventually produced Israel's withdrawal from the country on 24 May 2000.

The first Palestinian Intifada started on 8 December 1987 in the Jabalia refugee camp in Gaza, and it quickly spread throughout the occupied territories. It continued until the Oslo Accords were signed in 1993. The IDF responded to the riots with force, resulting in hundreds of Palestinian casualties. Israel also suffered significant losses during this period, both civilian and military, due to terror attacks.

Arafat declared the State of Palestine on 15 November 1988 in Algiers. Israel and the PLO began a series of secret negotiations in Oslo in 1993. These produced the Oslo Accords, endorsed by Israel's prime minister, Yitzhak Rabin, and the chair of the PLO, Yasser Arafat, on 13 September 1993 at the White House. The agreement provided for mutual recognition between Israel and the PLO, Israeli withdrawal from major Palestinian population centres in Gaza and the West Bank and limited Palestinian autonomy under a newly constituted Palestinian Authority. The agreement was widely expected to lead to the establishment of a Palestinian state in the West Bank and Gaza.

The Oslo Accords generated violent opposition from Hamas among Palestinians, and from the Israeli right on the other side. Hamas conducted a series of deadly suicide bombings within Israel during 1994, which served to undermine Rabin's popular support. Right-wing Israeli political groups, including Likud, and settlers' organizations organized mass rallies in which they portrayed Rabin as a traitor. Some of these featured placards with doctored photos of Rabin in an SS uniform. Netanyahu, then leader of the Likud opposition, spoke at several of these events, helping to intensify the growing atmosphere of incitement. On 4 November 1995 Yigal Amir, a far-right student at Bar-Ilan University, assassinated Rabin as he was leaving a peace rally in Tel Aviv. Netanyahu became prime minister in 1996, and the Oslo peace process slowed considerably under his government.

Ehud Barak formed a Labour-led government in 1999. He was determined to engage the PLO in negotiations for a two-state settlement, despite Arafat's reluctance to deal with final status issues. Bill Clinton invited both sides to a conference at Camp David, which lasted from 11 to 25 July 2000, but they failed to reach an agreement. They did express a willingness to continue the discussion at another venue. The second Intifada broke out on 28 September 2000, following the failure of the Camp David summit, and Ariel Sharon's (then leader of the opposition) visit to the Temple Mount. Despite the violence, talks between Israel and the PLO resumed in Taba from 21 to 27 January 2001.

During the negotiations Clinton proposed a set of parameters that included the establishment of a Palestinian state on approximately 95 per cent of the West Bank and Gaza, with land swaps between Israel and the Palestinian state of 1–3 per cent to compensate for annexed settlement blocks. The Arab neighbourhoods of East Jerusalem were to go to the Palestinians, and the Jewish neighbourhoods to Israel. The Palestinians would receive sovereignty over the Al Aqsa

Mosque compound on the Temple Mount, and Israel would have the Western Wall. The Palestinians were asked to waive the right of return of refugees to territory within Israel. Israel was to acknowledge its role in causing the refugee problem, accept a small number of refugees and assist in an international fund to compensate displaced Palestinians and their descendants. Israel was to retain a temporary security presence in the Jordan Valley, which would be augmented by an international force. The Israelis accepted the parameters with reservations. Arafat was initially evasive in his response, but in the end he refused to endorse them.[4]

The Clinton parameters constitute the third partition plan in the history of the conflict to fail. Had Arafat been seriously interested in the proposal but unhappy with some of its provisions, he could have insisted on negotiating other arrangements for those parts of the plan. His reasons for not accepting it remain obscure. It is not clear whether he was unable to compromise on the right of return, he feared Hamas reprisals should he agree to the parameters or he was unable to make the transition from guerrilla leader to head of state. All of these factors may have conditioned his response. The collapse of the Camp David-Taba talks effectively ended the Oslo process.

Sharon was elected prime minister in 2001. The violence of the second Intifada intensified considerably, with armed clashes between the IDF and Palestinian groups throughout the West Bank and Gaza. The uprising resulted in numerous casualties on both sides, many of them civilians. More than 1,000 Israelis died, most at the hands of Hamas suicide bombers. In excess of 5,000 Palestinians were killed in IDF actions. Israel constructed a security barrier, running close to the 1967 border, sealing off the West Bank from Israel, in an effort to reduce terror attacks. The barrier and associated security checkpoints have imposed considerable hardship on the Palestinian population, which is denied freedom of movement both within sections of the West Bank and into Israel. Arafat died on 11 November 2004, and Mahmoud Abbas replaced him as president of the Palestinian Authority (PA), and chair of the PLO. The second Intifada had run its course by early 2005.

Sharon unilaterally withdrew Israeli troops and settlements from Gaza in August 2005 without negotiating an arrangement with the PA. He also pulled back from several villages in the northern West Bank. The PA held presidential elections in January 2005, which Abbas won, and legislative elections in January 2006. Hamas was the clear victor in the latter. Hamas proceeded to evict the PLO from Gaza in a violent coup in June 2007. It established an Islamist regime, and it set up a military force in the territory that began rocket attacks on Israel in subsequent years. This marked the beginning of Hamas' career as a significant military and political force in the area. In response, Israel and Egypt closed their respective borders with Gaza and restricted travel into and out of the territory.

Ehud Olmert, heading a centrist government as leader of the Kadima Party, attempted to reach agreement with Abbas on a peace plan in 2008. The proposal improved on the Clinton parameters by offering the equivalent of 100 per cent of the territory of the West Bank and Gaza (with land swaps), international control of the Old City and the return of a small number of refugees to Israel. Olmert regarded an end to Israel's occupation of the West Bank as crucial to Israel's security, and its future as a democracy with a large Jewish majority. While Abbas took the proposal seriously, he did not accept it.[5] This was the fourth partition plan suggested as a solution to the conflict, and it too did not succeed. The first Gaza war started on 27 December 2008 and lasted until 18 January 2009. It put an end to the negotiations with the PA.

The Israeli peace movement and the mainstream left ceased to be a major political force after the collapse of the Oslo process and the second Intifada. Following Olmert's failure to negotiate an agreement with Abbas, it was largely marginalized. Netanyahu became prime minister again in 2009. He has remained in power since then, with the exception of a brief interregnum between June 2021 to the end of 2022, when Naftali Bennett and Yair Lapid led a broad coalition that included right-wing and left-wing factions, and an Israeli Arab party. Under Netanyahu political contact with the PA has virtually stopped, settlement activity has expanded and several military engagements have flared with Hamas and the Islamic Jihad in Gaza. However, military coordination between the IDF and the PA has continued. Hamas built up its forces in Gaza and entrenched its presence in the West Bank, threatening the position of the PA. Extremists among the settlers frequently terrorize Palestinian civilians with relative impunity. The incidence of Palestinians committing lethal individual terror actions against Israeli civilians has soared. Israelis and Palestinians settled into a violent stasis, with a continuing cycle of attacks and retaliation constituting the norm.

The situation changed radically on 7 October 2023. Hamas violated the ceasefire that had been in effect with a barrage of rockets on Israeli population centres. This was followed by a coordinated ground attack in which approximately 3,000 Hamas terrorists came across the fence. In the course of the day they took over several army bases and moved into twenty-two Israeli towns, villages and kibbutzim near the border. They also targeted a music festival that was taking place in the Negev near the border. They moved systematically from house to house, wiping out entire families. Their victims included infants, children, pregnant women and the aged. They mutilated bodies and raped women. The army was slow in responding, and in some cases help did not arrive for the better part of ten hours.

By the time the Israeli army regained control of the area and eliminated most of the terrorist force, approximately 1,200 Israelis had been killed, the large majority of them civilians. In addition, Hamas took at least 240 hostages back to Gaza.

Slightly over a hundred of the Israeli hostages, and several foreign workers taken by Hamas, were freed, in exchange for Palestinian prisoners in Israel, during a brief truce in the fighting. The army and the intelligence service had been taken by surprise. They had left the area largely undefended, and the initial response was slow and disorganized. This was the largest and bloodiest terrorist attack in the country's history. The extent of its savagery left the country in deep shock, as did the drastic failure of the government and the army to handle it effectively.

Israel responded with a massive air campaign followed by a large-scale ground offensive to take over Gaza. This campaign has produced thousands of Palestinian casualties, many of them civilian. It cut off water, food and fuel supplies in order to degrade Hamas' capacity to fight, later restoring water, and allowing limited humanitarian aid through the Egyptian border crossing at Rafah. The military operation has imposed immense suffering on Gaza's civilian population. Israel has vowed to uproot Hamas as an effective fighting force and as the government of Gaza. Limited engagements with Hezbollah have been taking place in the north, and there is deep concern at the possibility of a second front. Iranian-backed Houthi militias have been firing missiles at Israel from Yemen, which have been intercepted by both US and Israeli forces.

The Hamas terrorist attack is a watershed event. It has altered the terms of the conflict in ways that will have major consequences for the region, the Israeli political scene, the Palestinians and the Jewish world. We require a significant interval of time before we will be able to understand the full extent of these consequences.

Let us step back from the horrors of this latest round of fighting to regain a broader sense of perspective. Looking at the extended history of the conflict, one finds considerable justice on both sides. Large-scale Jewish immigration to Palestine came at a time when Jews were physically threatened with mass murder and then systematic genocide in Europe, and it continued through the absorption of refugees expelled from Arab countries, followed by those forced out of the former Soviet Union. The events of the twentieth century made it painfully obvious that the host societies in which Jews had lived in Europe, the Middle East and North Africa were both unable and uninterested in providing a secure home for their respective Jewish communities. This was not a one-time cataclysm, but the culmination of centuries of persecution and exclusion throughout these areas. The creation of a secure Jewish homeland became a matter of survival for many people, and so a historical imperative. The Zionist movement saw a rare opportunity to achieve this objective, and it took it. The cost of this homeland has been the displacement of most of the Palestinian Arab residents of the country, who have been dispossessed through the ongoing conflict, and the failure of successive partition plans. They continue to live under conditions of foreign occupation and repression. Each side has inflicted violence and suffering on the other, as the agony of the clash has dragged on over the years.

There is no perfect solution that will properly address the grievances of both sides. All that can be expected, and possibly achieved, is an arrangement that allows Israelis and Palestinians to satisfy their basic needs through uncomfortable compromises. Such an arrangement would enable them to live as sovereign peoples, dividing the country between them. Demonizing and delegitimizing one of the parties, taken as a people rather than a government or an organization, is not warranted by the facts, nor does it advance an end to the violence. Neither side can be made to disappear. Shrill propaganda that paints the issue in simplistic terms and promotes an agenda that seeks to eliminate one party to the dispute is very much part of the problem rather than a programme for resolving it. Above all, it is necessary to shed the cosmic iconographies in which the conflict has been wrapped, particularly by the far left on one side and some of Israel's more extreme supporters on the other. It is an encounter that bears striking similarities to other inter-ethnic disputes that have afflicted neighbouring countries, as well as more distant ones. Interestingly, these have not, in general, attracted the same widespread mythologizing, misrepresentation or feverishly partisan polemic from non-participants that the Israeli–Palestinian problem inspires.

6.2 Cyprus: A Partial Analogy

It is not necessary to go far to find a case of long-term ethnic strife that bears some resemblance to the Israeli–Palestinian issue. Cyprus is Israel's closest non-Arab neighbour, situated 293 miles to the north-east off Israel's Mediterranean coast.[6] It has been inhabited by Greek-speaking people for at least the past last three millennia, since the Bronze Age. It was ruled by a variety of Middle Eastern and European empires throughout its history. The Ottomans captured Cyprus from the Venetians in 1571, when it became a province of the Ottoman Empire. They introduced several thousand Turkish settlers to the island, to whom they gave land, and this population produced a sizeable Turkish presence over the three centuries of Ottoman rule. Turkey granted Britain control over Cyprus in 1878 after the Russo-Turkish war, in exchange for a promise of support opposing possible Russian action against Ottoman possessions in Asia. Cyprus became a protectorate, leased to Britain. With the outbreak of the First World War in 1914, Britain annexed the island outright.

During the first part of the twentieth century tensions between the Greek and Turkish communities in Cyprus intensified. Greek nationalists sought union (*enosis*) with Greece. Turkish Cypriots were interested in partition to protect their rights, and to achieve autonomy. The Greek nationalists initiated a revolt against British colonial rule in October 1931, which involved weeks of rioting. It was suppressed by British forces on the island in November. Nationalist violence also flared in the 1950s. Cyprus became an independent republic under President Archbishop Makarios III on 16 August 1960. Its constitution defined a system of power sharing between its two main constituent communities. At this time the population of Cyprus was 573,566, with 442,138 Greeks (77 per cent), 104,320 Turks (18.2 per cent) and 27,108 members of other groups (4.7 per cent) Both sides were dissatisfied with the constitution, and violent inter-communal violence erupted in 1963, causing hundreds of casualties among Turks and Greeks, with the destruction of numerous Turkish and mixed villages. Many Turkish Cypriots withdrew to protected enclaves for security. The capital city, Nicosia, was divided, and UN peacekeeping troops were deployed to separate the communities.

On 15 July 1974, a Greek Cypriot military junta, encouraged by the military regime in Greece, seized power in a coup, to implement *enosis*. Turkey invaded the northern part of Cyprus with the stated aim of protecting the island's Turkish population. The junta was deposed, a ceasefire reached and Makarios returned to power. In August, Turkey sent additional forces to Cyprus and extended its control to 37 per cent of the island's territory in the north. Approximately 170,000 Greeks were forced from their homes in northern Cyprus, while about 60,000 Turks were expelled from the south. The displaced Greek and Turkish residents were settled in the abandoned homes left by the refugees of each community. Turkey established the Turkish Republic of Northern Cyprus on 15 November 1983, and it remains the only country that recognizes it. Legally, the Republic of Cyprus has sovereignty over the entire island.

Since 1974, the Turkish government has imported large numbers of Turkish settlers from Anatolia and other areas of Turkey into the northern territory. The total current population of Cyprus is 1.25 million. Of the 382,836 people in the Turkish Republic of Northern Cyprus, an estimated 50 per cent are settlers from Turkey, or their descendants. When a foreign power introduces a civilian population into territory that it occupies as a result of armed conflict, this action violates Article 49, sixth paragraph, of the 1949 Geneva Convention IV.

Several attempts were made to negotiate a solution to the Cyprus conflict, none of which have succeeded to date. In 2004 the UN secretary general, Kofi Annan, proposed a confederation of two autonomous states on the island, with a collective presidency, and a joint legislature consisting of a senate and a house of deputies. Both chambers would have proportions of their seats allotted to each community. In a referendum on the plan two-thirds of the Turkish population approved it, but 74 per cent of the Greeks opposed it. In May 2004 the Republic of Cyprus joined the EU. The island remains divided, and there is little if any likelihood that the refugees from either side will return to their original homes. The situation in Cyprus continues to be a source of tension between Greece and Turkey.

In addition to the obvious differences between the Greek–Turkish dispute in Cyprus and the Israeli–Palestinian conflict, there are clear points of similarity between them. In each a population that immigrated in large numbers, initially under Ottoman rule, became permanently settled in the territory. Both countries were taken over by the British in the First World War, and tensions steadily grew between their respective constituent populations under British colonial administration. Attempts to solve these through either a federal model or partition failed, and inter-communal violence expanded. It erupted into an international conflict, with the involvement of regional armies. Each country was effectively partitioned by force, and one of the parties expanded its presence through settlement in territory that it had occupied. A UN-sponsored federal partition proposal was accepted by one side, but it was rejected by the other. A significant part of one population, and a smaller element of the second, were forced out of their respective homes and became refugees in the other part of the territory. Each conflict remains unresolved, with bitter acrimony between the two sides.

There is, however, a significant distinction worth noting. Progressive opinion has not, for the most part, invested the Cyprus dispute with the intense significance that it assigns to the Israeli–Palestinian problem. Greek Cypriot nationalists, Turkish Cypriot separatists and their respective sponsors in Greece and Turkey, have all remained largely free of the stigma that Israel, and its supporters in the Jewish Diaspora, now bear. Israel has increasingly been portrayed as a demonic actor, and the locus of a malicious international lobby that promotes reactionary colonialist causes everywhere. By contrast, Greeks and Turks in Cyprus are considered with detachment, and with sympathy for both parties to their dispute. Neither is asked to give up their core national interests for a simple 'one-state solution' that purports to be undefined relative to the collective identity of its two main populations.

There are other longstanding inter-ethnic conflicts that have become international problems, with analogies to the Israeli–Palestinian issue. The partition of the Indian sub-continent between India and Pakistan in 1947, the year before Israel was established, is an obvious one. It involved the creation of two states due to ethnic violence between Hindus and Muslims. This violence erupted under British colonial rule, and the partition accompanied the end of this regime. There were hundreds of thousands of casualties on both sides (a total of at least a million killed) and approximately 15 million refugees were displaced by the fighting. Few if any of them have returned to their original homes. The conflict continues, with territorial disputes between the two countries, and ongoing tension between Hindus and Muslims in India. Left-wing opinion may regret the dispute, and the partition that it generated. Progressives may criticize Modi's ethno-nationalist policies, or object to Pakistan's indulgence of Islamist politics. But at no point is either side to the conflict delegitimized, its right to exist as a sovereign state relentlessly questioned or its people portrayed as a malevolent collection of oppressors.

The Israeli–Palestinian problem resembles these other conflicts, but it is widely perceived in entirely different terms. It has a complex history, and both sides have justice on their side. The fact that large parts of the contemporary left have reduced it to a crude morality play has less to do with the facts of the case than with a perverse world view that is driving this reduction. Until this conflict is naturalized within its full historical context, it will not be possible to approach it rationally, or to appreciate the necessary conditions of a possible resolution.

6.3 Partition vs Binationalism: Two States or One?

For many years there was widespread agreement among moderate and progressive observers of the Middle East that the Israeli–Palestinian conflict requires a two-state solution. With the failure of the Oslo peace process and the Olmert proposal, the dominance of extremists on both sides and the expansion of the settlement enterprise in the West Bank, support for this model has steadily eroded. Large parts of the left and liberal opinion now endorse a one-state model that is described as a state that guarantees equal rights for all its residents. This is presented as a democratic alternative to a Jewish state that assigns privileged status to one of its ethnic groups. The dialectic between these options is a version of the debate between partition and binationalism, which preceded the creation of Israel.[7]

The programme for a binational Jewish–Arab state in Palestine was proposed by two main groups within the Yishuv.

One was Brit Shalom (1925–33), an organization of liberal Zionists that included Judah Magnes, Gershom Scholem, Haim Kalvarisky, Arthur Ruppin, Hugo Bergmann and Martin Buber. It was succeeded by the Ichud in the 1940s. Hashomer Hatzair, the left-wing socialist Kibbutz movement, was the second advocate of binationalism. It envisaged a joint Jewish–Arab workers country in all of western Palestine. After the 1929 riots binationalism was a minority option within the Zionist movement. However, Weizmann did offer sceptical encouragement to this approach as an avenue to explore. The mainstream Palestinian leadership opposed it as a Zionist programme that would sustain continuing Jewish immigration. Two moderate Palestinian leaders, Fawzi Darwish al-Husseini and the labour leader Sami Taha, were sympathetic to a binationalist approach in the 1940s, but they were assassinated by Palestinian rejectionists. The binationalists are generally regarded as having been a fringe group in the Yishuv. This was indeed the case for Brit Shalom and the Ichud, but not for Hashomer Hatzair. It constituted one of two main compo-nents of the political party Mapam (The United Workers Party), the second being Achdud HaAvodah. Mapam had the second-largest number of seats in the Knesset of 1949, and the third-largest representation in 1955.

In principle a binational model offers an attractive framework for solving the Israeli–Palestinian conflict. Both peoples would share the full territory of Israel-Palestine, and they would enjoy equal rights to it. Painful territorial conces-sions would be avoided, with immigrants and refugees from each side accommodated in a single country. A moment's reflection on the power-sharing arrangements required to implement such a programme should be sufficient to expose it as hopelessly devoid of any realistic prospect of success. The Middle East, and other regions, are littered with failed multi-ethnic countries that have dissolved into bitter chaos. They are racked by civil war, and the intervention of regional powers that frequently accompanies it. Lebanon, Iraq and Syria are prime examples of this phenomenon, as is the former Yugoslavia. Even binational states set up under far more auspicious conditions, such as Czechoslovakia, have split into their component nations due to nationalist competition. Ostensibly successful binational/multinational states, like Canada, Belgium and Spain, live under the constant centrifugal pressure of separatist movements.

In order for a binational venture to succeed, there must be a minimum of trust between its constituent nations, which must be willing to share power within common institutions of government. This condition is radically absent among most Israelis and Palestinians. After 150 years of strife, they regard one another as existential threats. Advocates of a one-state model for Israel-Palestine are seeking to inflict an arrangement of co-habitation on two peoples who, for the most part, have no interest in shared sovereignty. It is a recipe for civil war, and ongoing struggle for control of the military and political mechanisms of power. The advocates of the one-state model are generally unable to describe what it would look like, or how it could be realized, with any degree of detail or credibility. Therefore, it remains little more than a seductive, but empty slogan. Hamas' recent mass terrorist attack and the Israeli response highlight precisely how thoroughly devoid of substance a one-state model is in the present context. Why, then, has it become the rallying cry of putatively progressive opinion on the Israeli–Palestinian problem?

Several considerations come to mind. First, the growth of settlements and the discriminatory infrastructure that supports them has greatly complicated and undermined the prospects of a two-state model. This has caused many people to conclude that the approach is no longer viable, and so to opt for a one-state approach as the default alternative. While settlements are certainly a serious obstacle to a partition agreement, they by no means render it impossible. As of 2022 they take up 202 square kilometres, which is 3.6 per cent of the total land area of the West Bank (Owada, 2023). Most are concentrated close to the Green Line. Both the Clinton parameters and the Olmert proposals included land swaps to compensate the Palestinians for the territory of annexed settlement blocks. A Palestinian state comprising a contiguous West Bank and East Jerusalem, connected to Gaza by tunnels and/or a raised highway, remains feasible. It is the political dominance of rejectionists on both sides that is preventing such an arrangement, rather than the situation on the ground. The competition between the PA and Hamas seriously undermines the conditions for the two-state option. However, in the end the programme of two states for two peoples remains the only hope for an eventual agreement, despite the obvious difficulties involved in realizing it. A one-state framework offers no chance of a peaceful solution.

Second, one-state advocates frequently invoke South Africa's transition from apartheid to multi-ethnic democracy as the paradigm that they envisage for Israel-Palestine. In fact, the comparison is deeply flawed and inappropriate. Apartheid South Africa segregated its population on racial criteria to preserve the dominance of a White European elite. Both the White and the non-White South African populations are culturally diverse. The African and other non-White groups sought to participate in an existing nation state under conditions of equal citizenship. They saw themselves as belonging to the same national framework. The African National Congress was committed to building such a multi-ethnic society in a single country. By contrast the conflict between Jews and Arabs is not racial. It turns on differences in culture, national identity, language, religious identity and historical experience. These properties are constitutive of nations. In this case, both nations are multiracial. Each seeks independence within its own territory. Attempting to present a national conflict as a racial issue is an exercise in misrepresentation.

Finally, more extreme one-staters find the notion of a Jewish state unpalatable. They regard it as intrinsically racist and exclusionary. To the extent that Jewish privilege is sustained by coercive legislation or government policy, this claim has some point. But the original mainstream Zionist programme called for an egalitarian society with a large Jewish majority, that offers equal rights to all of its citizens, Jews and non-Jews alike. Israel has fallen short of this ideal. Few, if any countries fully realize democratic and egalitarian values. But they can be reformed to approach them more closely. However, militant one-state advocates oppose the existence of a Jewish polity of any kind, even if it is a model of liberal democracy. Interestingly, they have no difficulty with other ethnic states, either in the Middle East or elsewhere. They do not insist that Greek and Turkish Cypriots, or Indians and Pakistanis, give up their respective countries to live in unified states 'of all of their citizens'. They grant the complexity of other long-term historical struggles, and they recognize the need to accommodate competing national claims in those cases.

It is important to recognize that the country that extreme one-state advocates demand for Israel-Palestine is actually not binational. They describe it in the radically neutral republican language of the universal civil state that Bruno Bauer promoted. They are well aware of the fact that the Palestinians will sustain their ethnic national identity, and that they will seek to render it fully pervasive in this unitary framework. By contrast, Israeli Jews are required to disappear as a national collective for the country to qualify as democratic. This is, in contemporary terms, a version of Bauer's insistence that Jews give up their membership in a community in order to merit citizenship in the universal state, while tacitly acknowledging that other nations will retain their languages, cultures and national identities. Radical one-state enthusiasts regard the restoration of Palestinians to national dominance throughout all of Israel-Palestine as the fulfilment of historical justice.

Israeli Jews are an illicit people. They are not entitled to a national life, only civil rights as individuals. The historical forces that created Israel through the persecution, extermination and expulsion of Jews throughout the Diaspora remain invisible on this view. They are discounted as irrelevant to the discussion. Unlike the previous two variants of a one-state approach, this one is toxic, rather than naive or ill-informed. It is a programme for eliminating one side to the conflict.

The approval with which part of the radical left received Hamas' mass terrorist attack clearly indicates that it is entirely at ease with the violent destruction of the Jewish presence in Israel Palestine. In advocating a one-state model as the 'democratic' solution to the conflict, this group is using 'democratic' as a decorative euphemism for an eliminationist agenda. They are not committed to Nelson Mandela's inclusive view of liberation. Instead, they have shown themselves to be disciples of a movement that seeks to solve the conflict through expulsion and slaughter. They adhere to the mirror image of the programme that the extreme right in Israel pursues. Anyone genuinely committed to a just, realistic and peaceful resolution of the Israeli–Palestinian struggle will resist this view with the same vigour as that with which they ought to oppose Israel's continued occupation of the West Bank.

7

The Jewish Response to the Crisis

In the previous chapters I have considered antisemitism from socioeconomic, historical and cultural perspectives. I have attempted to understand its contemporary manifestations within the context of anti-globalist reactions to long-term economic trends that have caused major social crises throughout much of the world. These developments have produced fertile ground for different varieties of identity-driven political movements, in which conspiracy theories about the control of events to which these movements are responding have become increasingly influential. Such theories frequently express deeply rooted cultural attitudes to Jews that have taken shape over millennia. In this chapter I will briefly consider the different ways in which Jews have been reacting to the current patterns of antisemitism that they are encountering.

7.1 Collaborating with the Far Right

In America the right-wing Zionist Organization of America and part of the Orthodox Jewish community endorsed Trump.

As we noted in Chapter 3, Éric Zemmour ran to the right of Marine Le Pen and the National Rally in the 2022 French presidential election. Some Jews in other part of the Diaspora have also become supporters of far-right movements in their countries of residence. While these groups constitute small minorities within their respective communities, they are a vocal and highly visible presence within them. They cite the pro-Israel stance of far-right politicians as one of the main reasons for their support. They also regard them as a bulwark against radical Islamism.

There is a historical precedent for this phenomenon. A small minority of Italian Jews were active in the Italian Fascist Party in the 1920s and 1930s.[1] Initially Mussolini did not adopt a racist view of nationalism, and antisemitism was not part of his programme. This changed as his alliance with Hitler developed, and in 1938 he instituted a series of racial laws that targeted Jews for exclusion. Membership in the Fascist Party did not exempt Jews from these laws, nor was it of any consequence when Italy's Jews were deported to the Nazi extermination camps in the 1940s. Italian Jews who joined the Fascists in the first part of the twentieth century may have shown exceedingly poor political judgement, but they had no previous experience to serve as a guide as to where this movement would soon lead. Diaspora Jews who align themselves with far-right movements now cannot plead ignorance of the historical background from which these movements have emerged.

Alignment with the far right is a deeply misguided move for what should be glaringly obvious reasons. The ostensibly pro-Israel positions that such parties adopt is purely transactional. As we observed in Chapter 3, in Trump's case it is at least partly driven by a desire to curry favour with the large evangelical component of his base. It evaporated when his relationship with Netanyahu soured. Far-right support does not express concern for Jewish survival, or the wellbeing of Israel, but approval of the ethno-nationalist policies of the Netanyahu government. It blends seamlessly with the domestic antisemitism that these movements trade in. Their opposition to radical Islamism does not stem from concern with the threat that it poses to Jews and other minorities. It targets Muslims in general as an expression of hostility to immigrants, and of general xenophobia. Antisemitism is an integral element of this toxic mix. Jewish support for far-right political movements is a short-sighted, self-destructive exercise in assisting a dangerous enemy with a proven track record of anti-Jewish racism.

In Chapter 3 I argued that Netanyahu is a politician of the Alt Right whose policies are consonant with those of his allies in Europe and America. I also suggested that the rise of the far right in Israel is conditioned by the same economic and social forces that have propelled it to influence in other parts of the world, particularly in the West. Long-term levels of acute economic inequality and social marginalization have rendered working-class voters, particularly from Middle Eastern and North African Jewish backgrounds, receptive to Netanyahu's manipulation of their sense of grievance, through chauvinist, anti-elitist rhetoric. His current government is particularly extreme in policy and composition. It is a coalition dominated by radical religious Zionist parties from the most militant wing of the settlers' movement, ultra-Orthodox parties and the anti-liberal nationalist core of the Likud. Netanyahu has appointed Itamar Ben-Gvir, a disciple of Meir Kahane, as minister of internal security. Ben-Gvir has been indicted on numerous charges of anti-Arab violence, and he was convicted of racist incitement. In his current position he has sought to intervene personally in operational decisions concerning the activities of the police in Israel and the border police in the West Bank. Netanyahu also appointed Bezalel Smotrich as minister of finance. Smotrich has a history of anti-Arab agitation and religious extremism. As part of his ministerial role he has been given responsibility for the settlement and lands section of the Civil Administration of the West Bank.

The moderating pragmatic influences that partially constrained Netanyahu's previous governments in some areas of public policy are largely absent in his current coalition. This has produced reckless government initiatives that have precipitated several major political crises within the country. The most significant of these prior to October 7 is the emergence of a mass protest movement opposing the minister of justice Yariv Levin's proposed bills for restructuring the legal system. The legislation would, among other changes, subordinate Supreme Court decisions to an override by simple majority vote in the Knesset, thus abolishing the Court's role as an independent check on government power. It would also alter the system for appointing judges from the current arrangement in which a committee consisting of elected Members of Knesset and representatives of the legal profession determine the selections, to one that hands full control of the process to the ruling coalition's representatives within the committee.[2] The move is similar to the procedures that other right-wing authoritarian governments, such as those in Hungary and Poland, have invoked to destroy the independence of the judiciary and enlarge government power, by dispensing with constitutional oversight. In Israel's case, the changes would cancel the role of the Supreme Court in interpreting basic laws (a quasi-constitutional legal framework) and clauses of the country's Declaration of Independence, as restrictions on government actions and Knesset legislation. They would also permit the coalition to stock the courts with political appointees who share its views.

As part of their polemic on behalf of these proposals members of the coalition present them as an attempt to redress the domination of the courts by an Ashkenazi elite. This is a particularly clear instance of Netanyahu's use of ethnic grievance as a recruiting tool for his regime. It mirrors the anti-elitist appeal to socioeconomically disadvantaged groups that propels the far right in other countries.

The Kohelet Forum, an ultra-conservative Jerusalem think tank, has developed many of the policy positions that Netanyahu's current and past governments have pursued. It lobbied for the Nation State Law that I discussed in Chapter 3. It was responsible for formulating the principles of the judicial reform that Levin attempted to pass in the Knesset.[3] The Kohelet Forum is supported by anonymous contributions from American supporters. It describes itself as, among other things, 'libertarian'. This description refers to its advocacy of minimizing public regulation of the economy. They are, then, importing into the Israeli context many of the ideas that drive far-right American political movements. They combine religiously grounded ethno-nationalism with economic policies that promote corporate power and the political influence of private wealth. They seek to weaken independent judicial oversight of government in order to remove legal constraints on the way in which politicians govern.

The legal reform has been opposed by a sustained, large-scale popular protest movement. This movement held regular street demonstrations throughout the country that attracted hundreds of thousands of participants representing a large cross-section of the population. It has included high-ranking reserve army officers and pilots who said that they would refuse to report for military duty if the legislation is passed. Former prime ministers, past ministers of defence, heads of intelligence services, large parts of the legal profession, leading economists, members of Israel's high-tech industry, medical workers, academics and labour unions also joined.

The demonstrations were generally peaceful, but frequently militant in tone. They crossed party lines, with people from the centre right and religious Jews joining activists from the left and the liberal centre. They reached a climax on the evening of 26 March 2023, after Netanyahu dismissed his defence minister, Yoav Galant, for suggesting that the legal reform legislation be paused, due to the sharp internal divisions that it had provoked. Following the announcement massive street protests took place at night, and they continued through the following day. Netanyahu suspended passage of the legislation on the evening of 27 March, promising to reintroduce it in a later session of the Knesset. He eventually reinstated Galant as defence minister. The government organized a large right-wing demonstration at the end of April to support the legislation. It was dominated by the religious Zionist right and the settlers' movement. Interestingly Ultra-Orthodox religious and political leaders called on the members of their community to avoid it.

Part of the legal reform was implemented. On 23 July, the government succeeded in passing a bill that withdraws the Reasonableness Doctrine. This vaguely formulated constraint allowed the Supreme Court to overturn laws and government practices that it regarded as violating the norms of proper government. It was invoked in 2023 to overrule the appointment of Aryeh Deri, leader of the ultra-Orthodox Sephardi Shas Party, as a minister, on the grounds that he was convicted of bribery, fraud and breach of trust (with a three-year sentence) in 1999. He also entered into a plea bargain for tax crimes in 2021. Should the new legislation stand, the Doctrine will no longer be available to the courts as a basis for judicial oversight of government practice. Large-scale protests against this legislation, and proposed further moves, continued. The Supreme Court is considering several legal challenges to the government's legislation withdrawing the Reasonableness Doctrine. Should it rule against this legislation, then a constitutional crisis could ensue.

The protest movement constitutes a revival of Israel's mainstream liberal left. While it has coalesced around resistance to the current regime's assault on democratic institutions, it expresses long-term economic and social grievances. These include the growing influence of Israel's Ultra-Orthodox community in the public life of the country. Through their political parties within governing coalitions the Ultra-Orthodox have sustained exemption from army service for most of their members, and substantial amounts of financial assistance for their large families, while many of their adults are not active in the labour market. They have sought to impose additional religious restrictions on a variety of state-supported institutions. The settlements are also a major drain on government revenue at a time when resources for the secular education system and public services are under pressure. The cost of living is exceedingly high, and apartment ownership is out of reach for most young people. In a sense, the protest movement represents a revolt of the 'squeezed middle class' in Israel. This class bears the burden of taxation and military service, and it is largely secular, at least in its political commitments. Over the years its standard of living and its social space have been increasingly threatened by a variety of interest groups and factors.

It is possible to discern a line of continuity between the recent democratic protest movement and the wave of social justice demonstrations that swept Israel in August 2011. The latter were focused on the high cost of living, particularly housing. They also brought together a broad demographic of Israelis that crossed party and religious lines. The social justice movement dissipated after several months. Despite promises from Netanyahu and other government officials of the time, nothing of substance was done to accommodate the protesters' concerns. Nor did the movement succeed in translating the popular disaffection that it expressed into electoral terms. Netanyahu and his government remained in power, pursuing the same policies that had provoked the demonstrations.

There are at least three important differences between the current situation and the one that existed in 2011. First, the social justice movement of 2011 was explicitly addressing the consequences of the sharp inequality in income distribution that has become deeply entrenched in Israel over the past forty years. The basic institutions of the country were not then seen as under immediate threat. The recent protest movement was responding to an effort by a more extreme government to overturn some of the basic structures of Israel's democracy.

Second, unlike the regime of 2011, the current coalition is widely regarded as a danger to the country's national security. Netanyahu's willingness to grant wide-ranging powers to radical irredentist elements of the settler's movement has produced a pattern of serious provocation directed at the Palestinians in the West Bank and East Jerusalem. He has disregarded the advice of the leadership of the army and the police in granting Ben Gvir, Smotrich and their supporters considerably greater freedom than they had enjoyed in the past, to pursue extremist activities in sensitive areas. This has raised the level of violence in the territories, and it has created tensions with the American government. It has also undermined Israel's relations with the UAE and other Arab countries with which it has diplomatic relations.

Finally, while the economy was reasonably sound in 2011, the proposed judicial reform has produced deep unease among foreign investors, as well as serious criticism from leading economists. Both are troubled by the prospect of a regime that does not respect the rule of law within a liberal democratic framework damaging the political stability required for sustained growth. This worry is combined with concern over Netanyahu's promises of unrestrained spending for the partisan projects of his coalition partners. The current government is also considered to be a danger to the country's economic wellbeing.

These factors have caused the supporters of the democracy movement to see the coalition as an existential threat to the country's survival as a stable and prosperous democracy. They have brought together a broader range of people than the social justice movement of 2011. The movement has sustained large-scale protest over many months, which showed no sign of fading. It was a bottom-up phenomenon, without a single leadership figure, although many senior people from the highest ranks of the country's professional, business and military domains are actively involved. Whether the democracy movement will be more successful than the social justice protests of 2011 in generating change remains to be seen. It does, however, provide an impressive instance of popular resistance to the efforts of a far-right government to dismantle a liberal democracy in pursuit of an extreme ethno-nationalist vision. As such, its significance extends well beyond the Israeli political context.

The massive security failure of the government and the army in the face of the Hamas terrorist attack on 7 October confirmed the worst fears of the democracy movement that Netanyahu's far-right coalition posed a serious threat to the country's security and well being. Not only had the intelligence services and the military left the country completely exposed to the attack but many government agencies did not function effectively in dealing with its effects for days after it took place. Interestingly, the members of the democracy movement were often the first responders in the emergency. Reserve soldiers and pilots who had threatened not to serve if Levin's judicial reform was enacted rushed to their units on the southern border to defend against the terrorist assault. Others who had demonstrated every week against the reform quickly organised civic organizations to provide housing and services for the thousands of people displaced by the Gaza war. They filled a gaping void left by the government ministries that Netanyahu's political appointees were running.[4] These were the people who Netanyahu and his political allies had described as "traitors" and "anarchists" when they protested against his judicial programme.

It appears that one of the reasons that the army was stretched thin and unable to defend the southern border against the Hamas assault is that large numbers of troops had been moved to the West Bank to protect settlements. This was done at a time when extremist settlers were engaging in violent acts of provocation against Palestinian villagers, with the tacit support of far-right members of the governing coalition. It is also worth noting that, as Gorenberg (2023) observes, Netanyahu had pursued a long-term policy of strengthening Hamas and weakening the PA. The objective of this strategy was to marginalise the PA in order to avoid negotiations that might undermine his annexationist agenda in the West Bank.

7.2 Collaborating with the Far Left

A minority of Jews in the Diaspora and in Israel have joined the far left. They embrace its extreme anti-Zionism, and they actively support the Boycott, Divestment and Sanctions (BDS) campaign, including the cultural boycott of Israel. Jewish Voice for Peace and, in the UK, the pro-Corbynite Jewish Voice for Labour are representative of this group. Jewish academics involved in applying critical theory and cultural studies to political issues are prominent in the contemporary postmodernist anti-colonialist left.[5] Several members of these groups were among the cheerleaders for the Hamas mass terrorist attack on 7 October.

In many respects they are reprising the views and activities of Jewish political movements from the first half of the twentieth century. German Jewish liberals like Hermann Cohen regarded Zionism as tribalistic and opposed to the universalist values of an enlightened social order. They also felt that it degraded the moral vision that animates Jewish religious culture. The Bund sought to achieve Jewish cultural autonomy within the framework of a broader socialist federation. It saw Zionism as a distraction from the task of building Jewish workers' participation in the class struggle within the societies in which they lived. Jewish Communists identified the route to Jewish emancipation with a universal workers' revolution that would eradicate both class privilege and racism, including antisemitism. Jewish anarchists sought the abolition of nation states and the oppression that they embody. Ultra-Orthodox Jews opposed Zionism as a secular political movement that threatened the integrity of Jewish religious commitment and traditional observance.

Each of these responses to the Jewish situation enjoyed a certain plausibility within the turn-of-the-century European context. Their programmes could at least be imagined as possible ways of achieving a reasonable Jewish future in this environment. This plausibility was decisively eliminated by the successive cataclysms that followed. Nazism obliterated two-thirds of European Jewry within six years. Stalinism destroyed organized Jewish life within the Soviet Union, and the little that remained of this life within Eastern and Central Europe after the war. The expulsion of Jews from Arab countries in the second half of the twentieth century brought most of the Jewish Diaspora in the Islamic world to an end.

The new anti-Zionism of Jewish supporters of the contemporary far left calls for the cancellation of Israel as a Jewish state and a renewed focus on cultivating Jewish life in the Diaspora. This view can be described as a new Diasporism. It is bizarrely ahistorical in that it takes the catastrophes that rendered its own antecedent ideologies unworkable to be one-time events with no direct significance for the processes that led to the creation of Israel, or for the current situation of Jews in the Diaspora. New Diasporism does not seriously address the historical issue of Jewish survival in hostile host societies, that these events raise, but it reverts to past ideological models that have failed to solve this problem.

The following example illustrates the acute historical amnesia that permeates Jewish participation in the anti-Zionist far left. After the war Stalin resumed his purges and terror of the 1930s. He orchestrated show trials in the Soviet Union and its East European allies to conduct an antisemitic campaign that targeted Jewish Communists as agents of an international Zionist conspiracy and cosmopolitans disloyal to their countries. One of the most prominent of these was the Slánský trial in Prague in 1952.[6] A total of fourteen Czechoslovak Communist officials were indicted on charges of conspiracy against the regime in cooperation with imperialist powers, Israel primary among them. Of the fourteen defendants eleven were Jewish, with Rudolf Slánský, former secretary general of the Czechoslovak Communist Party, the main figure among them. The trial followed the usual Stalinist show trial template. Confessions were extracted from the accused through torture. Slánský and ten other defendants were executed, while three others received life sentences. A high-pitched anti-Zionist propaganda campaign preceded and followed the trial in the Soviet and East European Communist press. Western Jewish Communists and fellow travellers defended the trials and their attendant polemics in the Soviet media. They claimed that these were directed not at Jews, but at a Zionist conspiracy aimed at subverting Communist countries.

Harap (1953) is an instance of such an apologetic for the Slánský trial. Harap is at pains to argue that, unlike the imperialist West, the Soviet Union and its Communist allies were free of antisemitism. He claims that the charges against the defendants in the trial were well documented, and that they were deliberately misrepresented in the Western press. He insists that it is important not to conflate criticism of Israel's government (at the time, headed by Ben-Gurion) with antisemitism. Here is a representative quote.

The absence of any reference to Jews as such is easy to under-stand. In the Soviet Union and the people's democracies, anti-Semitism is a crime against the state, explicitly written into the constitution, together with a prohibition against all forms of racism and discrimination. What is more, this prohibition against anti-Semitism and racism is enforced.

The truth is that the general press and leaders of middle-class Jewish life, in their zeal to further hysterical war propaganda against the socialist countries, have promoted certain confusions that are not entirely innocent. Hatred of socialism, of the Soviet Union, of those who are fighting for negotiations and mutual concessions between the United States and the Soviet Union to achieve a desperately needed peace have led these forces to give the impression that anti-Zionism is tantamount to antisemitism, that opposition to the Ben-Gurion government is anti-Israel. In the course of this trial, the Czechoslovak press made quite clear that it considered Zionism an evil force. It is hard to deny them justification for this view in the light of the revelations of the Prague trial about the use of Zionist organizations for espionage. But *Rude Pravo*, official Czechoslovak Communist organ, on November 25, 1952, reaffirmed the Communist Party's implacable condemnation of anti-Semitism: 'It (the Party) must fight against Zionism. Lenin already pointed out that antisemitism and Zionism, or any form of fostering Jewish exceptionalism, are only head and tail of the same coin. Our Party has always emphasized that anti-Semitism is hostile to the working class, that it is base and beneath human dignity.' (pp. 6–7)

Harap's views anticipate the anti-Zionism of today's far left. The main difference is that the former are specified in terms of Communist ideology, while the latter are formulated as an expression of postmodernist anti-colonialism. Harap's pamphlet was published by *Jewish Life*, a New York-based periodical associated with the Communist Party USA. It broke with the party in 1956 and became *Jewish Currents*. The magazine was relaunched in 2018 as a forum of the Jewish radical left, and it is dominated by anti-Zionist opinion. Many of its articles on Israel and Zionism exhibit more than a passing resemblance to the attitudes of its original predecessor. The clear line of descent from the deeply racist character of Soviet anti-Zionist campaigns under Stalin and his successors to the obsessive anti-Zionist conspiracy theories of the postmodernist radical left seem to be invisible to the latter's Jewish participants. Jews who have embraced far-right politics have no difficulty in recognizing antisemitism on the left, but they are unable to identify it in their own constituency. Similarly, Jewish activists of the far left see the antisemitism of the far right clearly, but they are impervious to the extent to which it permeates their own movement.

At least three factors appear to be driving the new Diasporism of the Jewish far left. One is the high cost of any association with Israel in radical circles. The systematic criminalization of the country and its people renders it a major liability for anyone seeking to participate in progressive politics. Vigorous criticism of the misdeeds of the Israeli government, combined with commitment to Israel's right to exist, no longer suffice for acceptance among those who define fashionably radical opinion. Militant rejection of Zionism and the embrace of a one-state model have become the loyalty oath required of Jews wishing to identify as progressives. If historical precedent is a guide to the way in which this pattern evolves, the cost of acceptance of Jews by the radical left tends to escalate until even the most committed Jewish activists are subject to suspicion, and, eventually, to exclusion. Much of the far left's embrace of the Hamas terrorist atrocity of 7 October has marked a new escalation in the terms of membership required for Jewish participation. It will be interesting to see how many Jewish supporters will be prepared to satisfy these terms.

A second factor seems to be frustration that Zionism has not solved the problem of antisemitism, despite its promise to do so. Israel has provided a sanctuary for millions of Jewish refugees escaping persecution, but it has, in turn, become a target for intense hostility that frequently serves as a conduit for channelling hatred of Jews as a people. This has led to a sense among some, both in the Diaspora and in Israel itself, that it is more of a burden than an asset. The new Diasporists are anxious to free themselves of this burden. They assume that should Israel cease to exist as a Jewish state the rise in anti-Jewish racism that they are encountering among anti-globalist movements will disappear, or at least diminish. In its extreme form this approach leads to the perverse conclusion that Israel's existence is the cause of antisemitism, rather than a response to it.

Finally, the new Diasporists in America may be clinging to a notion of Jewish exceptionalism in that country. This view takes the Jewish experience in America to be outside of the normal patterns of Jewish history in the Diaspora. It sees it as exempt from the sequence of persecutions, expulsions and mass murder that have punctuated Jewish life in other parts of the Diaspora. Such a view is, of course, closely tied to notions of American exceptionalism.[7] But on the assumption that Jews in America are free of the threats to survival and security that they encountered in Europe, the Middle East and North Africa, then versions of the ideological solutions that failed abroad might yet succeed in America. Moreover, the focus of Jewish politics can, and should, shift from ensuring Jewish emancipation, which is now assured, to working for the liberation of other oppressed groups. Recent events have seriously undermined both notions of exceptionalism, but they remain deeply ingrained in American Jewish life.

American Jewish exceptionalism is linked to an issue that has run through American Jewish historiography over the past century. The great American Jewish historian Salo Baron criticized what he described as the lachrymose view of Jewish history as a tale of suffering and persecution. He argued that large periods of Jewish life in Europe were peaceful, productive and secure, particularly in the Middle Ages. He first proposed this perspective in Baron (1928), but it remained a theme throughout his extensive career (see, for example, Baron, 1963). According to Baron, earlier Jewish historians had distorted Jewish history by portraying it as an unrelieved series of disasters. A school of Baron-inspired Jewish historians developed that downplayed major Jewish persecutions, like the expulsions from Spain and Portugal, and the Khmelnytsky pogroms in the Ukraine. Instead they focused on continuity and flourishing within the European Diaspora. A positive view of Diaspora life emerges from this approach, in which Jewish persecution and survival are not at the centre of attention.

In fact, Baron's views are more nuanced than those of some of his disciples. He does not deny the reality of large-scale persecution as an important aspect of Jewish Diaspora life. Moreover, he characterizes the enlightenment and Jewish emancipation in the nineteenth century as a false dawn that led to repression, as well as to the loss of Jewish communal autonomy and the cultural independence that it provided. Baron's concern to emphasize the positive aspects of Jewish Diaspora life took shape in pre-war America, in the first part of the previous century. It seems to be at least partly conditioned by the apparent viability of the exceptionalist perspective on American society, and on the Jewish experience within in it, during that era. As an understanding of the Diaspora it was shattered by the cataclysms that befell Jews in the years that followed.[8]

Out of a total Jewish population of 15.3 million, 7,080,000 (46 per cent) now live in Israel. If current demographic trends continue, then it is reasonable to expect that within the next twenty to twenty-five years a majority of the world's Jews will be resident in Israel, for the first time in two and a half millennia. To dismiss Israel as a mistake and call for its annulment is to refuse to engage seriously with the contemporary realities of Jewish life. Many of the Jews who have joined the far left have retreated into a sentimentalized reverie of past Diaspora conditions in Eastern Europe and the Middle East, which has little, if any, basis in historical fact. The challenge for a genuinely progressive Jewish left, grounded in the current developments of Jewish history, is not to abolish Israel, but to support Israelis who are working to extend democracy and equality in their country. Such a left also has a responsibility to confront the antisemitism increasingly manifest in its own part of the political spectrum, as well as among its adversaries on the right. Not to do so is to deny the obvious, and to surrender its credibility.

7.3 Caught in the Middle

Most Jews in the Diaspora have not embraced the far right or the far left, but they inhabit a broad liberal centre. They are supportive of Israel, even if critical of its policies and actions. They generally endorse anti-racist and multicultural positions, as well as gender equality and LGBTQ rights, but they are suspicious of identity politics. Many are deeply concerned about the rise of antisemitism in recent decades, and they observe with dismay the seepage of anti-Jewish conspiracy theories into mainstream public discourse. They have become acutely aware of the threats that the three main streams of anti-globalist reaction pose to Jewish minorities in host countries where these movements have become influential. These threats pose challenges that most Jewish communities did not have to deal with during the period of relative security that the postwar era provided.

As the norms and arrangements of the postwar era have given way to increasing political polarization under stress of rapid economic and social change, Diaspora Jews have found themselves caught in the crossfire between far-right, far-left and radical Islamist groups, all of which target Jews as putative agents of malign power. To respond effectively to these threats, Jews require allies. But as identity politics increasingly fracture cross-ethnic solidarity, alliances have become difficult to sustain.

In the face of rising anti-Jewish violence Jewish communities have turned to the governments of their countries for support. Leaders of mainstream parties and political organizations invariably express their abhorrence of antisemitism, and of racism in general. They rarely take effective action to deal with it. Most countries have a variety of laws that criminalize racist speech and behaviour, but these are not consistently or effectively applied. The UK is a clear instance of this phenomenon. Hate crime of all types in England and Wales rose from 42,255 reported cases in 2013 to 155,841 in 2022 (369 per cent). The rate of prosecution for reported hate crime in England and Wales remained roughly constant over this period, with 13,070 prosecutions in 2013 (and a conviction rate of 83 per cent), and 13,073 in 2022 (and a conviction rate of 85 per cent). The proportion of prosecutions has declined significantly during this period.

In 2022, Jews in England and Wales suffered the highest rate of religiously identified crime, when normalized by population size, with 582 per 100,000, followed by Muslims, with 103 per 100,000.[9] These figures clearly indicate that racist violence has risen sharply in the UK over the past ten years, and that most acts of religious bigotry are directed at Jews. The Crown Prosecution Service has not expanded the small fraction of cases that it chose to bring to court during this period. In fact, some of the intervening years are marked by an increase in reported hate crime and a relative reduction in prosecutions.

Other countries exhibit a similar pattern. The Organization for Security and Cooperation in Europe (OSCE) examined US Department of Justice (DOJ) statistics to conclude that US Attorneys' offices investigated 8 per cent fewer reported hate crimes from the period of 2005–9 (647) to 2015–19 (597), despite an increase in such incidents over these years. In fact, the DOJ decided not to prosecute 83 per cent of suspected hate crimes from 2005 to 2019, which is a far lower rate of prosecution than the one applied to other federal offences.[10] The FBI reported that in 2021, 51.4 per cent of 1,591 religious hate crimes in the US were directed at Jews.[11]

The absence of serious commitment on the part of many government and public officials to dealing with the rising tide of explicit anti-Jewish racism has been strikingly clear in their weak response to the recent wave of hate rallies on American campuses, and to the mass demonstrations featuring anti-Jewish sloganeering in British and European cities. Despite strong rhetoric from political leaders and university administrators, little of substance has been done to constrain these eruptions. Had these events targeted other ethnic groups, one imagines that both the official and the popular reaction would have been quite different. In the current context, while these outbreaks are packaged together with legitimate concern for Palestinian suffering, little effective action has been taken to restrain the explicit antisemitism that they prominently feature.

Jewish communities have been forced to assume most of the burden of protecting their institutions and events from attack. Synagogues, schools and community centres have become guarded fortresses that one enters only by passing through rigorous security procedures. Few other ethnic communities need to sustain this sort of defensive regime. The majority populations of their host countries are largely unconcerned with the threat of violence that Jews deal with on a regular basis, and the impact that it has on organized Jewish life is not an issue of public discussion. Other ethnic and gender groups are subjected to horrific violence. People of colour, Asians, immigrants, women and LGBTQ people are regular targets. Fortunately a large array of progressive organizations and human rights groups provide advocacy in exposing and resisting this violence. By contrast, they tend to show little interest in the Jewish struggle against racist threats, beyond ceremonial assurances that they strongly disapprove of antisemitism. In part, this is due to the widespread perception of Jews as beneficiaries of White privilege and prosperity. This causes an acute sense of frustration and isolation among many members of the Jewish community.

One of the achievements of the #MeToo and Black Lives Matter movements is a heightened understanding of the importance of allowing the victims of bigotry to determine when they have been the targets of discrimination, and how they should describe their experiences. This is rightly understood as a process of empowering victims to deal with oppression by reclaiming their autonomy. It allows them to demand justice in a way that cannot be easily ignored within the broader social environment. In many cases this autonomy is denied Jews who encounter antisemitism. They are frequently told that they are smearing their adversaries with false charges in order to divert attention from legitimate criticism, either of Israel or of a nefarious abuse of power through lobbying. Vigorous objection to the Israeli government's behaviour is, in itself, certainly reasonable, and it is often warranted. Israel should be judged by the same standards as any other country. However, demonizing the entire nation, and its supporters, is a common vehicle for expressing racist hostility to Jews as a people. Extreme anti-Zionist rhetoric is frequently used as a set of dog whistles for Jew hatred. Encoding racism directed at other ethnic groups through mediating expressions has long been recognized as a technique for gaslighting victims and inciting bigotry, while claiming innocence of intent. It has now become pervasive in discourse concerning Jews, most prominently on the far left. It is invoked to deprive its targets of the power to identify the racism to which they are being subjected, and so to resist it.

The sharp rise in anti-Jewish incidents in the wake of the Hamas terrorist attack and its aftermath has greatly aggravated the sense of many Diaspora Jewish Communities that they are living in a hostile and dangerous environment. The relative silence of many political and cultural figures, particularly from the liberal left, in the face of these attacks, has intensified the feeling of isolation that large numbers of Jews are experiencing in the current turmoil of the Gaza conflict. This explosion of anti-Jewish racism throughout the West, in which large sections of enlightened opinion are looking on with relative indifference, has offered a dramatic view of the deep currents of bigotry that have been building up beneath the appearance of apparently normal social life, over many decades. When the current violence in Gaza ends, it is reasonable to expect that large-scale expressions of antisemitism will subside. The forces that generated them will continue to churn under the surface. This situation raises obvious questions about the long term viability of secure organised Jewish life in the European and American Diasporas.

The current situation of Diaspora Jews recalls earlier periods of Jewish history, particularly the turn of the last century. In both times they have been caught between the rising forces of far-right ethno-nationalist racism and far-left hostility to the class roles and cultural identity that Jews have evolved. In both instances small minorities sought to deflect these threats by actively collaborating with one of the sides. In the first incarnation this was done in wishful innocence, while in the second it has been pursued with historical blindness.

Mainstream Diaspora communities are struggling to cope with the breakdown of the postwar political consensus, and the dangers to which this process has exposed them. The governments and official agencies of their host countries express sympathy and support, but they do little of substance to alleviate the growing threats that Jewish communities face. The left, and ethnic and gender groups targeted by bigotry, should be natural allies in this struggle. Many of their members are at best ambivalent, and frequently they are explicitly hostile to Jewish concerns.

In Israel the far right has been in power for more than a decade, and the current regime is engaged in an unrestrained assault on the democratic institutions of the country. A large cross-section of the population has resisted this attempted coup through a sustained campaign of mass popular protest. The war in Gaza has put this contest on hold. It has also aroused deep and widespread anger at Netanyahu and his coalition for their failure to prevent the security disaster at the start of the war. Once the fighting ends, a serious political upheaval is likely to accompany the reckoning of responsibility for this failure. The outcome of that process will decide the character of the country for many years to come.

These events in Israel and the Diaspora are taking place within the larger context of the massive instability unleashed by decades of intensifying economic inequality throughout much of the world. In order to fully understand the issues that both Diaspora Jews and Israelis are confronting, it is necessary to recognize them as elements of these more general patterns. It requires seeing the challenges that Jews are currently facing, not in isolation, but in the broader political and economic environment within which they arise. To address the causes that are generating these challenges requires a new progressive politics that offers the hope of overcoming the social problems provoking the anti-globalist responses that feed chaos and extremism. In the next chapter I will briefly consider, in outline, what such a politics might look like.

8

Notes for a New Progressive Politics

In this chapter I will briefly consider some of the elements that, it seems to me, a new progressive politics must contain in order to respond effectively to the forces that are propelling the extremism of current anti-globalization reactions. These ideas are not detailed policy proposals. They are offered as directions to be explored in working out a reasonable programme for redistributing income to reduce the sharp inequality that is driving the crisis, while restoring the viability of liberal democratic institutions.

8.1 From Identity Back to Class

We have seen that each of the three main anti-globalization movements considered in previous chapters is pursuing a version of identity politics. The far right has resorted to ethno-nationalism to recruit an economically and socially displaced constituency to a nativist programme directed against minorities, with Jews, Muslims, immigrants and people of colour prominent among them in different places. The postmodernist far left has taken the descendants of victims of slavery and colonialism and marginalized gender groups as their focus of social action. Radical Islamists seek to enlist the Ummah in an international struggle to establish a new Islamic theocratic order. Identity politics has intensified polarization within the societies in which these movements are active. It has balkanized the public domain into hostile camps among which communication has become increasingly difficult. It has disrupted many of the broad coalitions that previously spanned ethnic and cultural differences for the pursuit of common political goals.

Vigorous opposition to racism and gender exclusion is integral to any society governed by liberal values and a commitment to social equality. Cultural and religious autonomy for the members of such a society follow directly from these values. But an ideology focused on ethnic and gender identity leads to the destructive consequences that we have observed. The sharp rise in income inequality that has played a central role in generating the current threat to democracy is largely an issue of economic class. There are, of course, important ethnic and gender aspects to inequality, but the core of this phenomenon is the concentration of wealth in an increasingly small part of the population. Formulating a progressive politics in terms of class rather than identity goes back to older traditions of the left. It allows a variety of ethnic and social groups to develop alliances within a unifying framework. This is the demand for an equitable distribution of resources to avoid the extreme monopolization of wealth and power by a small elite, with the attendant dispossession of increasing numbers of people.

A progressive left that takes class as its primary interest would in no way abandon the struggle for racial justice and gender equality. These objectives are central to achieving equality. However, an obsession with ethnic and gender identity would not be the driving force of its activism. Identity politics is the specialty of the far right, and pursuing it provides right-wing demagogues with a convenient weapon with which to incite their constituents. The resulting 'culture wars' divide groups of people who may share common interests in progressive reform.

Similarly, such a left would not give up its commitment to anti-colonialism. But it would support groups that claim to represent the struggle against colonialism not because of their ethnic background, or solely because of the countries against which they are acting. It would endorse them by virtue of their commitment to democracy and equality within their own societies. Putative anti-colonialists who do not sustain these conditions do not warrant the backing of a genuinely progressive left. Democracy and equality are the same principles that the postmodernist far left claims to be animated by at home. When it suspends them abroad in deference to cultural relativism it presents an incoherent and indefensible view. Defending radical Islamist regimes and organizations while selling out labour organizers and women's rights activists in the Middle East is an example of the faux anti-colonialism that identity politics generates. Celebrating acts of mass murder embellished as "anti-colonial resistance" is a betrayal of democratic values, and a violation of basic decency.

Throughout the mid twentieth century labour unions were highly effective vehicles for improving the wages and working conditions of wage earners, particularly in Europe and North America. Farber et al. (2021) present a study covering eighty years of the economic effects of union membership in the United States, from 1936 until the present time. They find that union members consistently enjoy better income and benefits than their non-union counterparts, across periods of varying levels of participation. They also report that unions contribute to narrowing the income gaps between White and non-White workers, and between men and women. The study identifies a strong negative correlation between union activity and inequality as measured by the Gini coefficient. It argues that they played a major role in achieving the significant reduction in the disparity of wealth in the US that characterized the postwar era.

Union membership has declined sharply in the period corresponding to the second wave of globalization. In the US more than 30 per cent of the workforce was unionized in the mid-1950s, but only 10.1 per cent in 2022. There is also a large disparity between membership in the public and the private sectors. In 2022, 33.1 per cent of public sector workers were unionized, but only 6 per cent of employees in private companies.[1] Similarly, union membership fell in the UK from a high of 13 million in 1981 to 7 million in 2021, with most union members working in public services.[2]

The anti-union policies of the Reagan and Thatcher governments contributed to this decline. But the effects of globalization on the manufacturing industries in which private sector unions were concentrated were decisive in undermining the power of organized labour in most Western economies. Collective bargaining empowered the working class in much of the West to overcome poverty and achieve a secure middle-class lifestyle. With the erosion of manufacturing and the rise of service-based economies the balance of power has shifted radically to owners of capital. Increasingly, wage earners without advanced education or high-demand skills have been subjected to the vicissitudes of freelance and temporary employment, absent occupational benefits. There has recently been renewed public support for unions, and attempts have been made to unionize large private companies, like Amazon and Starbucks. These have enjoyed limited success to date, and union membership remains historically low.

I suggested in Chapter 1 that globalization in itself did not create the inequality driving anti-globalist extremism. In fact, it produced a significant expansion of wealth, which economic and social policies have distributed in a way that creates inequality. Labour activism should be one of the priorities of a new progressive politics. Expanding unions in service industries that employ the bulk of low-paid workers is an effective method for combatting poverty and the decline of the middle class in the West. It also offers a more promising route to eliminating the income differentials, and the differences in employment opportunities, among ethnic and gender groups, than the pursuit of identity-focused culture wars.

Actively supporting independent labour movements in developing countries responds to the rise of within-country inequality that has accompanied the rapid growth of industry in their economies. It also enhances the struggle for democracy and human rights in developing nations ruled by autocratic regimes. Labour organizers are often prime targets for persecution by these regimes. They need strong international backing, but do not always receive it. Western consumers enjoy inexpensive imports from these countries, manufactured under highly exploitative conditions. While the companies that produce and market these imports pay lip service to fair labour practices, they frequently ignore them. Consumer pressure can help to improve the situation to a limited extent. It is no substitute for strong local unions that defend workers on site.

8.2 Socializing Globalization

International trade agreements provide essential mechanisms for economic globalization. Advocates of free trade point out that these agreements generally increase growth and GDP for all contracting parties. This is indeed the case. But this observation passes over the fact that free trade affects different sectors of a country's economy in distinct ways. It frequently lowers the price of imported products and increases corporate profits for companies that can relocate production to a low-wage country. It may also cause an increase in investment in high-tech industries, with an expansion in high-skill jobs. But lower-wage industries will contract, and many may disappear. The result is that the benefits of free trade are distributed in a radically uneven way among workers, consumers, corporations and private investment agencies.

The North American Free Trade Act (NAFTA), which went into effect in 1994, is a case in point. It integrated the markets of Canada, the US and Mexico. In the nearly three decades that it has been in force trade between the three countries has expanded considerably. However, manufacturing in the US has declined, with a significant loss of lower-skilled jobs and a reduction of wages in these parts of the economy. NAFTA contributed to this pattern, even if it is not solely responsible for it. Average wages did not increase in Mexico, despite the growth of high-skill manufacturing along its northern border with the US. The rate of poverty in the country rose above that in many other Latin American countries. Mexican farmers have been adversely affected by imports of subsidized American produce. The fact that the flow of illegal immigration from Mexico to the US has expanded in this period is at least partially due to the failure of NAFTA to improve conditions for the poorer segments of the Mexican population. The Canadian and American economies were highly integrated prior to NAFTA, and their wage and price levels more closely aligned. Therefore, the effect of the agreement on the two countries has been less substantial.[3]

I noted in Chapter 1 that the recent wave of globalization created rapid growth in parts of Asia, with the effect that China has been able to largely eliminate extreme poverty in its population. However, together with growth it has also experienced a sharp rise in inequality. Bin et al. (2023) report that China now has a Gini coefficient of close to 0.5, which is comparable to that of the US. This indicates that the distribution of the wealth created by the significant rise in its

GDP is skewed towards a small urban class of entrepreneurs and tech professionals. They point out that a high degree of income inequality correlates with different levels of access to health care, education and other public services. Lower-income groups receive significantly less of these benefits.

High inequality is not an inevitable consequence of the growth that free trade produces. It is generated by specific public policies. So, for example, corporate tax rates in Western countries have been reduced during the current wave of globalization. In the US they were more than 50 per cent in the 1950s, and they are currently 21 per cent. In the UK they went down from 52 per cent in 1982 to 19 per cent in 2017. They were recently raised to 25 per cent in 2023. Similarly, top rates of personal income tax for very high earners declined substantially in both countries from postwar highs of 91 per cent during the 1950s to 43.4 per cent now in the US, and from 90 per cent through the 1950s to 45 per cent now in the UK. Governments have found themselves under pressure to reduce the tax burden in order to attract foreign investment and skilled labour. The result is that revenue for public services that improve opportunities for the poorer part of the population has declined.

One of the primary reasons that trade agreements have the economic results that we observe is that their terms are, in large measure, determined by the interests of corporate lobbyists. These arrangements are designed to serve their interests. An obvious priority for a new progressive politics should be to rewrite trade agreements to more equitably represent the concerns of workers and consumers in the countries among which they are concluded. This would involve strong fair labour and wage conditions as a requirement for foreign companies to do business in the markets that they are entering. Such an approach would also incorporate stricter environmental controls on these companies. It would insist that foreign companies pay reasonable rates of corporate tax on the profits that they make, in the countries in which they earn them. It would also demand that foreign companies invest in the social and educational infrastructure of the country that they are operating in. This is the market that supplies their wealth. Helping to support its people's wellbeing is part of a fair exchange.

As we saw in Chapter 1, the decline of the welfare state has accompanied the second period of globalization since 1980. Even when social democratic parties are elected to government, they find themselves under pressure to pursue a low-tax regime, with privatization and cutbacks in public services as part of this package. These actions are forced by the need to attract foreign investment, and to sustain international competitiveness. Individual nation states are increasingly limited in their power to resist this pattern. A cooperative programme among social democrats in different countries is a necessary condition for achieving socialized trade agreements that will reverse the continuing drift to extreme inequality.

A new progressive politics has no alternative but to adopt an internationalist perspective. This does not entail disregarding the legitimate interests of one's own country, or abandoning membership in one's nation. It requires that one build cross-border political alliances with social democrats abroad for concerted action to achieve common objectives through federative arrangements.

8.3 Refugees and Immigration

Immigration is one of the most polarizing issues in countries throughout the world, particularly in the West. The far right uses it as an instrument for xenophobic incitement. The liberal centre and the left have not succeeded in developing an effective response to this campaign, nor have they formulated a coherent alternative policy on immigration. Some parties of the left have adopted an anti-immigrant stance in order to compete with the far right. So, for example, the Danish Social Democrats have introduced severe restrictions on non-EU immigration, and on refugees seeking asylum. The Biden administration has modified some of Trump's punitive measures for handing asylum seekers at the Mexican border, but it has left many of his immigration policies intact.[4]

Far-right advocates rely on several claims to promote hostility to immigration. First, they state that immigrants create waves of crime and violence. Second, they say that they lower wages, take jobs from home workers and place a strain on the network of social welfare and public services. Finally, they maintain that they destroy the native culture of the country. All three assertions can be shown to be false.

Recent studies on the correlation of migration and crime have indicated that for almost all categories of serious criminal activity immigrants do not have higher rates than native-born citizens. Light et al. (2020) report a comparative examination of crime levels in Texas between 2012 and 2018. They show that, with the exception of traffic violations, both legal and undocumented migrants commit significantly fewer offences than native US citizens. The crime rate among undocumented migrants is even lower than that of legal immigrants. Bell (2013) cites results that indicate no significant relationship between the proportion of foreign-born people in an area and its crime rate in the UK.

Immigration to advanced economies has a marginal impact on wages, affecting primarily lower-paid workers. It does not cause a significant drop in wages at any level, nor does it generate substantial unemployment. Quite the contrary, it can increase growth. Immigrants contribute more in tax revenue than they receive in benefits and services. In net terms, immigration to developed countries tends, in many cases, to be an economic asset.[5]

Immigration introduces cultural and demographic diversity, but it does not displace the native language(s) or established culture of the host country. Many people grossly overestimate the number of immigrants in their country, and the effect that they have on its lifestyle. As of 2022, a total of 14.8 per cent of the population of the UK was foreign born (Immigrant Advice Service at https://iasservices.org.uk/how-many-immigrants-are-in-the-uk/). In the US immigrants constituted 13.6 per cent of the population in 2021 (Migration Policy Institute at https://www.migrationpolicy.org/article/frequently-requested-statistics-immigrants-and-immigration-united-states). Immigrants generally integrate and become committed citizens by the first generation.

A new progressive politics needs to respond vigorously to far-right misrepresentations concerning immigration by making the relevant facts widely known. It also has to suggest rational policies for dealing with both immigration and refugees that offer a credible response to the hate campaigns of the far right. For the most part, people do not choose to leave their home country except to escape a serious threat to their security, or to avoid extreme poverty. A progressive politics would promote policies that ameliorate violence, poverty and environmental disaster in those areas that refugees are fleeing. Socialized trade agreements of the sort sketched in the previous section may be one way of doing this effectively. They would encourage development and stability in those areas. To the extent that they are successful, the flow of refugees would be reduced.

However, there are actually compelling reasons for encouraging immigration to the West, and parts of Asia. The birth rate in these areas is declining, and longevity is increasing. As a result the ratio of older people on pensions to those in employment is rising quickly.[6] This pattern is placing a strain on health, welfare and public services, which is increasing in relation to the demographic trend. It poses a long-term threat to economic growth and prosperity. Reversing the trend through an expansion of local birth rates is not likely to happen. Increasing immigration among younger people from the developing world is a viable way of sustaining growth and the provisions of the welfare state.

A new progressive politics must learn how to market increased immigration as an economic necessity. It provides an alternative to permanent decline and attendant social dysfunction. It is precisely those parts of the population who have suffered dislocation through globalization that are most vulnerable to the effects of this demographic trend, as they have the least resources with which to deal with it. They are the target audience of the right-wing assault on immigrants. Persuading them that immigration is in their interests, rather than opposed to it, is a major challenge.

8.4 Artificial Intelligence, Big Tech and Disinformation

On 22 March 2023 a group of high-tech researchers and entrepreneurs signed an open letter urging a six-month halt in work on large artificial intelligence (AI) systems, such as the ChatGPT chatbot series that OpenAI has produced.[7] One of the main fears that they raise concerning this work is that it will eventually create super-intelligent AI agents whose cognitive abilities surpass those of humans. Such devices will not be constrained by moral or other human considerations, and they would pose an existential threat to civilization. Such fears have frequently been expressed in the past. In my view, they are not well motivated by the nature of AI systems. While impressive progress has been made in developing systems that approach, and in some cases surpass, human performance, they are task specific, and they do not exhibit general intelligence or reasoning power. There is also no obvious basis for the worry that they could develop autonomous volition and so achieve independence from human control.

In particular, the chatbots causing excitement now are large language models (LLMs), trained on vast amounts of data to produce surprisingly natural text in response to linguistic prompts. They are highly effective as question-answering systems. When the multimodal versions of these models are fully online, they will also be able to describe visual images and generate graphic representations from descriptions. They will perform a certain amount of inference that is semantically grounded in non-linguistic entities. But LLMs are not capable of complex reasoning by analogy, across different domains, a distinctively human ability that people exercise effortlessly.[8]

It is important not to confuse the threat of super-intelligent AI agents with the danger involved in misusing AI technology. The former is a purely theoretical concern, and it has a low probability of occurrence. The latter is very real, but it attaches to any technology. Allowing AI expert systems to make hiring decisions, or to operate weapons without human supervision, is indeed dangerous, not because these systems are super-intelligent, but precisely because they are not. We have, however, been relying on automatic pilots to fly planes for many decades, and they generally perform very well.

There are, however, other more immediate dangers that AI poses. The success with which current systems already handle a variety of high-level tasks, such as automatic translation, medical diagnostics, tax return calculation, image and voice recognition, text generation, text summarization and question answering, will allow for the automation of many jobs now performed by humans. AI-driven robots are already doing industrial production and certain types of surgery, and autonomous vehicles are appearing on the roads. Human participation is still involved in supervising these devices, but it is increasingly minimal. Should the rapid development of sophisticated AI systems continue at its current pace, automation of a wide range of skilled professions will become a realistic prospect.

This could lead to large-scale unemployment, not just in low-skilled industrial tasks, but across significant swaths of the labour market. If not properly managed, this process will result in an even greater concentration of wealth and power in a small elite that owns the companies creating AI systems. The economic and social consequences of such a development would be significant.[9] A new progressive politics must develop an approach to this issue that involves public intervention to accommodate that part of the labour market that will be displaced by AI-driven automation. It must also devise methods for properly regulating the tech industry that is producing and marketing these systems.

In Chapter 1 I briefly mentioned the abuse of social media for disseminating disinformation and extremist views. Powerful multimodal chatbots are rendering this problem even more acute. They have now reached the level where, in many cases, it is not possible to distinguish human from computer-generated text and images. This is giving rise to a new dimension of disinformation through the internet. News reports, scholarly articles, scientific papers, government statements, photographs, videos, music and art work can all be easily fabricated by multimodal chatbots. Therefore, it will become increasingly difficult to know when the information that one is accessing online is reliable.

Large tech companies have a monopoly on the LLMs that drive chatbots. They are the only agencies that can afford the vast amount of data and computing power required to train them. To date these companies have largely avoided responsibility for the content that they host on their social media sites. They have managed to escape much of the legal accountability that constrains print and broadcast media. One of their arguments for sustaining this arrangement is that they are socially responsible companies that are capable of regulating themselves. This is a fiction. Private companies are in business to make money. They cease to exist when they are not profitable, and so they are willing to apply almost any practice required to make a profit. Their algorithms have been shown to amplify extremist and racist posts in order to maximize advertising revenue. There is little reason to think that they will act to prevent the abuse of their chatbots for disinformation. It is imperative that a new progressive politics develop a clear and workable programme for regulating large tech companies in the public interest. The integrity of information exchanged in the digital domain depends on such regulation being effective.

8.5 Conclusion

I have explored the politics of contemporary antisemitism within the context of globalization and the three main forms of extremist reaction against it. I have argued that it is necessary to consider this context in order to understand the nature of the threat to democracy that these reactions pose. I have suggested that the source of the problem is not globalization itself, but the sharp rise in economic inequality that has accompanied it. This is largely the result of the way in which the architects of international commercial agreements have liberalized trade, and the conservative economic and social programmes that governments have implemented during this period. In order to address the inequality driving extreme anti-globalist movements it is necessary to refocus progressive political action on measures to redistribute wealth, while strengthening democratic institutions.

An obvious extension of this conclusion is that it is not possible to combat antisemitism in isolation. Effective resistance requires recognizing it as closely associated with other forms of racism and intolerance that have been intensified by the rise of extremism. However, antisemitism is unique in that it crosses ideological lines in a way that other forms of bigotry do not. It is prominent in all three anti-globalist movements that we have explored here. The sharp rise in antisemitism across these movements indicates the depth of the threat to democracy and stability that they pose. One minimizes the threat, and the extent to which antisemitism is a clear symptom of it, at one's peril.

Groups that present themselves as anti-racist frequently append antisemitism to the end of the list of evils that they oppose, as an afterthought. Their statement to the effect that of course they also stand against antisemitism is often little more than an incantational performance in which the utterance constitutes the sum total of their commitment on this matter. As we observed in Chapter 4, the postmodernist far left emphasizes the need to understand the history of racism and gender discrimination in order to take effective action against it. It displays little, if any, interest in the history of antisemitism. Its main concern is to exhibit it as a disease of the far right and to deny its presence in its own ranks.

Much education against antisemitism highlights the Holocaust as a lesson in the horrors that racism can produce. This can, and often does, generate the impression that the Nazi genocide is outside the rest of Jewish history, and of history in general, as a unique one-time event. While it was certainly unprecedented as a case of ideologically motivated, industrialized mass murder, it cannot be set apart from the rest of Jewish history. It was possible only because of the centuries of systematic incitement, violence and exclusion that preceded it. The Holocaust was the culmination of a long history of antisemitism, rather than an event that stands on its own, without antecedence.

I have argued that the primary reason that the current outbreak of anti-Jewish racism is manifest across the political spectrum is that it is so deeply embedded in Western culture, and easily imported into radical Islamism. The root of this racism is the idea that the Jews are an illicit people, which has been central to the religious and political traditions of the West for millennia. The demonic cosmic role assigned to Jews in both religious and secular messianic movements over the centuries has created a rich mythology of conspiratorial power that renders them an obvious defendant when a deep crisis destabilizes the prevailing social order. It is necessary to explore this history in detail if one is to understand the dynamics of antisemitism. Most self-styled progressive anti-racists have no interest in it. As a result, the acute anti-Jewish bigotry of the far left is invisible to them. It is now on vivid display in the mass rallies and social media torrent that has accompanied the situation in Gaza.

The mythology that feeds antisemitism has infected the discussion of the Israeli–Palestinian conflict, obscuring its causes and its nature. I have argued that it must be re-naturalized within its historical context. This involves recognizing that it is a clash between two nations in the same territory, with considerable justice on each side. Such an approach requires seeing the obvious parallels between this conflict and other protracted ethnic disputes in the region, as well as in other parts of the world. I have also suggested that the rise of the far right in Israel follows the same pattern that holds in many other places, showing Israel to be a normal country, rather than a locus of exceptionalism. An enlightened and unprejudiced view requires that it be treated as such.

We are living through a period of rapid change and deep instability. These developments have unleashed irrational political forces that threaten the foundations of democracy and social cohesion. The environment that they are shaping is confronting Jews both in Israel and in the Diaspora with unfamiliar challenges. The traditional solutions of the past do not suffice to meet these challenges. New approaches are required to deal with them. There is a pressing need for searching discussion of these issues among people committed to liberal values and egalitarian principles. If this book helps to promote such a discussion, then it will have achieved its purpose.

Notes

Chapter 1: Introduction: Democracy in Crisis

1 For reports, with data, see the Anti-Defamation League (ADL), *Audit of Antisemitic Incidents*, 3 May 2022 (https://www.adl.org/audit2021) for the US; the Community Security Trust (CST), *Antisemitic Incidents Report*, 4 August 2022 (https://cst.org.uk/news/blog/2022/08/04/antisemitic-incidents-report-january-june-2022) for the UK; and the Center for the Study of Contemporary European Jewry, Tel Aviv University, *Antisemitism Worldwide Report 2021*, 27 January 2022 (https://cst.tau.ac.il/wp-content/uploads/2022/04/Antisemitism-Worldwide-2021.pdf) for an international overview. The 7 October 2023 Hamas terrorist attack, and Israel's response to it, have produced a record number of anti-Jewish hate crimes, as well as assaults on Muslims, throughout the West.

2 Butter (2020) provides a historical study of conspiracy theories.

3 See, for example, Alarcón et al. (2017), ch. 2, for an economic description of this period.

4 Markus (2022) provides a summary of this chain of events.

5 See Canola (2008) for a discussion of the role that Clinton's deregulation played in facilitating the financial crash of 2007–8.

6 See Posen (2022) for a description of the impact of Brexit on the British economy, with evidence that it has reduced both

the UK's international trade openess and its level of foreign direct investment. Helm et al. (2022) offer a vivid portrait of the economic disruptions that Brexit is causing.

7 I am grateful to Peter Nicholas for invaluable discussion and guidance on the economic issues addressed in this section.

8 See Nayyar (2006) for a discussion of the parallels and differences between the two periods of globalization.

9 The Gini index (Gini coefficient) is a widely used measure of income inequality. For a formal definition and explanation of this measure see *Gini Coefficient: Simple Definition* (https://www .statisticshowto.com/gini-coefficient/).

10 See *How Does Trade Affect Inequality?*, Centre for Inclusive Trade Policy, July 2022 (https://citp.ac.uk/publications/how-does -trade-affect-inequality), for a summary of recent work on how globalization has adversely affected lower-wage workers in the West. The World Bank report on manufacturing as a percentage of GDP for 2019/21, available at https://data.worldbank.org /indicator/NV.IND.MANF.ZS?most_recent_value_desc=true, indicates the move of European and North American economies away from industry and the rise of manufacturing in China and India. Interestingly, Germany has not succumbed to this trend, retaining a level of manufacturing that is a comparatively high percentage of its GDP.

11 Lakner and Milanovic (2013) first introduced the elephant curve in their discussion of global growth and income distribution.

12 Waldenström (2021) argues that increased house ownership and pension provision has greatly reduced inequality in the West over the past 150 years. Maclennan and Long (2023) present evidence that while rising house ownership did reduce inequality until the end of the 1970s, the rapid rise in housing prices that accompanied deregulation of the lending market has reversed this trend. They observe that since the 1980s there has been a significant increase in inequality associated with house purchases among regions, generations and income groups. Houses in rural areas have considerably less value than those in cities. Younger wage earners are finding it increasingly difficult to secure the large down payments required for a mortgage, since

the tightening of lending conditions after the financial crash of 2007–8. Mortgage payments take up a disproportionately large share of lower incomes than higher ones. Housing purchases have declined among lower-income and younger people. Also the houses that these two groups own have increasingly lower value, and the mortgages that they carry constitute greater risks, than the housing assets of high-income owners. Some of the papers in Kuitto et al. (2021) describe the rising inequality in pension income in the West due to the increase in privatized pension schemes and the reduction of state pensions. In this situation pensions are directly conditioned by pre-retirement income and savings. Osakwe and Solleder (2023) show that the there is a direct positive correlation between income inequality and wealth inequality. This correlation holds across all global regions. It is weaker in the West, but still significant.

13 See Roberts and Lamp (2021) for a discussion of different perceptions of globalization among distinct social and political groups.

14 See Dubhashi and Lappin (2021) for a brief discussion of the role of large tech companies in facilitating the rise of extremism, racism and disinformation through social media.

15 See Wistricht (1995) for a detailed discussion of political antisemitism in France and Germany in the nineteenth century.

16 See *A Hoax of Hate: The Protocols of the Learned Elders of Zion*, Anti-Defamation League, 5 January 2013 (https://www.adl.org /resources/backgrounders/a-hoax-of-hate-the-protocols-of-the -learned-elders-of-zion) for a brief summary of the career of the *Protocols* since its publication.

17 In Haubtmann (1960–1), vol. II, pp. 337–8, quoted in Wistricht (1995), p. 117.

18 A translation from the French original is available on the anarchist website libcom.org (https://libcom.org/article/translation -antisemitic-section-bakunins-letter-comrades-jura-federation). The editors of the site strongly reject Bakunin's antisemitism.

19 Lappin (2019) considers the view of the Jews as an illicit collectivity, common to both the left and the right, in the context of contemporary antisemitism.

20 McGeever and Virdee (2017) address antisemitism in the Second International.

21 Lappin (2003) suggests a connection between replacement of this kind and antisemitism.

Chapter 2: The Roots of Antisemitism in Western Culture

1 See Hezser (2023) for a summary of these writings, and references to scholarly work on pre-Christian anti-Jewish attitudes in the classical world.

2 See Grüen (2016), ch. 12, 'Tacitus and the Defamation of the Jews', for a critical discussion of Tacitus' anti-Jewish views.

3 Reinhartz (2022) provides an overview of Christian anti-Jewish religious beliefs in the New Testament.

4 Garroway (2022) offers a summary of this evolution of Christian theological anti-Judaism in late antiquity.

5 See Teter (2020) for a detailed history of the blood libel in medieval and modern European history.

6 See Kaplan (2022) for a discussion of Luther's attitudes to Jews.

7 Cohen (2014) discusses Jewish–Muslim relations in the early period of Islam.

8 See Ravitzky (1996) for a critical account of this messianic wing of religious Zionism.

9 See Peled (1992) for a discussion of this debate.

10 Marx's 'On the Jewish Question' appears in O'Malley (1994), pp. 28–56.

11 Toynbee (1961), pp. 515–16.

12 Toynbee (1961), p. 517.

13 See Lappin (2008) for a description, with references, of British immigration policy on Jewish refugees before and immediately after the Second World War.

14 Toynbee (1969), pp. 266–7.

15 By *postmodernist* left I intend that part of the current far left whose main attitudes have their historical roots in some of the ideas of critical theory, as characterized by the writings of Gramsci, the thinkers of the Frankfurt School, such as Adorno and Marcuse, and their followers in the New Left. Bohman (2005) offers an overview of the history of critical theory. The

current postmodernist left focuses on ethnic, racial and gender identity, rather than economic class, as key factors of privilege and power. It substitutes a particular variety of anti-colonialism for class struggle. Many of its adherents regard scientific objectivity and liberal values as instruments of manipulation that a reactionary elite uses to suppress marginalized cultural and social groups. See Burston (2022) for a discussion of critical theory and left-wing antisemitism.

Chapter 3: The View from the Right

1 See Maizland (2022) for a description of the BJP's assault on India's Muslims. Ganguly (2021) documents the case that the BJP is also promoting intolerance against non-Muslim religious minorities.

2 Diamond (2020) reviews the racist background of the Immigration Act of 1924.

3 See Pietsch (2022) on Stanford's history of excluding Jewish applicants.

4 Lappin (2021) discusses how Trump's cultivation of White supremacism as a central force of the MAGA Republican Party, and the increase in left-wing antisemitism in academic and cultural environments, has disrupted the escape of American Jews from Diaspora history and thrust them back into it.

5 Roose (2021) gives a detailed description of the history and beliefs of QAnon.

6 Kabaservice (2020) traces the connections between the Tea Party and Trump.

7 These figures are from the Jewish Agency for Israel, 2022 (https://www.jewishagency.org/jewish-population-rises-to-15 -3-million-worldwide-with-over-7-million-residing-in-israel/).

8 See Gates (2009) on the Supreme Court's role in the movement to overturn Reconstruction.

9 Buruma (2021) presents a profile of Zemmour's views, and he attempts to understand them in the context of his North African Jewish background.

10 Orbán propagates the second-order replacement theory that George Soros, the Hungarian Jewish financier and civil society

philanthropist, is seeking to promote Muslim immigration to Europe in order to undermine native Christian societies. He has emphasized this anti-Jewish conspiracy theory in his election campaigns. Witte (2018) describes the role of this idea in Orbán's assault on democratic institutions and human rights organizations. A curious precursor to the theory is advanced in Bat Ye'or's 2005 book *Euroabia: The Europe–Arab Axis*. Bat Ye'or (Gisèle Littman), an Egyptian Jewish writer, claims that a group of EU leaders concluded a secret agreement with several Arab states to facilitate large-scale Muslim immigration to Europe and Islamization of the continent.

11 See the ADL's *Pat Buchanan in His Own Words*, 2 July 2017 (https://www.adl.org/resources/profile/pat-buchanan-his-own -words).

12 See Merrit (2017) on the role of dispensationalism in motivating American evangelical support for Israel.

13 See Arnsdorf (2023) on Trump's initial response to the Hamas terrorist attack.

14 See Raoul Wootliff, 'Final Text of Jewish Nation-State Law, Approved by the Knesset Early on July 19,' *Times of Israel*, 19 July 2018 (https://www.timesofisrael.com/final-text-of-jewish-nation -state-bill-set-to-become-law/) for an English translation of the full text of the Nation-State Law.

Chapter 4: The View from the Left

1 See Lappin (2006) for a discussion of the radical left's transition from class to identity politics, which started in the 1960s.

2 In *Judith Butler on Hamas, Hezbollah & the Israel Lobby (2006)*, posted on *Radical Archives* (https://radicalarchives.org/2010/03 /28/jbutler-on-hamas-hezbollah-israel-lobby/).

3 See Bernstein (2016) for details and testimony of the emergence in 'progressive' circles of the idea that the Holocaust was an instance of White on White violence.

4 Lewis (1987) provides a detailed historical account of Jewish life in Islamic countries over the many centuries in which Jews lived in these regions.

5 Weinstock (2008), Julius (2018) and Green and Stursberg (2022)

present histories of the expulsion of Middle Eastern and North African Jews in the second half of the twentieth century.

6 See Gansinger (2016) for a detailed description of the Polish Communist government's anti-Zionist campaign of 1968–9.

7 See Laqueur (2003) for a definitive history of Zionism.

8 The archives of the Bund are available online at YIVO, the Institute for Jewish Research (http://www.yivoarchives.org /index.php?p=collections/controlcard&id=33762).

9 See Lappin (2008) for a discussion of this issue, and references.

10 See Julius (2022) for a detailed and illuminating discussion of both the facts and the legal issues of the Miller case.

11 See Alter (2023) for an account of the left's support for the Hamas attack. Mitchell (2023) reports that Jeremy Corbyn pointedly refused to condemn the atrocity.

Chapter 5: The View from Radical Political Islamism

1 See Hathaway (2005) for a description of the Mawza exile in its cultural and geopolitical context.

2 Dawisha (2016) provides a history of Arab nationalism. Spyer (2014) discusses the rise of nationalism throughout the Middle East, including Turkey, Iran, the Arab world and Israel-Palestine.

3 See Linfield's (2019) chapter on Memmi for a discussion of his views on Israel and Zionism.

4 Shavit (2015) presents a detailed account of the development of Ridas' views on Jews and Zionism.

5 See Küntzel (2005) on the Muslim Brotherhood's historical connections with Nazism, and its virulently anti-Jewish attitudes.

6 Tibi (2010) gives a detailed account of Qutb's transformation of antisemitism from a European import into a core feature of Islamist ideology.

7 Yaakov Lappin (2011) discusses the role that Qutb's ideas have played in shaping modern jihadi movements. He also demonstrates how the Sunni wing of jihadists have largely moved online to wage their campaign.

8 See the report 'Argentina Court Drops Jewish Center Bombing Cover-Up Claim Against Ex-President' in the *Times of Israel*, 8 October 2021 (https://www.timesofisrael.com/argentina

-court-drops-jewish-center-bombing-cover-up-claim-against-ex
-president/). The federal prosecutor who brought the charge
against Kirschner, Alberto Nisman, was found dead in his
apartment the day before he was due to testify at a congressional
panel on the case.

9 *Left Foot Forward*, 21 September 2010 (https://leftfootforward
.org/2010/09/livingstone-al-qaradawi-is-a-leading-progressive
-voice-in-muslim-world/).

10 *The Guardian*, 4 July 2016 (https://www.theguardian.com
/politics/2016/jul/04/jeremy-corbyn-says-he-regrets-calling
-hamas-and-hezbollah-friends).

11 *Times of Israel*, 26 September 2018 (https://www.timesofisrael
.com/irate-corbyn-refuses-to-say-if-he-regrets-working-for
-irans-press-tv/).

12 *The Guardian*, 3 August 2009 (https://www.theguardian.com
/media/2009/aug/03/george-galloway-ofcom-press-tv).

13 *Alliance for Securing Democracy*, 20 October 2022 (https://
securingdemocracy.gmfus.org/british-commentators-iran
-russia-ukraine-conspiracy-theories/).

14 See Lappin (2006) for detailed discussion of this substitution of
Islamist anti-colonialism for revolutionary working-class politics
in the contemporary radical left.

15 *The Times of Israel*, 4 October 2022 (https://www.timesofisrael
.com/leading-us-jewish-groups-blast-berkeley-law-school-amid
-anti-zionism-uproar/).

Chapter 6: The Israeli–Palestinian Conflict Re-naturalized

1 The historiography of the Israeli–Palestinian conflict is
populated by a variety of sharply divergent accounts. Rather
than try to summarize them or adjudicate among them, I will
cite several representative references of the major streams
in this debate. Interested readers are encouraged to consult
these sources and to arrive at their own conclusions. I am
not claiming to be a detached observer in this debate, given
my clear connection to one side of the dispute. Gelber (2006)
and Shapira (2014) offer a more traditional Israeli view of the
conflict, and of Israeli history in general. Morris (2004) presents

a revisionist account of the origins of the Palestinian refugee problem, which overturns the now widely discarded Zionist claim that the refugees left of their own volition, due to the influence of the propaganda calls of the Palestinian Higher Committee and invading Arab countries. Morris (2009) gives a critically balanced treatment of the 1948 war. Khalidi (2020) presents a Palestinian historical narrative. Pappe (2022) and Shlaim (2010) argue for radically revisionist views of Israeli history that promote the Palestinian perspective. This debate is very much ongoing, and all of these accounts remain controversial. In addition to arguments over the facts themselves, these historians also disagree on methodology. Morris, Gelber and Shapira regard archival documentation as crucial for establishing the reliability of any historical claim. Pappe and many other pro-Palestinian historians insist that oral testimony and postmodernist notions of personal narrative are of equal significance as sources of evidence. Gelber (2011) offers a critique of postmodernist historiographical methods in the context of the Israeli–Palestinian struggle.

2 The following historical demographic estimates are from DellaPergola (2003).

3 See Sheffer (1996) for a discussion of the tensions that emerged between Sharett and Ben-Gurion after the 1948 war. This divergence developed into a radical split between them over Ben-Gurion's pursuit of the 1956 Sinai Campaign against Egypt.

4 See Ross (2004) and Sher (2006) for accounts of the Camp David and Taba talks. Ross was involved in both meetings as an American negotiator. Sher participated in them as Barak's chief of staff. They each agree that while Israel accepted the Clinton parameters, with conditions, Arafat rejected them, and he refused to negotiate possible alternatives.

5 See Khoury (2009) and Federman (2015) on the details of Olmert's peace plan, and Abbas' rejection of it.

6 See Ker-Lindsay (2011) for a brief history of the Greek–Turkish conflict in Cyprus.

7 See Lappin (2004) for a discussion of binationalism as a Zionist proposal within the Yishuv, and Laqueur (2003) on the reception

of binationalism among different Palestinian Arab factions in the pre-state period.

Chapter 7: The Jewish Response to the Crisis

1 Sarfatti (2017) presents a set of articles describing the history of Jewish participation in the Italian Fascist Party.
2 See Sharon (2023) for a description of Levin's legislative proposals.
3 See Sharon (2023a) on the role of the Kohelet Forum in formulating Yariv's judicial reform legislation.
4 See Hendrix (2023) on the role that the democracy movement has been playing in running volunteer organizations responding to the Gaza crisis.
5 See Butler (2012), Diner and Feld (2016), Robin (2018) and Boyarin (2023) for American Jewish activists who represent different aspects of this trend. In the British context Rose (2005) argues against Israel and Zionism. Lappin (2006a) presents a critical review of Rose's book. Rose (2006) and Lappin (2006b) continue the debate. The radical Israeli revisionist historians cited in Chapter 6, n. 72, as well as several Israeli postmodernist academics and journalists, adopt many elements of the far left's anti-Zionist perspective.
6 See Michal Frank's description of the Slánský trial in the *YIVO Encyclopedia of Jews in Eastern Europe* (https://yivoencyclopedia.org/article.aspx/Slansky_Trial).
7 See Lappin (2021) for a discussion of recent challenges to the notion of American Jewish exceptionalism.
8 See Teller (2014) for a critique of Baron's approach to violence against Jews in the Diaspora, and of the Panglossian attitudes of some of his disciples.
9 The UK statistics on hate crime are from Allen and Zayed (2022).
10 The OSCE report on hate crime reporting in the USA is at https://hatecrime.osce.org/united-states-america, and Lynch (2019) provides the rate of DOJ prosecution of suspected hate crimes.
11 The FBI's 2021 Updated Hate Crimes Statistics is at https://www.justice.gov/crs/highlights/2021-hate-crime-statistics.

Chapter 8: Notes for a New Progressive Politics

1 See Gurley (2022), US Bureau of Labour Statistics, *Union Members Summary*, 19 January 2023 (https://www.bls.gov/news.rclease/union2.nr0.htm), and The White House, *The State of Our Unions*, 5 September 2022 (https://www.whitehouse.gov/cea/written-materials/2022/09/05/the-state-of-our-unions/), for the statistical profiles of the decline in union membership in the USA.

2 The relevant data is presented in Department for Business, Energy and Industrial Strategy, *Trade Union Membership, UK 1995–2021: Statistical Bulletin*, 25 May 2022 (https://www.gov.uk/government/statistics/trade-union-statistics-2021).

3 Baker (2013) summarizes the impact of NAFTA on wages in US manufacturing. Weisbrot et al. (2017) present a profile of the impact of the agreement on the Mexican economy. Chatzky et al. (2020) give an overview of different economists' views on how NAFTA has affected each of the three economies.

4 See Poulsen's (2021) description of the Danish Social Democrats' embrace of rigorous restrictions on immigration, and Chotiner (2023) on Biden's continuation of many elements of Trump's border controls.

5 Vargas-Silva and Sumption (2023) provides data on the impact of immigration on wages in the UK. Damas de Matos (2021) discusses the economic effects of immigration in OECD countries, with reference to GDP, tax revenue and consumption of public services. Engler et al. (2020) assesses the role of immigration in promoting growth in advanced economies.

6 See the papers in Goerres and Vanhuysse (2021). Sciubba (2021) discusses this trend in Canada and the US. Naumann and Hess (2021) analyse it for Western Europe.

7 *Pause Giant AI Experiments: An Open Letter*, Future of Life Institute, 22 March 2023 (https://futureoflife.org/open-letter/pause-giant-ai-experiments/).

8 See Lappin (2021a) for an introduction to large language models in natural language processing.

9 See Dubhashi and Lappin (2017) for a discussion of this issue, with relevant references.

References

Ahad Ha'am (1891), 'Emet mi-Eretz Israel' (Truth from the Land of Israel), *Hamelitz*, 19–30 June 1891.

Alarcón, Diana et al. (2017), *World Economic and Social Survey 2017: Reflecting on Seventy Years of Policy Analysis*, Department of Economic and Social Affairs, United Nations.

Allen, Grahame and Yago Zayed (2022), *Hate Crime Statistics*, House of Commons Library, UK Parliament, London.

Alter, Charlotte (2023), 'How the Activist Left Turned On Israel', *Time*, 14 October 2023 (https://time.com/6323730 /hamas-attack-left-response/).

Alvaredo, Facundo, Lucas Chancel, Thomas Piketty, Emmanuel Saez and Gabriel Zucman (2018), *World Inequality Report 2018*, World Inequality Lab.

Arnsdorf, Isaac (2023), 'Trump Faults Netanyahu, Calls Hezbollah "Very Smart" amid Israel War', *The Washington Post*, 12 October 2023 (https://www.washingtonpost.com /politics/2023/10/12/trump-israel-netanyahu-comments/).

Baddiel, David (2022), *Jews Don't Count*, William Collins, Glasgow.

Baker, Dean (2013), 'Nafta Lowered Wages, as It Was Supposed to Do', *The New York Times*, 5 December 2013

(https://www.nytimes.com/roomfordebate/2013/11/24
/what-weve-learned-from-nafta/nafta-lowered-wages-as-it
-was-supposed-to-do).

Baron, Salo (1928), 'Ghetto and Emancipation', *The Menorah Journal*, June.

Baron, Salo (1963), 'Newer Emphases in Jewish History', *Jewish Social Studies*, vol. 25, no. 4, pp. 235–48.

Bauer, Otto (1924), *Die Nationalitätenfrage und die Sozialdemokratie*, Verlag der Wiener Volksbuchhandlung, Vienna.

Bell, Brian (2013), *Immigration and Crime: Evidence for the UK and Other Countries*, The Migration Observatory, University of Oxford Centre on Migration, Policy and Society, 13 November 2013 (https://migrationobservatory
.ox.ac.uk/resources/briefings/immigration-and-crime
-evidence-for-the-uk-and-other-countries/).

Berend, Ivan (2006), *An Economic History of Twentieth-Century Europe*, Cambridge University Press, Cambridge.

Bernstein, David (2016), 'The Holocaust as "White on White Crime" and Other Signs of Intellectual Decay', *Washington Post*, 5 February 2016.

Bin, Simon Xiao Zhao, Wong David Wai Ho, Shao Chen Han and Liu Kai Ming (2023), 'Rising Income and Wealth Inequality in China: Empirical Assessments and Theoretical Reflections', *Journal of Contemporary China*.

Birnbaum, Pierre (2008), 'The French Radical Right: From Anti-Semitic Zionism to Anti-Semitic Anti-Zionism', *The Journal of Israeli History*, vol. 25, no. 1, pp. 161–74.

Bland, Benjamin (2019), 'Holocaust Inversion, Anti-Zionism and British Neo-Fascism: The Israel–Palestine Conflict and the Extreme Right in Post-War Britain', *Patterns of Prejudice*, vol. 53, no. 1, pp. 86–97.

Bogdanor, Paul (2016), 'An Antisemitic Hoax: Lenni Brenner on Zionist "Collaboration" with the Nazis', *Fathom*, 20 June 2016.

Bohman, John (2005), 'Critical Theory', *Stanford Encyclopedia of Philosophy* (https://plato.stanford.edu/entries/critical-theory/).

Boyarin, Daniel (2023), *The No State Solution: A Jewish Manifesto*, Yale University Press, New Haven, CT.

Burston, Daniel (2022), 'Critical Theory, Left-Wing Authoritarianism, and Anti-Semitism', in John Mills and Daniel Bursdon (eds), *Critical Theory and Psychoanalysis*, Routledge, London, pp. 158–84.

Buruma, Ian (2021), 'Éric Zemmour and the Revenge of Vichy', *Project Syndicate*, 3 November 2021 (https://www.project-syndicate.org/commentary/zemmour-french-far-right-extremist-jew-by-ian-buruma-2021-11).

Butler, Judith (2012), *Parting of the Ways: Jewishness and the Critique of Zionism*, Columbia University Press, New York.

Butter, Michael (2020), *The Nature of Conspiracy Theories*, Polity Press (John Wiley and Sons), Cambridge and Medford, MA.

Canola, Timothy (2008), 'The Legacy of the Clinton Bubble', *Dissent*, Summer, pp. 41–50.

Chancel, Lucas and Thomas Piketty (2021), *Global Income Inequality, 1820–2020: The Persistence and Mutation of Extreme Inequality*, HAL, Open Science, halshs-03321887.

Chancel, Lucas, Thomas Piketty, Emmanuel Saez, Gabriel Zucman et al. (2022), *World Inequality Report 2022*, World Inequality Lab, wir2022.wid.world.

Chatzky, Andrew, James McBride and Mohammed Aly Sergie (2020), *NAFTA and the USMCA: Weighing the Impact of North American Trade*, Council on Foreign Relations (https://www.cfr.org/backgrounder/naftas-economic-impact).

Chiarini, Roberto (2008), 'Anti-Zionism and the Italian Extreme Right', *Modern Italy*, vol. 13, no. 1, pp. 21–35.

Chotiner, Isaac (2023), 'Are Biden's Immigration Policies Stuck in the Trump Era?', *The New Yorker*, March 2023.

Cohen, Mark R. (2014), 'Islamic Policy toward Jews from the Prophet Muhammad to the Pact of 'Umar', in Meddeb and Stora (2014), pp. 58–71.

Crenshaw, Kimberle (1991), 'Mapping the Margins: Intersectionality, Identity Politics, and Violence against Women of Color', *Stanford Law Review*, vol. 43, no. 6, pp. 1241–99.

Damas de Matos, Ana (2021), 'The Fiscal Impact of Immigration in OECD Countries Since the Mid-2000s', in *International Migration Outlook 2021*, OECD Publishing, Paris (https://www.oecd-ilibrary.org/social-issues-migration-health/international-migration-outlook-2021_4ccb6899-en).

Davis, David Brion (1994), 'The Slave Trade and the Jews', *The New York Review of Books*, 22 December 1994.

Dawisha, Adeed (2016), *Arab Nationalism in the Twentieth Century: From Triumph to Despair*, Princeton University Press, Princeton, NJ.

DellaPergola, Sergio (2003), 'Demographic Trends in Israel and Palestine: Prospects and Policy Implications', *The American Jewish Year Book*, vol. 103, The American Jewish Committee and Springer, pp. 3–68.

Diamond, Anna (2020), 'The 1924 Law That Slammed the Door on Immigrants and the Politicians Who Pushed It Back Open', *Smithsonian Magazine*, 19 May 2020.

Diner, Hasia and Marjorie Feld (2016), 'We're American Jewish Historians. This Is Why We've Left Zionism Behind', *Haaretz*, 1 August 2016 (https://www.haaretz.com/opinion/were-american-jewish-historians-this-is-why-weve-left-zionism-behind-1.5418935).

Dubhashi, Devdatt and Shalom Lappin (2017), 'AI Dangers: Imagined and Real', *Communications of the ACM*, vol 60. no. 2, February 2017, pp. 43–5.

Dubhashi, Devdatt and Shalom Lappin (2021), 'Scared About the Threat of AI? It's the Big Tech Giants that Need Reining In', *The Guardian*, 16 December 2021.

Engler, Philipp, Margaux MacDonald, Roberto Piazza and

Galen Sher (2020), *Migration to Advanced Economies Can Raise Growth*, IMF Blog, 19 July 2020 (https://www.imf.org/en/Blogs/Articles/2020/06/19/blog-weo-chapter4-migration-to-advanced-economies-can-raise-growth).

Faber, Eli (2000), *Jews, Slaves, and the Slave Trade: Setting the Record Straight*, NYU Press, New York.

Farber, Henry, Daniel Herbst, Ilyana Kuziemko and Suresh Naidu (2021), *Unions and Inequality over the Twentieth Century: New Evidence from Survey Data*, National Bureau of Economic Research, April 2021 (https://www.nber.org/papers/w24587).

Federman, Josef (2015), 'Abbas Admits He Rejected 2008 Peace Offer from Olmert', *The Times of Israel*, 19 November 2015 (https://www.timesofisrael.com/abbas-admits-he-rejected-2008-peace-offer-from-olmert/).

Fouquin, M. and J. Hugot (2016), 'Back to the Future: International Trade Costs and the Two Globalizations', *CEPII Working Paper*, no. 13, Centre d'études prospectives et d'informations internationales (CEPII), Paris.

Frazer, Jenni (2016), 'Top Historians Take Down Ken Livingstone's Claim that "Hitler Supported Zionism"', *The Times of Israel*, 21 June 2016 (https://www.timesofisrael.com/top-historians-take-down-livingstons-claim-that-hitler-supported-zionism/).

Fredrikson, Paula and Oded Irshai (2022), 'Christian Anti-Judaism: Polemics and Policies', in Katz (2006), ch. 38, pp. 977–1034.

Fukuyama, Francis (1992), *The End of History and the Last Man*, Free Press, New York.

Ganguly, Sumit (2021), 'India's Religious Minorities Are Under Attack', *Foreign Policy*, 30 December 2021 (https://foreignpolicy.com/2021/12/30/india-religious-minorities-under-attack-christian-muslim-modi-bjp/).

Gansinger, Simon (2016), 'Communists Against Jews: The Anti-Zionist Campaign in Poland in 1968', *Fathom*, Autumn.

Garroway, Joshua (2022), 'Church Fathers and Antisemitism from the 2nd Century through Augustine (end of 450 CE)', in Katz (2022), ch. 4, pp. 66–82.

Gates, Henry Louis (2019), 'The "Lost Cause" That Built Jim Crow', *The New York Times*, 8 November 2019 (https://www.nytimes.com/2019/11/08/opinion/sunday/jim-crow-laws.html).

Gelber, Yoav (2006), *Palestine 1948: War, Escape and the Emergence of the Palestinian Refugee Problem*, second edition, Liverpool University Press, Liverpool.

Gelber, Yoav (2011), *Nation and History: Israeli Historiography Between Zionism and Post-Zionism*, Valentine Mitchell, London and Portland, OR.

Goerrcs, Achim and Pieter Vanhuysse (eds) (2021), *Global Political Demography*, Palgrave Macmillan, London.

Gorenberg, Gershom (2023), 'Netanyahu Led Us to Catastrophe. He Must Go', *The New York Times*, October 18, 2023 (https://www.nytimes.com/2023/10/18/opinion/netanyahu-israel-gaza.html).

Green, Henry and Richard Stursberg (2022), *Sephardi Voices: The Untold Expulsion of Jews from Arab Lands*, Figure 1 Publishing, Vancouver, BC.

Grüen, Erich S. (2016), *The Construct of Identity in Hellenistic Judaism: Essays on Early Jewish Literature and History*, De Gruyter, Berlin.

Gurley, Lauren Karol (2023), 'Union Membership Hit Record Low in 2022', *The Washington Post*, 19 January 2023 (https://www.washingtonpost.com/business/2023/01/19/union-membership-2022/).

Haag, Matthews (2018), 'Robert Jeffress, Pastor Who Said Jews Are Going to Hell, Led Prayer at Jerusalem Embassy', *The New York Times*, 14 May 2018 (https://www.nytimes.com/2018/05/14/world/middleeast/robert-jeffress-embassy-jerusalem-us.html).

Harap, Louis (1953), *The Truth About the Prague Trials*,

published by *Jewish Life*, January (https://www.marxists.org/subject/jewish/harap-prague.pdf).

Hathaway, Jane (2005), 'The Mawza Exile at the Juncture of Zaydi and Ottoman Messianism', *The Association for Jewish Studies Review*, vol. 29, no. 1, pp. 111–28.

Haubtmann, Pierre (ed.) (1960–1), *Carnets de P.-J. Proudhon*, vol. 2, *1847–1846*, Paris.

Helm, Toby, Robin McKie, James Tapper and Phillip Inman (2022), '"What Have We Done?": Six Years on, UK Counts the Cost of Brexit', *The Observer*, 25 June 2022.

Hendrix, Steve (2023), 'Israel's Massive Democracy Movement is Ready for War', *The Washington Post*, 24 October 2023 (https://www.washingtonpost.com/world/2023/10/24/israel-democracy-protesters-war-aid/).

Herf, Jeffrey (2014), 'Haj Amin al-Husseini, the Nazis and the Holocaust: The Origins, Nature and Aftereffects of Collaboration', *Jewish Political Studies Review*, vol. 26, no. 3/4, pp. 13–37.

Hezser, Catherine (2023), 'Anti-Semitism, Pagan', *Oxford Classical Dictionary* (https://oxfordre.com/classics/display/10.1093/acrefore/9780199381135.001.0001/acrefore-9780199381135-e-528;jsessionid=E22635B839B4A0B953BFA2AFA5111832).

Hirsh, David (2017), *Contemporary Left Antisemitism*, Routledge, Abingdon.

Hope, David and Julian Limberg (2020), *The Economic Consequences of Major Tax Cuts for the Rich*, Working Paper 55, LSE International Inequalities Institute.

Inbari, Motti, Kirill M. Bumin and M. Gordon Byrd (2021), 'Why Do Evangelicals Support Israel?', *Politics and Religion*, vol. 14, no. 1, pp. 1–36.

Jefferson, Thomas (1785), *Notes on the State of Virginia*, Paris.

Johnson, Alan (2019), *Institutionally Antisemitic: Contemporary Left Antisemitism and the Crisis in the British Labour Party*, Fathom (http://fathomjournal.org

/wp-content/uploads/2019/03/Institutionally-Antisemitic -Report-for-event.pdf).

Julius, Anthony (2010), *Trials of the Diaspora: A History of Anti-Semitism in England*, Oxford University Press, Oxford.

Julius, Anthony (2022), 'Willed Ignorance: Reflections on Academic Free Speech, Occasioned by the David Miller Case', *Current Legal Problems*, vol. 75, pp. 1–44.

Julius, Lyn (2018), *Uprooted: How 3000 Years of Jewish Civilization in the Arab World Vanished Overnight*, Valentine Mitchell, London and Portland, OR.

Kabaservice, Geoffrey (2020), 'The Forever Grievance', *The Washington Post*, 4 December 2020 (https://www .washingtonpost.com/outlook/2020/12/04/tea-party -trumpism-conservatives-populism/).

Kaplan, Debra (2022), 'Martin Luther and the Reformation', in Katz (2022), ch. 15, pp. 273–90.

Katz, Steven (ed.) (2006), *The Cambridge History of Judaism*, Cambridge University Press, Cambridge and New York.

Katz, Steven (ed.) (2022), *The Cambridge Companion to Antisemitism*, Cambridge University Press, Cambridge and New York.

Ker-Lindsay, James (2011), *The Cyprus Problem: What Everyone Needs to Know*, Oxford University Press, Oxford and New York.

Khalidi, Rashid (2020), *The Hundred Years' War on Palestine: A History of Settler Colonial Conquest and Resistance*, Profile Books, London.

Khoury, Jack (2009), 'Abbas: Olmert Offered PA Land Equaling 100 per cent of West Bank', *Haaretz*, 20 December 2009 (https://www.haaretz.com/1.4883092).

Kuitto, Kati, Susan Kuivalainen and Katja Möhring (eds) (2021), *Social Policy and Administration*, vol. 55, no. 3, special issue on inequalities in pensions and retirement from a life course perspective (https://onlinelibrary.wiley.com /doi/full/10.1111/spol.12663).

Küntzel, Matthias (2005), 'National Socialism and Anti-Semitism in the Arab World', *Jewish Political Studies Review*, vol. 17, no. 1/2, pp. 99–118.

Lakner, Christoph and Branko Milanovic (2013), 'Global Income Distribution: From the Fall of the Berlin Wall to the Great Recession', *Policy Research Working Paper Series 6719*, The World Bank.

Lappin, Shalom (2003), 'Israel and the New Antisemitism', *Dissent*, vol. 50, no. 3, pp. 18–24.

Lappin, Shalom (2004), 'Israel/Palestine: Is There a Case for Bi-Nationalism?', *Dissent*, vol. 51, no. 1, pp. 13–17.

Lappin, Shalom (2006), 'How Class Disappeared from Western Politics', *Dissent*, vol. 53, no. 1, pp. 73–8.

Lappin, Shalom (2006a), 'The Caricature of Zion', *Democratiya*, 6, September–November.

Lappin, Shalom (2006b), 'A Question of Zion: A Rejoinder to Jacqueline Rose', *Democratiya*, Winter.

Lappin, Shalom (2008), *This Green and Pleasant Land: Britain and the Jews*, Working Paper, Institute for the Study of Global Antisemitism and Policy (https://isgap.org/wp-content/uploads/2013/08/ISGAP-Working-Papers-Booklet-Lappin-copy.pdf).

Lappin, Shalom (2019), 'The Re-Emergence of the Jewish Question', *Journal of Contemporary Antisemitism*, pp. 29–46.

Lappin, Shalom (2021), 'We Shall Be as a City on a Hill: Trump, "Progressive" Antisemitism, and the Loss of American Jewish Exceptionalism', *Fathom*, September 2021 (https://fathomjournal.org/we-shall-be-as-a-city-on-a-hill-trump-progressive-antisemitism-and-the-loss-of-american-jewish-exceptionalism/).

Lappin, Shalom (2021a), *Deep Learning and Linguistic Representation*, CRC Press, Taylor & Francis, Boca Raton and Oxford.

Lappin, Yaakov (2011), *The Virtual Caliphate*, Potomac Books, Washington DC.

Laqueur, Walter (2003), *A History of Zionism: From the French Revolution to the Establishment of the State of Israel*, Schocken, Tel Aviv.

LeTourneau, Nancy (2019), 'A More Twisted Form of Anti-Semitism', *Washington Monthly*, 12 February 2019 (https://washingtonmonthly.com/2019/02/12/a-more-twisted-form-of-anti-semitism/).

Levin, Ines, Alexandra Filindra and Jeffrey S. Kopstein (2022), 'Validating and Testing a Measure of Anti-Semitism on Support for QAnon and Vote Intention for Trump in 2020', *Social Science Quarterly*, vol. 103, pp. 794–809.

Lewis, Bernard (1987), *Jews of Islam*, Princeton University Press, Princeton, NJ.

Light, Michael T., Jingying He and Jason P. Robey (2020), 'Comparing Crime Rates Between Undocumented Immigrants, Legal Immigrants, and Native-Born US Citizens Texas', *PNAS* (https://www.ncbi.nlm.nih.gov/pmc/articles/PMC7768760/pdf/pnas.202014704.pdf).

Linfield, Susie (2019), 'Albert Memmi: Zionism as National Liberation', in Susie Linfied (2019), *The Lions' Den: Zionism and the Left from Hannah Arendt to Noam Chomsky*, Yale University Press, New Haven, CT, pp. 165–96.

Lipstadt, Deborah (2018), *Antisemitism: Here and Now*, Schocken Books, New York.

Lynch, Sarah (2021), 'U.S. Chose Not to Prosecute 82 per cent of Hate-Crime Suspects from 2005–2019', *Reuters*, 9 July 2021 (https://www.reuters.com/world/us/us-chose-not-prosecute-82-hate-crime-suspects-2005-2019-2021-07-08/).

Maclennan, Duncan and Jinqiao Long (2023), *How Does the Housing Market Affect Wealth Inequality*, UK Collaborative Centre for Housing Evidence, 1 March 2023 (https://housingevidence.ac.uk/how-does-the-housing-market-affect-wealth-inequality/).

Maizland, Lindsay (2022), 'India's Muslims: An Increasingly

Marginalized Population', *Council on Foreign Relations*, 22 July 2022 (https://www.cfr.org/backgrounder/india-muslims-marginalized-population-bjp-modi).

Markus, Stanislav (2022), 'Meet Russia's Oligarchs, a Group of Men Who Won't Be Toppling Putin Anytime Soon', Davis Center for Russian and Euroasian Studies, Harvard University, 4 March 2022.

Mason, Lilian, Julie Wrongly and John V. Kane (2021), 'Activating Animus: The Uniquely Social Roots of Trump Support', *American Political Science Review*, vol. 115, no. 4, pp. 1508–16.

Meddeb, Abdelwahab and Benjamin Stora (eds) (2014), *A History of Jewish–Muslim Relations From the Origins to the Present Day*, Princeton University Press, Princeton, NJ and Oxford.

Memmi, Albert (2021), *The Colonizer and the Colonized*, Beacon Press, Boston, MA.

Menard, Louis (2001–2), 'Morton, Agassiz, and the Origins of Scientific Racism in the United States', *The Journal of Blacks in Education*, no. 34, Winter, pp. 110–13.

Merrit, Jonathan (2017), 'Understanding the Evangelical obsession with Israel', *American Magazine*, 11 December 2017 (https://www.americamagazine.org/politics-society/2017/12/11/understanding-evangelical-obsession-israel).

Milanovic, Branko (2023), 'The Great Convergence: Global Equality and Its Discontents', *Foreign Affairs*, 14 June 2023 (https://www.foreignaffairs.com/world/great-convergence-equality-branko-milanovic).

Mitchell, Archie (2023), 'Jeremy Corbyn Refuses to Condemn Hamas after Militant Group Carries out Deadly Attack on Israel', *The Independent*, 9 October 2023 (https://www.independent.co.uk/news/uk/politics/jeremy-corbyn-hamas-israel-palestine-b2426364.html).

Morris, Benny (2004), *The Birth of the Palestinian Refugee*

Problem Revisited, second edition, Cambridge University Press, Cambridge.

Morris, Benny (2009), *1948: A History of the First Arab–Israeli War*, Yale University Press, New Haven, CT.

Naumann, Elias and Moritz Hess (2021), 'Population Ageing, Immigration and the Welfare State: The Political Demography in Western Europe', in Goerres and Vanhuysse (2021), pp. 351–71.

Nayyar, Deepak (2006), 'Globalisation, History and Development: The Tale of Two Centuries', *Cambridge Journal of Economics*, vol. 30, pp. 137–59.

O'Malley, Joseph (ed.), assisted by Richard Davis (1994), *Marx: Early Political Writings*, Cambridge University Press, Cambridge.

Osakwe, Patrick N. and Olga Solleder (2023), *Wealth Distribution, Income Inequality and Financial Inclusion: A Panel Data Analysis*, United Nations Conference on Trade and Development, Working Paper no. 4, April 2023 (https://unctad.org/system/files/official-document/wp-2023d3-no4_en.pdf).

Owada, Reham (2023), 'How Israeli Settlements Impede the Two-State Solution', *Carnegie Endowment for International Peace*, 7 March 2023 (https://carnegieendowment.org/sada/89215#:~:text=blocking per cent20agricultural per cent20development.-,Violating per cent20Palestinian per cent20Sovereignty,area per cent20of per cent20the per cent20West per cent20Bank).

Pappe, Ilan (2022), *A History of Modern Palestine*, third edition, Cambridge University Press, Cambridge.

Peled, Yoav (1992), 'From Theology to Sociology: Bruno Bauer and Karl Marx on the Question of Jewish Emancipation', *History of Political Thought*, vol. 13, no. 3, pp. 463–85.

Petri, Peter and Meena Banga (2020), 'The Economic Consequences of Globalisation in the United States', *ERIA Discussion Paper Series*, ERIA-DP-2019-25.

Pietsch, Bryan (2022), 'Stanford Apologizes for Limiting Admissions of Jewish Students in 1950s', *The Washington Post*, 13 October 2022.

Piketty, Thomas (2014), *Capital in the Twenty-First Century*, The Belknap Press of Harvard University Press, Cambridge, MA and London.

Posen, Adam (2022), 'The UK and the Global Economy after Brexit', *PIIE Charts*, Peterson Institute for International Economics, 27 April 2022 (https://www.piie.com/research /piie-charts/uk-and-global-economy-after-brexit).

Poulsen, Regin Winther (2021), 'How the Danish Left Adopted a Far-Right Immigration Policy', *Foreign Policy*, 12 July 2021 (https://foreignpolicy.com/2021/07/12/denmark-refugees -frederiksen-danish-left-adopted-a-far-right-immigration -policy/).

Ravitzky, Aviezer (1996), *Messianism, Zionism, and Jewish Religious Radicalism*, University of Chicago Press, Chicago, IL.

Reinhartz, Adele (2022), 'New Testament Origins of Christian Anti-Judaism', in Katz (2022), ch. 2, pp. 42–56.

Rich, Dave (2016), *The Left's Jewish Problem: Jeremy Corbyn, Israel and Anti-Semitism*, Biteback Publishing, Hull.

Rich, Dave (2023), *Everyday Hate*, Biteback Publishing, London.

Roberts, Anthea and Nicolas Lamp (2021), *Six Faces of Globalisation: Who Wins, Who Loses, and Why It Matters*, Harvard University Press, Cambridge, MA.

Robin, Michael (2018), 'American Jews Don't Need Israel to be Jewish', *Forward*, 21 February 2018 (https://forward .com/opinion/394903/american-jews-have-never-needed -israel/).

Roose, Kevin (2021), 'What Is QAnon, the Viral Pro-Trump Conspiracy Theory?', *The New York Times*, 3 September 2021.

Rose, Jacqueline (2005), *The Question of Zion*, Princeton University Press, Princeton, NJ.

Rose, Jacqueline (2006), 'A Reply to Shalom Lappin', *Democratiya*, Winter.

Ross, Dennis (2004), *The Missing Peace: The Inside Story of the Fight for Middle East Peace*, Farrar, Straus and Giroux, New York.

Sarfatti, Michele (ed.) (2017), 'Italy's Fascist Jews: Insights on an Unusual Scenario', *Quest. Issues in Contemporary Jewish History*, no. 11, October (https://www.quest-cdecjournal.it/?issue=11).

Sciubba, Jennifer D. (2021), 'Intergenerational Controversy and Cultural Clashes: Political Consequences of Demographic Change in the US and Canada Since 1990', in Goerres and Vanhuysse (2021), pp. 325–50.

Shapira, Anita (2014), *Israel: A History*, Weidenfeld and Nicholson, London.

Sharon, Jeremy (2023), 'Levin Unveils Bills to Remove Nearly All High Court's Tools for Government Oversight', *The Times of Israel*, 11 January 2023 (https://www.timesofisrael.com/levin-unveils-bills-to-weaken-top-court-enable-laws-to-be-immune-to-judicial-review/).

Sharon, Jeremy (2023a), 'Kohelet, Right-Wing Think Tank That Inspired Overhaul, Calls for Partial Compromise', *The Times of Israel*, 14 March 2023 (https://www.timesofisrael.com/right-wing-think-tank-that-inspired-judicial-overhaul-calls-for-compromise/).

Shavit, Uriya (2015), 'Zionism as Told by Rashid Rida', *The Journal of Israeli History*, vol. 34, no. 1, pp. 23–44.

Sheffer, Gabriel (1996), *Moshe Sharett: Biography of a Political Moderate*, Clarendon Press, Oxford.

Sher, Gilead (2006), *Israeli–Palestinian Peace Negotiations, 1999–2001: Within Reach*, Routledge, Abingdon.

Shlaim, Avi (2010), *Israel and Palestine: Reappraisals, Revisions, Refutations*, Verso Books, New York.

Snyder, Timothy (2018), 'Ivan Ilyin, Putin's Philosopher of Russian Fascism', *The New York Review of Books*, 16 March 2018.

Spyer, Jonathan (2014), *The Rise of Nationalism: The Arab World, Turkey, and Iran*, Mason Crest, Broomall PA.

Stanley, Jason and Eliyahu Stern (2022), 'Putin's Fascism', *Tablet*, 21 March 2022.

Teller, Adam (2014), 'Revisiting Baron's "Lachrymose Conception": The Meanings of Violence in Jewish History', *Association for Jewish Studies Review*, vol. 38, no. 2, pp. 431–9.

Teter, Magda (2020), *Blood Libel: On the Trail of an Antisemitic Myth*, Harvard University Press, Cambridge, MA.

Tibi, Bassam (2010), 'From Sayyid Qutb to Hamas: The Middle East Conflict and the Islamization of Antisemitism', *The Yale Initiative for the Interdisciplinary Study of Antisemitism Working Paper Series* (https://isgap.org/wp-content/uploads/2011/10/bassam-tibi-online-working-paper-20101.pdf).

Toynbee, Arnold (1961), *The Study of History*, vol. 12, Oxford University Press, Oxford.

Toynbee, Arnold (1969), *Experiences*, Oxford University Press, Oxford.

Vargas-Silva, Carlos and Madeleine Sumption (2023), *The Labour Market Effects of Immigration*, COMPAS, Centre on Migration Policy and Society, Oxford University (https://migrationobservatory.ox.ac.uk/wp-content/uploads/2016/04/MigObs-Briefing-The-Labour-Market-Effects-of-Immigration.pdf).

Waldenström, Daniel (2021), *Wealth and History: An Update*, Research Institute of Industrial Economics, IFN Working Paper no. 1411 (https://www.ifn.se/en/publications/working-papers/2021/1411/).

Walker, Peter and Jessica Elgot (2020), 'Jeremy Corbyn Rejects Overall Findings of EHRC Report on Antisemitism in Labour', *The Guardian*, 29 October 2020.

Weinstock, Nathan (2008), *Une Si Longue Présence*, PLON, Paris.

Weisbrot, Mark, Lara Merling, Vitor Mello, Stephan Lefebvre

and Joseph Sammut (2017), *Did NAFTA Help Mexico: An Update After 23 Years*, Center for Economic and Policy Research (https://cepr.net/images/stories/reports/nafta -mexico-update-2017-03.pdf?v=2).

Wistricht, Robert (1995), 'Radical Antisemitism in France and Germany (1840–1880)', *Modern Judaism*, vol. 15, pp. 109–35.

Witte, Griff (2018), 'Once-Fringe Soros Conspiracy Theory Takes Center Stage in Hungarian Election', *The Washington Post*, 17 March 2018 (https://www.washingtonpost.com /world/europe/once-fringe-soros-conspiracy-theory-takes -center-stage-in-hungarian-election/2018/03/17/f0a1d5ae -2601-11e8-a227-fd2b009466bc_story.html).

Ye'or, Bat (2005), *Euroabia: The Europe–Arab Axis*, Fairleigh Dickinson, Madison NJ.

Zeldin, Alex (2022), 'The Other History of the Holocaust', *The Atlantic*, 4 April 2022.

Index

Abbas, Mahmoud, 143–4
academia, 4, 104–5, 125–6, 166
Achdud HaAvodah, 152
Action Française, 28
Adler, Viktor, 26
Adversous Judaeos, 37–8
Afghanistan, 124
African Americans, 59, 60, 102
African National Congress (ANC), 154
Against Apion (Josephus Flavius), 35
Agassiz, Louis, 27
agriculture, 13, 62, 84, 100, 101, 184
Åkesson, Jimmie, 65
Al Qaeda, 118, 119, 120
Alexandria, 34–6
Algeria, 63, 71, 113, 114
Algerian War, 71, 114
Allen, Jim, 97
Almohads, 110–11
Altneuland (Herzl), 130
Alvaredo, Facundo, 17
Amir, Yigal, 141
Anan, Kofi, 149
anarchism, 24, 29–30, 99, 167

anti-colonialism, 4, 81, 83–8, 90–1, 94–108, 113–14, 117, 118, 123–4, 166, 169, 180–1
Anti-Defamation League, 2
anti-elitism, 5, 21, 22, 33, 52, 59, 159, 160–1
anti-globalism, 3, 10, 21–2, 32, 33–4, 88–9, 157, 171, 173, 178, 179, 192–3
anti-racism, 1, 193–4
Antisemiten-Liga, 24
Antisemitic League of France, 28
anti-Zionism, 6, 51, 70–1, 93, 95–108, 116, 166–72, 176
anusim, 40, 111, 112
apartheid, 56, 154
Apion, 35
al-Aqsa Mosque, 116, 131, 141–2
Arab Higher Committee, 132, 134
Arab Israelis, 77, 135–6
Arab League, 134, 136, 137
Arab Liberation Army, 134
Arab nationalism, 28, 71, 95–6, 97, 112–15, 117, 118, 130–1, 133, 137
Arabic language, 75, 112

Arafat, Yasser, 137, 139, 140–3
Argentina, 98, 119
aristocracy, 23, 82
artificial intelligence (AI), 189–92
Ashkenazi Jews, 94, 160–1
al-Assad, Bashar, 69, 118
assassinations, 116, 117, 139–40,
141, 152
assimiliation, 30, 52, 63, 65, 82, 99,
100
Atatürk, Mustafa Kemal, 113
Augustine, 38
Auschwitz, 63
austerity, 9
Australia, 83, 98
Austria, 26, 30, 67, 100
Austrian Social Democratic
Workers Party, 26, 30, 86
Austro-Hungarian Empire, 30, 31
authoritarianism, 3–4, 6, 60, 66–7,
8183
Auto-Emancipation (Pinsker), 100

Baath Parties, 114–15
Back to Africa movement, 102
Baddiel, David, 2
Baghdad, 95
Bakunin, Mikhail, 30
Balfour Declaration, 129, 131, 137
Banga, Meena, 11
banks, 9–10, 28
al-Banna, Hassan, 116
Banu Nadir, 42–3
Banu Qaynuqa, 42–3
Banu Qurayza, 42–3
Bar Kochva rebellion, 109
Barak, Ehud, 141
Bardella, Jordan, 63
Baron, Salo, 171–2
Barris, Kenya, 92
Bauer, Bruno, 46–9, 64–5, 155
Bauer, Otto, 30, 49
Begin, Menachem, 72, 138–40
Beirut, 139–40

Bell, Brian, 187
Ben Gurion, David, 132, 134, 136,
168, 169
Ben-Gvir, Itamar, 159, 164
Bennet, Naftali, 73, 144
Berbers, 110, 112, 113
Bergman, Hugo, 152
Berkeley Law School, 125
Bevin, Ernest, 102
Bharatiya Janata Party (India), 54–5
Biden, Joe, 57, 68, 73, 187
bin Laden, Osama, 118
binationalism, 151–6
Birnbaum, Pierre, 70–1
Black Book of Soviet Jewry, 90
Black Lives Matter movement, 176
Blair, Tony, 9
Bland, Benjamin, 71
blood libel, 36, 40–1
Bolshevik revolution, 40, 84, 101
Bolsonaro, Jair, 4
Boycott, Divestment and Sanctions
(BDS) movement, 107, 166
Brazil, 4, 40
Brenner, Lenny, 97
Bretton Woods system, 7
Brexit, 10
Bristol University, 104–5
Britain *see* United Kingdom
Brit Shalom, 152
British National Party, 71
British Union of Jewish Students,
104
Brothers of Italy (FdI), 66
Brown, Gordon, 9
Buber, Martin, 152
Buchanan, Pat, 59–60, 70
Buenos Aires, 119
Butler, Judith, 86–7, 122
Byzantium, 39, 128, 129

Cain, 38
Cairo, 110, 115–16, 139
Caligula, 35

Camp David Accords, 138–9
Camp David-Taba talks, 141–2
Canada, 51, 52, 98, 153, 184
Capital (Marx), 83
capital-owning classes, 13, 85–6, 182
capitalism, 30, 48, 65, 83–6, 91, 123
Carlson, Tucker, 68
Catholicism, 26, 27, 40, 41–2, 69
censorship, 61, 90
centre right, 62, 161
Chamberlain, Houston Stewart, 27, 45
Chancel, Lucas, 13, 17, 79
Chappelle, Dave, 1–2
Charlottesville demonstrations, 1
Chechnya, 67
Chiarini, Roberto, 70
China, 3, 11, 16, 17, 84, 125, 184–5
Christian Social Party, 26
Christianity
    anti-Judaism, 36–42, 46, 50
    Catholicism, 26, 27, 40, 41–2, 69
    Christian population in Israel-Palestine, 128–9
    conversion to, 38, 40, 45, 47
    dispensationalism, 47, 72
    established as religion of Roman Empire, 38–9
    evangelical Christianity, 71–2, 158
    fundamentalism, 60, 61
    Maronite Christianity, 139
    Orthodox Christianity, 37–9
    Protestantism, 41–2, 72
    Reformation, 41
    religious texts, 29, 36–7, 41
    and replacement, 29, 36–7, 47
    spread of, 38
    theology, 36–42, 46, 50
Civic Platform Party (Poland), 69
civil rights, 61, 64–5, 156
civil society, 52, 68

civil state, 46–7, 155
civil wars, 8, 152–3
civilians, 67, 69, 106, 119, 122, 140, 142
class, 13, 16–17, 20–1, 23, 48, 62–3, 74, 81–6, 91, 93, 122–3, 159, 163, 167, 169, 177, 180–3
class consciousness, 91
class struggle, 48, 83, 85–6, 123, 167
Clermont-Tonnerre, Stanislas-Marie-Adélaide de, 46, 64
climate change, 5, 9
Clinton, Bill, 9, 141–2
Clinton parameters, 141–2, 143, 154
Cohen, Hermann, 166
collective bargaining, 182
colonialism
    British, 51, 83, 98, 113, 129, 131–4, 147–8, 149
    cultural and linguistic suppression, 98
    decolonization, 7, 113–14
    and dispossession, 51, 83, 98, 99, 103, 128
    European mandates in Middle East, 31, 51, 97, 113, 129, 131–4, 149
    and the far left, 4, 81, 83–8, 90–1, 94–5, 96–108
    French, 113, 133
    and globalization, 13
    Israel depicted as colonialist, 50–1, 96–108, 128
    justified through racial theories, 27
    and labour, 13, 83
    neo-colonialism, 123
    and privilege, 89, 94–5
    Spanish, 98
    and trade, 13
    and Zionism, 50–1, 95, 96–108
    see also anti-colonialism

Colonizer and the Colonized
    (Memmi), 114
communications technology,
    11–13, 22
Communism, 7, 8, 73, 84, 97, 99,
    101, 116, 124, 167, 168–70
Congress Party (India), 55
conservatism, 8, 62, 69, 78, 192
conspiracy theories, 2, 5–6, 22,
    28–9, 32–6, 52, 57–8, 89–92,
    103–8, 116–18, 127, 157,
    168–70, 173
Constantine I, 38
Constitution of Medina, 43
conversion, 38, 40, 45, 47, 111, 112
Corbyn, Jeremy, 87, 103–4, 122,
    166
Cordoba, 110
corruption, 24, 28, 36, 44–6, 52, 77,
    115, 117, 121, 123, 162
cosmopolitanism, 21, 68, 73, 96,
    168
cost of living, 163
coups, 117, 143, 148
Covid pandemic, 9, 10, 11
Crenshaw, Kimberle, 92–3
crime rates, 187
Crimea, 67
critical race theory, 93
critical theory, 84–8, 92–4, 166; *see
    also* academia; postmodernism
Crusades, 39, 129
cultural autonomy, 30, 99, 101, 109,
    166, 172, 180
cultural exchange, 110
cultural relativism, 123–4, 181
culture wars, 21, 181, 183
Cyprus, 125, 133, 147–51
Czechoslovakia, 67, 153, 168–9

Darwin, Charles, 26–7
Davis, David Brion, 91
decadence, 67, 116, 117, 121
decolonization, 7, 113–14

deicide, 29, 36–7, 41, 43
democracy, 3–4, 6, 23–4, 32, 46–8,
    55, 61, 66–9, 143, 154–6,
    162–5, 178, 180–1, 183, 192–3
Democratic Party (US), 57–8, 59
Democratic Socialists of America
    (DSA), 87, 106
Denmark, 187
deregulation, 9–10, 161
Deri, Aryeh, 162
Dhimmi, 43, 109, 110
Diasporism, 167, 170–1
digital revolution, 13, 22
disinformation, 22–3, 191–2
dispensationalism, 47, 72
displacement, 23, 32, 50–1, 96, 99,
    128, 134–6, 142, 146, 148, 150
dispossession, 51, 83, 98, 99, 103,
    128, 146, 180
dog whistles, 176
Donbas, 67
Dreyfus, Alfred, 28, 63
Drumont, Édouard, 28
Du Bois, W. E. B., 102
Dugin, Aleksandr, 67–8

economic growth, 7, 8, 11–20, 23,
    25, 164, 184, 187, 188–9
economic recession, 7, 9, 11
education, 7, 16, 56, 61, 79, 89–90,
    163, 182, 185, 186, 193
Edward I, 39
Egypt, 76, 110, 113, 115–17, 119,
    133, 134, 135, 136–9, 143
Egyptian civilization, 34–6
Ehrenburg, Ilya, 90
1848 revolutions, 23, 24
elites, 21, 22, 52, 59, 78, 154, 160–1,
    180, 191; *see also* anti-elitism
employment, 7, 8, 16, 20, 79, 163,
    182–3, 191; *see also* labour
    market
entertainment industry, 2, 4, 92
environment, 9, 185, 188

Equality and Human Rights
Commission, 103–4
Erdoğan, Recep Tayyip, 4
Ethiopia, 94
ethnic cleansing, 85, 135; see also
genocide
ethnic conflicts, 4, 124–5, 147–51,
150
ethnic identity, 5–6, 21, 30, 52, 74,
77–8, 85, 86, 93, 105, 113, 123,
155, 180
ethno-nationalism, 4, 21, 24, 44–6,
52–5, 58, 62–6, 75–9, 121, 151,
159–61, 165, 177, 179
European Union, 9, 10, 62, 68, 149
evangelical Christianity, 71–2, 158
exceptionalism, 60–1, 79, 169, 171
exclusion, 24, 39, 55, 76, 81–2, 86,
89, 91, 99, 109, 126, 130, 146,
158, 193
Exodus narrative, 34–6
expansionism, 3, 118–19
exploitation, 21, 29, 30, 48, 81, 82,
83
expulsions, 39–40, 43, 45–6, 51,
55, 65, 95–6, 102, 111, 134–5,
145–6, 156, 167, 172

Faber, Eli, 91
Falwell, Jerry, 72
far left
    alliances with radical Islamism,
    121–6
    anti-colonialism, 4, 81, 83–8,
    90–1, 94–108, 123–4, 166, 169,
    180–1
    anti-elitism, 5, 52
    anti-West ideology, 85, 87–8
    anti-Zionism, 6, 93, 95–108,
    166–72, 176
    and class struggle, 48, 83, 85–6,
    123
    conspiracy theories, 5, 52, 89,
    91–2, 103–5, 107, 168, 170

Diasporism, 167, 170–1
    in Europe, 65, 66, 81, 83, 91
    Holocaust historiography, 89–90
    Holocaust inversion, 71
    identity politics, 4, 5, 52, 84–8,
    93–4, 107, 122–3, 179–81
    and intersectionality, 92–4
    in Israel, 134, 152
    Jewish collaboration with,
    166–73, 177
    moral relativism, 123–4
    position on Israel–Palestine
    conflict, 106–7, 124, 126, 146,
    151, 156, 170
    position on Ukraine, 68, 87–9,
    93, 124
    postmodernism, 4, 52, 84–96,
    103, 107, 122–3, 166, 169–70,
    179–80, 181, 193
    in the UK, 71, 87–8, 103–7, 122,
    166
    in the US, 87–8, 169–70, 171–2
    White privilege narratives, 52,
    86, 89–96, 107
far right
    anti-elitism, 5, 52, 59, 159, 160–1
    anti-Zionism, 70–1
    in Brazil, 4
    conspiracy theories, 5, 28–9, 52,
    57–8
    in Europe, 3–4, 61–71, 73, 158
    Holocaust inversion, 71
    hostility to European Union, 10,
    62
    identity politics, 5, 179, 180–1
    in Israel, 72, 74, 75–80, 101, 134,
    141, 156, 159–66, 178, 194
    Jewish collaboration with,
    157–66, 177
    opposition to radical Islamism,
    158, 159
    political parties, 3, 61–6, 68–9,
    71, 74
    position on Ukraine, 68–9

far right (*cont.*)
  potential backlashes from, 107
  pro-Israel antisemitism, 70–4
  recruitment techniques, 121
  in Russia, 3, 66–70, 73–4
  support for Putin, 68–9
  targeting of immigrants, 5–6, 33,
    54, 57, 59, 62, 63, 65, 159, 179,
    186–9
  targeting of Muslims, 5–6, 54–5,
    62, 63, 65, 125, 159, 179
  in the UK, 71
  in the US, 1, 3, 55–61, 70, 157, 161
  and the welfare state, 26, 63, 66
al-Farabi, 110
Farhud, 95
Farrakhan, Louis, 91–2
fascism, 7, 31, 61–2, 66, 67, 71, 90,
  158
financial deregulation, 9–10, 161
financial institutions, 6, 9–10
financial services sector, 79
First Aliya, 100, 130
first Gaza war, 143
first Intifada, 140
First World War, 11, 31, 113, 131,
  147, 149
folkist autonomism, 99
foreign investment, 10, 164, 185–6
Fox News, 68
France
  and the Algerian War, 71, 114
  colonialism, 113, 133
  Dreyfus affair, 28, 63
  expulsions of Jews in twelfth to
    fourteenth centuries, 39
  far left, 65
  far right, 3, 63–5, 70–1, 158
  invasion of Egypt, 136
  Islamist attacks, 119
  Jewish immigrants, 65, 94, 114
  laïcité, 64–5
  mandates in Middle East, 113,
    133

National Rally party, 63–4, 158
nationalism, 64, 71
political antisemitism, 28, 29
radical Islamism, 65
republicanism, 46, 63–5
Vichy government, 28, 63
fraud, 77, 162
Fredrikson, Paula, 37
Free Officers Movement coup
  (Egypt), 117
free speech, 104–5, 125
free trade, 8, 183–5
Fukuyama, Francis, 8

Galant, Yoav, 162
Galilee, 128, 131, 132, 135
Galloway, George, 122
Gaon, Saadya, 110
Garvey, Marcus, 102
al-Gaylani, Rashid Ali, 95, 97,
  132–3
Gaza, 78, 118, 124, 135–7, 138–9,
  140–4, 154, 177, 194
Gemayel, Bashir, 139–40
gender, 5, 52, 77, 85, 86, 88, 91, 93,
  105, 122, 123, 173, 180, 193;
  see also women's rights
General Jewish Workers Bund, 30,
  101–2, 166–7
generative language models
  (LLMs), 190
Geneva Conventions, 149
genocide, 31, 41, 46, 85, 87, 89–90,
  97, 106, 145, 193; *see also*
  Holocaust
gentrification, 21, 78
Georgia, 67
Germany
  Arab nationalist support for,
    132–3
  comparisons of Israel with Nazi
    Germany, 97
  expulsion of Jews from Upper
    Bavaria, 39

al-Husseini and al-Gaylani flee
to, 132–3
invasion of Soviet Union, 88
nationalism, 24–6
Nazism, 26–8, 31, 41, 46, 66,
88–90, 97, 102, 132–3, 167
non-aggression pact with Soviet
Union, 88
occupation of Poland, 69
pan-Germanism, 24, 26
plot to overthrow government,
58
political antisemitism, 24–8, 31
QAnon, 58
ghettos, 30
Gini inequality index, 13, 14, 182,
184
global financial crisis, 9, 11
globalization, 10, 11–23, 33, 88–9,
91, 182–6, 189, 192
gnostics, 37
Golan Heights, 71, 137, 138
Gorbachev, Mikhail, 8
Gorenberg, Gershom, 166
Gramsci, Antonio, 84–5
Granada, 110
Graves, Philip, 28
Greece, 147–50
Greek civilization, 34–6, 110
grievances, 4–5, 62, 78, 146, 159–63
Grossman, Vasily, 90
Grundlagen des neunzehnten
Jahrhunderts (Chamberlain),
27
gun rights, 59

Ha'am, Ahad (Asher Ginsberg), 130
Hagee, John, 71–2
Haifa oil refinery, 135
Hamas, 73–4, 78–9, 86–7, 106–7,
118, 122, 124, 126, 141–5,
153–4, 156, 165–6, 170
HaNagid, Joseph, 110
HaNagid, Shmuel, 110

Harap, Louis, 168–9
Hashemites, 131
Hashomer Hatzair, 134, 152
hate crimes, 2, 57, 73, 106, 174–5
healthcare, 185, 188
Hebrew Immigrant Aid Society
(HIAS), 57
Hebron, 131, 138
hegemony, 6, 37, 120, 123
Herzl, Theodor, 100, 130
Heyer, Heather, 1
Hezbollah, 73, 86–7, 118, 119, 122,
140, 145
Hill, Jonah, 92
Hindu nationalism, 54–5, 151
Hinduism, 4, 54–5, 150
Hirsh, David, 2
Histadrut Labour Federation, 101
Histories (Tacitus), 35
historiography, 34–5, 69, 89–92,
107, 171–2
Hitler, Adolf, 26, 67, 68, 97, 158
Holocaust, 41–2, 50, 62, 63, 68, 71,
72, 73, 89–90, 92, 97, 119, 158,
167, 193
Holocaust denial, 97, 119
Holocaust inversion, 71
Hope, David, 20
hostage taking, 145
housing, 17, 79, 163
Houthi militias, 118, 145
Hovevei Tzion, 100
Hugh of Lincoln, 40
human rights, 81, 82, 97, 124–5, 183
humanitarian aid, 145
Hungary, 3–4, 68, 73, 77, 160
Hussein, King of Jordan, 139
al-Husseini, Fawzi Darwish, 152
al-Husseini, Haj Amin, 97, 116, 131,
132–3

Ibn Gabirol, Solomon, 110
Ibn Rushd, 110
Ibn Saud, 113

Ibn Sina, 110
Ichud, 152
identity politics, 4, 5, 33, 52, 84–8,
    93–4, 107, 122–3, 157, 173–4,
    179–81
Iggeret Teiman (Maimonides), 111
Ilyan, Ivan, 67
immigration
    far-right targeting of immigrants,
        5–6, 33, 54, 57, 62, 63, 65, 159,
        179, 186–9
    Jewish immigrants in France, 65,
        94, 114
    Jewish immigrants in the US,
        55–6, 60–1
    Jewish immigration to Israel, 54,
        65, 100, 105, 128–31, 133, 136,
        145–6, 152
    management of, 5, 56, 102, 133,
        186–9
    from Mexico to the US, 57, 184,
        187
    non-EU immigration, 69, 187
    numbers of immigrants, 21, 188
    and replacement, 29, 52, 57
    see also refugees
Immigration Act (US), 56
Inbari, Motti, 72
income distribution, 13–21, 33, 79,
    159, 164, 179–86, 192
India, 3, 4, 16, 17, 54–5, 83, 125,
    150–1
indigenous peoples, 50–1, 83, 87,
    89, 98
industrialization, 13–16, 23, 24, 99
inequality
    between-country inequality,
        13–17
    Gini inequality index, 13, 14, 182,
        184
    and globalization, 11–23, 33,
        182–3, 192
    income inequality, 11, 13–21, 33,
        79, 159, 164, 179–86, 192

integrated international
    approaches to, 32, 186
    in Israel, 79, 159, 164
    in the UK, 79, 182
    in the US, 79, 181–2
    wealth inequality, 17–20, 21, 180,
        184–5, 191, 192
    within-country inequality, 13–21,
        33, 183
inflation, 8, 9, 20
integrationism, 102
intelligence services, 79, 145, 161,
    165
intersectionality, 92–4
Iran, 70, 74, 112, 118–20, 124, 145
Iranian Revolution, 118, 124
Iraq, 70, 95, 97, 113, 114–15, 118,
    120, 132–3, 134, 153
Irshai, Oded, 37
Islam
    conflict with Hinduism in India,
        150–1
    conversion to, 111, 112
    far-right targeting of Muslims,
        5–6, 54–5, 62, 63, 65, 125, 159,
        179
    Jews in traditional Islamic
        societies, 109–12
    Muslim population in Israel-
        Palestine, 128–9
    philosophy, 110
    radical Islam *see* radical
        Islamism
    religious texts, 29, 43–4
    and replacement, 29, 43–4
    Sharia law, 6, 43, 117
    Shia Islam, 111, 112, 118, 119–20
    Sunni Islam, 115–16, 119–20
    teachings on Judaism and
        Christianity, 42–4
    theology, 42–5
    Uyghur Muslims, 125
Islamic State, 120
isolationism, 10, 56, 59

Israel
annexationist policies, 71, 78, 166
Arab citizens, 77, 135–6
Barak government, 141
Begin government, 72, 138–40
Ben Gurion governments, 132, 134, 136, 168, 169
Bennet–Lapid government, 73, 144
Camp David-Taba talks, 141–2
Christian and Muslim populations, 128–9
civilian casualties, 73, 106, 119, 122, 135, 136, 140, 142, 144–5
comparisons with Nazi Germany, 97
cost of living, 163
creation of, 44, 96, 99, 121, 134
Declaration of Independence, 75, 160
depicted as colonialist, 50–1, 96–108, 128
displacement of Palestinians, 96, 99, 128, 134–6, 142, 146
education, 79, 163
employment, 79, 163
far left, 134, 152
far-left positions on, 106–7, 124, 126, 146, 151, 156, 170
far right, 72, 74, 75–80, 101, 134, 141, 156, 159–66, 178, 194
first Aliya, 100
first Gaza war, 143
foreign investment, 164
Hamas terror attacks, 73–4, 79, 106–7, 124, 126, 141–5, 153, 156, 165–6, 170
historical overview, 127–47
housing, 79, 163
income inequality, 79, 159, 164
intelligence services, 79, 145, 161, 165
Israel Defence Force (IDF), 134, 137, 140, 142, 144–5, 165–6

Israeli–Palestinian conflict, 32, 44–5, 71, 78, 96, 124, 127–56, 194
Jewish immigration, 54, 65, 100, 105, 128–31, 133, 136, 145–6, 152
judicial reforms, 74, 77, 160, 161–2, 164
Kadima Party, 143
Kibbutz movement, 101, 152
labour movement, 44, 101
Labour Party, 78–9, 80, 134, 138, 141
liberal left, 77–9, 162–3
Likud party, 80, 138, 141, 159
Mapam party, 152
military service, 78, 163
Nation State Law, 75–7, 161
nationalism, 44, 75–7, 79, 159–61, 165
Netanyahu governments, 71, 72–3, 74–80, 141, 144, 158–66, 178
1948 war, 96, 116, 128, 134–6, 138
1967 war, 45, 71, 115, 137–8
1973 war, 80, 138
1982 Lebanon war, 139–40
non-European Jewish population, 94–5, 97–8
occupation of southern Lebanon, 118
Olmert peace proposal, 78, 143–4, 151, 154
one-state solution, 150, 151–6, 170
Oslo peace process, 78, 140–2, 143–4, 151
Ottoman rule, 100, 128, 129
partition plans, 44, 129, 132, 133–4, 135, 142, 143, 146, 153–4
PLO terror attacks on, 139, 140
position on Ukraine, 74

Israel (cont.)
  press restrictions, 74
  privatization, 79
  protest movement, 161–5, 178
  public services, 79, 163
  Rabin government, 140–1
  Reasonableness Doctrine, 77, 162
  relocation of US embassy, 71–2
  Revisionist Zionist party, 132, 134
  right-wing militias, 134
  security barriers and checkpoints, 142–3
  Sephardi Shas Party, 162
  settler movement, 44–5, 130, 138, 141, 144, 159–60, 162, 164, 166
  7 October attack, 73, 74, 79, 106–7, 124, 126, 144–5, 153, 156, 165–6, 170
  Sharon government, 142–3
  Sinai Campaign, 136–7
  social justice movement, 163–5
  socialist-Zionist parties, 100–1
  Supreme Court, 75, 77, 160, 162
  targeting of civilians, 135, 140
  taxation, 163
  Tochnit Dalet, 134–5
  two-state solution, 78, 141, 151, 153–4
  2006 Lebanon war, 78
  ultra-Orthodox community, 77–8, 159–60, 162, 163, 167
  unions, 78–9, 161
  US support for, 70, 71–3
  welfare system, 79
  withdrawal from Gaza, 78, 143
Israel Defence Force (IDF), 134, 137, 140, 142, 144–5, 165–6
Italian Fascist Party, 158
Italian Social Movement (MSI), 66, 70
Italy, 3, 39, 66, 70, 113, 133, 158

Jabalia refugee camp, 140
Jabotinsky, Ze'ev, 132
Japan, 7, 58
Jefferson, Thomas, 27
Jeffress, Robert, 71–2
Jerusalem, 34, 71–2, 116, 129, 131, 133, 135, 137, 141–2, 143, 154, 164
Jesus, 36–7, 38, 41, 72
Jewish Agency for Israel, 74
Jewish Agency in Palestine, 132, 134
Jewish collectivity, 30, 31, 49–52, 64–5, 90, 155–6
Jewish control, 2, 6, 45, 70
Jewish Currents, 169–70
Jewish emancipation, 24–6, 40, 46–9, 65, 167, 172
Jewish exceptionalism, 60–1, 79, 169, 171–2
Jewish Life, 169
'Jewish lobby', 6, 70, 103–5, 127, 150, 176
Jewish particularism, 49, 82, 89–90
Jewish Voice for Labour, 166
Jewish Voice for Peace, 166
Jews and Their Lies (Luther), 41
jihadism, 116, 117–21
job security, 7, 16, 182, 187
John XXIII, 41
Johnson, Alan, 103
Jordan, 76, 113, 131, 134, 135, 136, 137, 139
Jordanian Legion, 135
Josephus Flavius, 34–5
Judenfrage, Die (Bruno Bauer), 46
Judenstaadt (Herzl), 100
judicial independence, 3–4, 69, 74, 77, 160, 161–2, 164
Julius, Anthony, 2

Kaczyński, Jarosław, 77
Kadima Party (Israel), 143
Kahan Commission, 140

Kahane, Meir, 159
Kalvarisky, Haim, 152
Kfar Etzion kibbutz, 135
Khmelnytsky pogroms, 172
Khomeini, Ayatollah, 118, 124
Kibbutz movement, 101, 152
Kielce pogrom, 40
al-Kindi, 110
King, Martin Luther, 102
Kirchner, Christina, 119
Kohelet Forum, 161
Kurds, 112, 113, 125

labour market, 7, 10, 13, 20, 102,
    163, 182–3, 185, 191; see also
    employment
labour movement, 44, 101, 102,
    124, 181–3
Labour Party (Israel), 78–9, 80, 134,
    138, 141
Labour Party (UK), 9, 102, 103–4,
    122, 166
labour unions see unions
laïcité, 64–5; see also secularism
land swaps, 141, 143, 154
Lapid, Yair, 73, 144
Lavrov, Sergei, 68
Law and Justice Party (Poland), 69,
    73, 77
Le Pen, Jean-Marie, 63
Le Pen, Marine, 63, 158
League of Nations, 131
Lebanon, 78, 113, 115, 118, 133,
    139–40, 153
LeTourneau, Nancy, 72
*Letter to the Comrades of Jura
    Federation* (Bakunin), 30
Levin, Ines, 58
Levin, Yariv, 160, 161, 165
Lewis, Bernard, 109
LGBTQ people, 68, 69, 87, 122, 124,
    173, 175
liberal left, 9, 77–9, 83, 162–3, 177
libertarianism, 8, 59, 62, 161

Libre Parole, 28
Libya, 113
Light, Michael T., 187
Likud party (Israel), 80, 138, 141,
    159
Limberg, Julian, 20
Linz programme, 26
Lipstadt, Deborah, 2
literary representations, 42
living standards, 7, 16, 84, 163
Livingstone, Ken, 97, 122
London, 40, 106, 119, 122
Lueger, Karl, 26, 30, 86
Luther, Martin, 41

Maccabean revolt, 35
Macias, Enrico, 114
Macron, Emmanuel, 63
MAGA movement, 59–60, 61, 62,
    71
Magnes, Judah, 152
al-Mahdi Ahmad, 111
Maimonides, Moses, 110, 111
mainstream media, 5, 22, 66–7, 68;
    see also press
Makarios III, 148
Malcolm X, 102
al-Manar, 115–16
Mandela, Nelson, 156
Manetho of Alexandria, 34–5
manufacturing, 7, 11–13, 16, 21, 23,
    182, 183, 184
Mapam party (Israel), 152
Marcion, 37
markets, 8, 13, 47, 48, 98
Maronite Christianity, 139
Marr, Wilhelm, 24, 45
Marshall Plan, 7
Marx, Karl, 30, 46–9, 65, 83–4
Marxism, 85–6, 96–7, 107, 123
Mashhad, 112
Mason, Lilian, 58
massacres, 39, 110, 135, 140
Maurras, Charles, 28

Mawza exile, 111
media *see* mainstream media; press; state media
Medina, 42–3
Meloni, Georgia, 66
Memmi, Albert, 114
Menard, Louis, 27
messianism, 29, 31, 44–5, 194
#MeToo movement, 176
Mexico, 40, 57, 184, 187
middle classes, 16, 17, 20–1, 23, 81, 163, 169, 182, 183
Milanovic, Branko, 17
Milestones (Qutb), 117
military service, 78, 163
Miller, David, 104–5, 122
Moderate Party (Sweden), 66
Modi, Narendra, 4, 55, 125, 151
moral relativism, 123–4, 181
Morocco, 110, 113
Morris, Benny, 135
Morton, Samuel George, 27
Moses, 34
moshavim, 101
Mosley, Oswald, 71
Mubarak, Hosni, 139
Muhammad, 42–3
multiculturalism, 52, 63, 65, 109, 173
Muslim Brotherhood, 116, 120, 122
Muslims *see* Islam; radical Islamism
Mussolini, Benito, 67, 158

Naples, 39
Nasser, Gamal Abdel, 115, 117, 136–8
Nation of Islam, 91–2
Nation State Law, 75–7, 161
National Front (UK), 71
national liberation movements, 113–14
National Rally (France), 63–4, 158
nationalism
  Arab nationalism, 28, 71, 95–6,
    97, 112–15, 117, 118, 130–1,
    133, 137
  in Egypt, 116
  ethno-nationalism, 4, 21, 24,
    44–6, 52–5, 58, 62–6, 75–9,
    121, 151, 159–61, 165, 177, 179
  in Europe, 23–6, 31–2, 64, 66, 69,
    71, 147–8, 150, 158
  Hindu nationalism, 54–5, 151
  in Israel, 44, 75–7, 79, 159–61,
    165
  and radical Islamism, 44
  rise of in nineteenth century,
    23–6, 113
  in Russia, 67–8
  and secularism, 4, 114–15, 117,
    118
  in Turkey, 4, 95, 113, 115
  in the UK, 10
  in the US, 1, 58, 62
  White nationalism, 1, 60
nativism, 52, 56, 59, 60, 64, 65–6,
  69, 107, 179
NATO, 62, 68, 87–8
natural resources, 13, 98
Nazism, 7, 26–8, 31, 41, 46, 66, 68,
  73, 88–90, 97, 102, 116, 129,
  132–3, 158, 167
Negev, 135, 137, 144
neo-colonialism, 123
neo-Confederacy, 60, 61
neo-fascism, 4, 61–71, 73–4
neoliberalism, 88
neo-Nazism, 57, 65, 97
Netanyahu, Benjamin, 71, 72–3,
  74–80, 141, 144, 158–66, 178
new Diasporism, 167, 170–1
New Left, 84
New Testament, 36–7, 41
New York, 106, 119, 169
New York Daily Tribune, 83
New York Times, 92
Nicosia, 148
9/11 attacks, 119

1948 war, 96, 116, 128, 134–6, 138
1967 war, 45, 71, 115, 137–8
1973 war, 80, 138
1982 Lebanon war, 139–40
North American Free Trade Act
     (NAFTA), 184
Nuremberg rallies, 41

Obama, Barack, 59
oil prices, 8
Old Testament, 37–8, 41
oligarchs, 8–9, 66
Olmert, Ehud, 78, 143–4, 151, 154
one-state solution, 150, 151–6, 170
oppression, 5, 38, 47, 50, 61, 84–5,
     88, 89, 93–4, 109, 111, 123–4,
     167
Orbán, Viktor, 3–4, 68, 73, 77
Organization of Security and
     Cooperation in Europe
     (OSCE), 174–5
orientalism, 123
Origin of Species (Darwin), 26–7
Orthodox Christianity, 37–9
Orthodox Judaism, 47, 77–8,
     157–8, 167, 157
Oslo Accords, 140–1
Oslo peace process, 78, 140–2,
     143–4, 151
Ottoman Caliphate, 44, 113, 116
Ottoman Empire, 31, 44, 85, 95,
     100, 111, 112–13, 116, 128,
     129, 130, 147, 149
Our Battle Against the Jews (Qutb),
     117

Pact of Umar, 43
paganism, 35, 37, 38
Pahlavi dynasty, 112
Pakistan, 150–1
Pale of Settlement, 40
Palestine
     Arab Higher Committee, 132,
          134

British mandate, 51, 97, 113, 129,
     131–4, 149
British withdrawal from, 133
Camp David-Taba talks, 141–2
Christian and Muslim
     populations, 128–9
civilian casualties, 135, 140, 142,
     145
demonstrations in support of,
     106–7, 124, 126, 175, 194
depicted as colonised, 50–1,
     96–108, 128
displacement of Palestinians, 96,
     99, 128, 134–6, 142, 146
establishment of Palestinian
     state, 140–2
far-left positions on, 106–7, 124,
     126, 146, 151, 156, 170
first Intifada, 140
first Gaza war, 143
Gaza, 78, 118, 124, 135–7, 138–9,
     140–4, 154, 177, 194
Hamas, 73–4, 78–9, 86–7, 106–7,
     118, 122, 124, 126, 141–5,
     153–4, 156, 165–6, 170
historical overview, 127–47
irregular troops, 134, 135
Israeli–Palestinian conflict, 32,
     44–5, 71, 78, 96, 124, 127–56,
     194
Israeli settlements, 44–5
Olmert peace proposal, 78,
     143–4, 151, 154
one-state solution, 150, 151–6,
     170
Oslo peace process, 78, 140–2,
     143–4, 151
Palestine Liberation Organization
     (PLO), 137, 139–43
Palestinian Authority, 78, 140,
     143–4, 154, 166
partition plans, 44, 129, 132,
     133–4, 135, 142, 143, 146,
     153–4

Palestine (*cont.*)
  refugees, 96, 128, 134–6, 140,
    142, 143
  riots, 116, 131–2
  second Intifada, 78, 141, 142–3,
    144
  security barriers and
    checkpoints, 142–3
  7 October attack, 73, 74, 79,
    106–7, 124, 126, 144–5, 153,
    156, 165–6, 170
  targeting of civilians, 73, 106,
    135, 136, 140, 144–5
  two-state solution, 78, 141, 151,
    153–4
  West Bank, 103, 135–8, 140–4,
    151, 154, 156, 159–60, 164,
    166
Palestine Liberation Organization
  (PLO), 137, 139–43
Palestinian Authority, 78, 140,
  143–4, 154, 166
pan-Arabism, 113, 114–15, 117,
  137; *see also* Arab nationalism
pan-Germanism, 24, 26
pan-Slavism, 67–8
partition
  Cyprus, 147–50
  India, 150–1
  plans for Israel-Palestine, 44,
    129, 132, 133–4, 135, 142, 143,
    153–4
patriarchy, 86, 88, 123
peacekeeping troops, 136–7, 148
Peel Commission, 132
Perdition (Allen), 97
Pétain, Philippe, 63
Petri, Peter, 11
Philo, 35
philosophy, 110, 121
Piketty, Thomas, 11, 13, 17
Pilate, Pontius, 36
Pinsker, Leon, 100
pluralism, 6, 54, 62, 64, 66

pogroms, 26, 39–40, 56, 89, 95, 98,
  100, 106, 112, 172
Poland, 40, 67, 69, 73, 77, 97, 101,
  160
polarization, 33, 52, 173, 180, 186
polemics, 28, 34–6, 37–8, 41
political antisemitism, 23–32
political parties
  centre right parties, 62
  collapse of trust in, 5
  far-right parties, 3, 61–6, 68–9,
    71, 74
  lack of effective action against
    antisemitism, 174
  social democratic parties, 26, 30,
    49, 62, 186
  socialist parties, 30, 101
  socialist-Zionist parties, 100–1
political rights, 46–7, 65
population transfer, 132, 133–4, 135
populism, 5, 22
Portugal, 39–40, 55, 172
postmodernism, 4, 52, 84–96,
  103, 107, 122–3, 166, 169–70,
  179–80, 181, 193
postwar era, 5, 7–8, 10–11, 52, 56,
  84, 102, 115, 118, 173
poverty, 16, 82, 182, 184, 188
power-sharing, 148, 152–3
pre-Christian era, 34–6
press, 4, 6, 28, 30, 69, 74, 77, 104,
  168–70; *see also* mainstream
  media
press freedom, 69, 74
Press TV, 122
privatization, 8–9, 17, 79, 186
privilege, 52, 81, 85, 86, 89–96, 107,
  155, 167, 176
profession restrictions, 39, 40
pro-Israel antisemitism, 70–4, 158
propaganda, 23, 28, 35, 56, 67–8, 71,
  116, 119, 128, 133, 146, 168–9
pro-Palestine demonstrations,
  106–7, 124, 126, 175, 194

protectionism, 59, 62, 66
Protestantism, 41–2, 72
Protocols of the Elders of Zion, 28, 58, 92, 116
Proudhon, Pierre-Joseph, 29
public services, 17, 79, 163, 185, 186, 187, 188
Putin, Vladimir, 3, 8–9, 66–70, 73–4, 87–8, 124, 125

QAnon, 57–8
al-Qaradawi, Yusuf, 122
Qatar, 122
quotas, 56
Quran, 43
Qutb, Sayyed, 117–18

Rabin, Yitzhak, 140–1
racial theories, 26–7
radical Islamism
  alliances with the far left, 121–6
  anti-colonialism, 117, 123–4
  anti-elitism, 5, 52
  anti-Zionism, 116
  and the collapse of the Ottoman Empire, 44
  conspiracy theories, 5, 6, 52, 116, 117–18
  in Egypt, 139
  emergence of, 115–21
  in Europe, 65, 66
  far-right opposition to, 158, 159
  identity politics, 5, 180
  introduction of anti-Jewish views, 44–5
  jihadism, 116, 117–21
  Jewish control narratives, 6
  and nationalism, 44, 117, 118
  in Pakistan, 151
  and Sharia law, 6, 117
  support for Nazism, 116
  theocracy, 87, 123, 180
  in Turkey, 4
  see also Islam

Rafah, 145
Reagan, Ronald, 8, 59, 182
Reasonableness Doctrine, 77, 162
redistribution, 8, 20, 179, 192
Reform Judaism, 47
Reform Party (US), 59
Reformation, 41
refugees
  Central American, 57
  countering far-right narratives about, 186–9
  in Cyprus, 148–50
  Jewish, 26, 50, 65, 73, 89, 97–9, 102, 129–30, 133, 136, 145–6, 171
  Palestianian, 96, 128, 134–6, 140, 142, 143
  Ukrainian, 69
religious freedom, 38, 47, 109
replacement, 28–9, 31, 43–4, 45–53, 57; *see also* supersession
Republican Party (US), 3, 57–60, 62, 68, 78
republicanism, 46, 63–5
Respect Party (UK), 122
Revisionist Zionist party (Israel), 132, 134
revolution, 23–4, 30, 31, 48, 65, 83, 84, 86, 101, 120, 123, 167
Rich, Dave, 2
Rida, Muhammad Rashid, 115–16
Roman Empire, 34–6, 38–9, 128, 129
Roosevelt, Franklin D., 9
Rothschild family, 58
Ruppin, Arthur, 152
rural populations, 16, 20–1, 23, 84, 93
Russia
  alliance with Iran, 70, 74
  annexation of Crimea, 67
  authoritarianism, 66–7
  Bolshevik revolution, 40, 84, 101

Russia (*cont.*)
  Czarist Empire, 40, 100
  dismantling of democracy, 66–7
  far right, 3, 66–70, 73–4
  ghettoization of Jews, 40
  immigrants from in the West,
    125
  nationalism, 67–8
  neo-fascism, 66–70, 73–4
  oligarchs, 8–9, 66
  opposition politicians, 124
  pan-Slavism, 67–8
  pogroms, 26, 100
  political antisemitism, 28, 30
  privatization, 8–9
  propaganda, 67–8
  Putin regime, 3, 8–9, 66–70,
    73–4, 87–8, 124, 125
  sanctions against, 68, 74
  state media, 66–7
  support for Assad regime, 69, 118
  targeting of civilians, 67, 69
  war against Ukraine, 3, 9, 67,
    68–70, 74, 87–9, 124, 125
  war in Syria, 69, 74, 118
  wars in Chechnya and Georgia,
    67
  Yeltsin regime, 8, 66
  Zionism, 100
  see also Soviet Union
Russo-Turkish war, 147

Sadat, Anwar, 138–9
Salahadin, 129
Sana'a, 111
sanctions, 68, 74
Saturday Night Live, 1–2
Saudi Arabia, 113, 118, 119
Scholem, Gershom, 152
science, 85, 110, 121
Second Aliya, 130
second coming, 72
second Intifada, 78, 141, 142–3, 144
Second Temple, 109

Second World War, 11, 28, 56, 62,
  69, 88, 89–90, 95, 97, 113, 129;
  see also Holocaust
*Secret Relation Between Blacks and
  Jews, The* (Nation of Islam),
  91–2
sectarianism, 4, 54–5
secularism, 4, 29, 30, 31, 45–53, 55,
  64–5, 113, 114–15, 117, 163,
  167
Seleucid Empire, 35
self-determination, 75, 81, 88, 100
separatism, 30, 82, 96, 102, 150, 153
Sephardi Shas Party (Israel), 162
service industries, 16, 182, 183
settler movement, 44–5, 130, 138,
  141, 144, 159–60, 162, 164, 166
7 October attack, 73, 74, 79, 106–7,
  124, 126, 144–5, 153, 156,
  165–6, 170
7/7 bombing, 119
Sharett, Moshe, 136
Sharia law, 6, 43, 117
Sharon, Ariel, 139–40, 141, 142–3
Shia Islam, 111, 112, 118, 119–20
show trials, 96, 168
Sicily, 39
Sinai, 34, 136–7, 138
Slánský trial, 168–9
slavery, 13, 27, 43, 51, 81, 83, 85, 89,
  91–2, 179–80
Smotrich, Bezalel, 159–60, 164
Snyder, Timothy, 67
social control, 84–5
social democracy, 26, 30, 62, 78–9,
  84, 86, 186, 187
Social Democrats (Denmark), 187
social media, 1, 22–3, 106, 191–2,
  194
social welfare, 20, 26, 63, 66, 79, 84,
  186, 187, 188
socialism, 24, 29–30, 48, 83–4, 99,
  100–1, 102, 115, 120, 130, 152,
  166–7

Soros, George, 58, 73
South Africa, 56, 154
sovereignty, 10, 51, 62, 114, 146
Soviet Union
  anti-Zionism, 96–7
  censorship, 90
  collapse of, 8, 67
  Communist Party, 101
  expulsions, 146
  German invasion of, 88
  Gorbachev presidency, 8
  historiography, 89–90
  Holocaust, 89–90
  non-aggression pact with Nazi
    Germany, 88
  political antisemitism, 31
  propaganda, 168–9
  purges, 96, 101, 168
  replaces Czarist Russia, 31
  show trials, 96, 168
  Stalinism, 7, 31, 88, 90, 96–7,
    101, 167, 168
  see also Russia
Spain, 39–40, 55, 109, 110–11, 153,
  172
Spanish Inquisition, 39–40
'Speech on Religious Minorities'
  (Clermont-Tonnerre), 64
Stalin, Joseph, 7, 31, 88, 90, 96–7,
  101, 120, 167, 168
Stanley, Jason, 67–8
Starmer, Keir, 104
state media, 66–7, 122
Stern, Eliyahu, 67–8
Stop the War Coalition, 87–8
Suez Canal, 136, 138
suicide bombings, 119, 122, 141,
  142
Sunni Islam, 115–16, 119–20
supersession, 29, 36–7, 43–4; see
  also replacement
Supreme Court (Israel), 75, 77, 160,
  162
Supreme Court (US), 61

Sweden, 3, 65–6
Sweden Democrats (SD), 65–6
Switzerland, 67, 100
Syria, 69, 74, 113, 114–15, 118, 120,
  134, 137, 138, 139, 153

Tacitus, 35
Taha, Sami, 152
Taliban, 124
Talmud, 41
taxation, 8, 11, 20, 59, 62, 82, 163,
  185–6
Tea Party, 59–60, 62
tech sector, 79, 161, 184, 189–92
technological innovation, 7, 11–13,
  189–92
Tel Aviv, 74, 140, 141
Temple Mount, 131, 141, 142
territorialism, 99
terrorism, 57, 73, 74, 79, 106, 119,
  126, 139, 140, 141, 142, 143,
  144–5, 153, 156, 165–6
Tertullian, 37–8
Thatcher, Margaret, 8, 182
theocracy, 87, 123, 180
Theodosius I, 38–9
Times of London, 28
Tochnit Dalet, 134–5
Toynbee, Arnold, 49–51
trade, 10, 11–13, 183–6, 188, 192
trade unions see unions
transportation, 11–13
trauma, 106, 111
Tree of Life Synagogue attack, 57, 73
trickle-down economics, 20
Trotsky, Leon, 120
Trump, Donald, 1, 3, 6, 56–61, 62,
  68, 71–3, 78, 157, 158, 187
Trump supporters, 3, 56–61, 62, 71
Tudeh Party (Iran), 124
Tunisia, 113, 114, 139
Turkey, 4, 31, 95, 113, 115, 125,
  147–50
Tusk, Donald, 69

two-state solution, 78, 141, 151,
    153–4
2006 Lebanon war, 78

Ukraine, 3, 9, 40, 67, 68–70, 74,
    87–9, 90, 93, 124, 125, 172
ultra-Orthodox Judaism, 77–8,
    159–60, 162, 163, 167
unemployment, 7, 8, 187, 191
unions, 7, 78–9, 161, 181–3
Unite the Right, 1
United Arab Emirates, 164
United Kingdom
    academia, 104–5, 125–6
    austerity, 9
    Blair government, 9
    Brexit, 10
    British National Party, 71
    colonialism, 51, 83, 98, 113, 129,
        131–4, 147–8, 149
    conspiracy theories, 57–8, 103–5
    Covid pandemic, 10
    decline of manufacturing, 16
    denies entry to Jewish refugees,
        50, 102, 133
    economic recession, 9
    expulsion of Jews in 13th century,
        39, 40
    far left, 71, 87–8, 103–7, 122, 166
    far right, 71
    fascism, 71
    financial deregulation, 9
    foreign investment, 10
    hate crimes, 2, 106, 174
    housing, 17
    immigration management, 102,
        133
    income inequality, 79, 182
    invasion of Egypt, 136
    Iranian regime television, 122
    labour market, 10, 102
    labour movement, 102
    Labour Party, 9, 102, 103–4, 122,
        166

mandates in Middle East, 51, 97,
    113, 129, 131–4, 149
National Front, 71
nationalism, 10
pogroms, 39, 40
privatization, 17
pro-Palestine demonstrations,
    106–7, 124, 126, 175, 194
Respect Party, 122
rule over Cyprus, 147–8, 149
rule over India, 150
7/7 bombing, 119
and the slave trade, 51
taxation, 8, 185
Thatcher government, 8, 182
trade, 10
union membership, 182
withdrawal from Palestine,
    133–4
United Nations
    General Assembly, 134
    partition plan, 129, 133–4, 135
    peacekeeping troops, 136–7, 148
    Special Committee on Palestine
        (UNSCOP), 133–4
United States
    academia, 105, 106, 125–6
    African Americans, 59, 60, 102
    Biden administation, 57, 68, 73,
        187
    British colonialism, 51, 83, 98
    Capitol riots, 57, 58, 60
    censorship, 61
    Christian fundamentalism, 60, 61
    Clinton administration, 9, 141–2
    crime rates, 187
    decline of manufacturing, 16, 184
    Democratic Party, 57–8, 59
    dispossession of indigenous
        peoples, 50–1
    education, 61
    entertainment industry, 2, 92
    entry into Second World War,
        56, 88

evangelical Christianity, 71–2,
    158
exceptionalism, 60–1, 171–2
far left, 87–8, 169–70, 171–2
far right, 1, 3, 55–61, 70, 157, 161
financial deregulation, 9
gun rights, 59
hate crimes, 2, 57, 73, 106, 174–5
historiography, 171–2
immigration management, 56,
    187
income inequality, 79, 181–2
Iraq invasion, 70, 118
isolationism, 56, 59
Jewish immigrants, 55–6, 60–1
MAGA movement, 59–60, 61,
    62, 71
multiculturalism, 52
nationalism, 1, 58, 62
9/11 attacks, 119
Nixon administration, 59
QAnon, 57–8
pro-Palestine demonstrations,
    106–7, 124, 126, 175, 194
protectionism, 59
Reagan administration, 8, 59, 182
Reform Party, 59
relocates embassy in Israel, 71–2
Republican Party, 3, 57–60, 62,
    68, 78
support for Israel, 70, 71–3
support for Ukraine, 68
Supreme Court, 61
taxation, 8, 59, 62, 185
Tea Party, 59–60, 62
trade, 184
Tree of Life Synagogue attack,
    57, 73
Trump, 1, 3, 6, 56–61, 62, 68,
    71–3, 78, 157, 158, 187
Trump supporters, 3, 56–61, 62,
    71
2020 elections, 6, 57, 60
union membership, 181–2

White supremacism, 1, 56–7
Zionism, 157
urban populations, 16, 21, 78, 185
Uyghurs, 125

Vichy France, 28, 63
Vienna, 26, 27, 39, 100
von Schönerer, Georg Ritter, 26, 45

wages, 16, 23, 79, 181, 184, 185,
    187
Wagner, Richard, 27
Washington Post, 92
wealth distribution, 17–20, 21, 180,
    184–5, 191, 192
Weg zum Siege des
    Gaermanenthums über das
    Judenthum (Marr), 24
Weizman, Chaim, 132, 152
welfare state, 20, 26, 63, 66, 79, 84,
    186, 187, 188
West, Kanye, 1–2
West Bank, 103, 135–8, 140–4, 151,
    154, 156, 159–60, 164, 166
Western Wall, 131, 142
White nationalism, 1, 60
White privilege, 52, 86, 89–96, 107,
    176
White supremacism, 1, 56–7
William of Norwich, 40
Williamson, Chris, 122
women's rights, 69, 81, 122, 124,
    173, 181; see also gender
working classes, 16, 17, 20–1, 23,
    30, 62, 63, 74, 81–2, 85–6, 93,
    123, 159, 169, 182
working conditions, 16, 181, 183
World Zionist Organization, 100,
    132

Yeltsin, Boris, 8, 66
Yemen, 111, 118, 145
Yevsektsiya, 101
Yiddish language, 101

York, 39, 40
You People (Netflix), 92
Young Turks revolution, 116
Yugoslavia, 8, 153

Zeldin, Alex, 90
Zelenskyy, Volodymyr, 68, 70, 90
Zemmour, Éric, 63–4, 158
Zionism
    anti-Zionism, 6, 51, 70–1, 93,
        95–108, 116, 166–72, 176
    and colonialism, 50–1, 95,
        96–108
    Hitler depicted as supporter of,
        97
    increased radicalism of, 44–5

political movement, 99–103, 146,
    152, 155
Revisionist Zionist party, 132,
    134
Rida's writings on, 116
socialist-Zionist parties, 100–1
rise of, 44–5
in Russia, 100
and the settler movement, 44–5,
    130, 159–60, 162
in the US, 157
Zionism in the Age of the Dictators
    (Brenner), 97
Zionist Organization of America,
    157–8
'Zur Judenfrage' (Marx), 47–8